D1030959

The Business Cycle in a Changing World

Arthur F. Burns

THE BUSINESS CYCLE
in a CHANGING WORLD

ESSAYS reprinted to honor Dr. Burns for his 38 years of active involvement in the research and administration of the National Bureau of Economic Research and on the occasion of his election as Honorary Chairman of the Bureau's Board of Directors.

NATIONAL BUREAU OF ECONOMIC RESEARCH

New York   1969

DISTRIBUTED BY

Columbia University Press   New York and London

HB
3711
B88

NATIONAL BUREAU OF ECONOMIC RESEARCH
STUDIES IN BUSINESS CYCLES

RELATION OF THE DIRECTORS TO THE WORK AND PUBLICATIONS OF THE NATIONAL BUREAU OF ECONOMIC RESEARCH

1. The object of the National Bureau of Economic Research is to ascertain and to present to the public important economic facts and their interpretation in a scientific and impartial manner. The Board of Directors is charged with the responsibility of ensuring that the work of the National Bureau is carried on in strict conformity with this object.

2. The President of the National Bureau shall submit to the Board of Directors, or to its Executive Committee, for their formal adoption all specific proposals for research to be instituted.

3. No research report shall be published until the President shall have submitted to each member of the Board the manuscript proposed for publication, and such information as will, in his opinion and in the opinion of the author, serve to determine the suitability of the report for publication in accordance with the principles of the National Bureau. Each manuscript shall contain a summary drawing attention to the nature and treatment of the problem studied, the character of the data and their utilization in the report, and the main conclusions reached.

4. For each manuscript so submitted, a special committee of the Board shall be appointed by majority agreement of the President and Vice Presidents (or by the Executive Committee in case of inability to decide on the part of the President and Vice Presidents), consisting of three directors selected as nearly as may be one from each general division of the Board. The names of the

special manuscript committee shall be stated to each Director when the manuscript is submitted to him. It shall be the duty of each member of the special manuscript committee to read the manuscript. If each member of the manuscript committee signifies his approval within thirty days of the transmittal of the manuscript, the report may be published. If at the end of that period any member of the manuscript committee withholds his approval, the President shall then notify each member of the Board, requesting approval or disapproval of publication, and thirty days additional shall be granted for this purpose. The manuscript shall then not be published unless at least a majority of the entire Board who shall have voted on the proposal within the time fixed for the receipt of votes shall have approved.

5. No manuscript may be published, though approved by each member of the special manuscript committee, until forty-five days have elapsed from the transmittal of the report in manuscript form. The interval is allowed for the receipt of any memorandum of dissent or reservation, together with a brief statement of his reasons, that any member may wish to express; and such memorandum of dissent or reservation shall be published with the manuscript if he so desires. Publication does not, however, imply that each member of the Board has read the manuscript, or that either members of the Board in general or the special committee have passed on its validity in every detail.

6. Publications of the National Bureau issued for informational purposes concerning the work of the Bureau and its staff, or issued to inform the public of activities of Bureau staff, and volumes issued as a result of various conferences involving the National Bureau shall contain a specific disclaimer noting that such publication has not passed through the normal review procedures required in this resolution. The Executive Committee of the Board is charged with review of all such publications from time to time to ensure that they do not take on the character of formal research reports of the National Bureau, requiring formal Board approval.

7. Unless otherwise determined by the Board or exempted by the terms of paragraph 6, a copy of this resolution shall be printed in each National Bureau publication.

(*Resolution adopted October 25, 1926, and revised February 6, 1933, February 24, 1941, and April 20, 1968*)

Acknowledgments

I owe the publication of this volume to the urging of two friends—Gottfried Haberler and Geoffrey Moore. I did not give my consent quickly. But when I finally agreed, I did so with the conviction that even a collection of scattered essays such as this may convey something of the spirit that has long marked the National Bureau's effort to inform public policy through the disinterested study of business cycles.

The present essays are concerned with the business cycle in our rapidly changing world. They were written during a stage of life when, finding myself heavily engaged in administrative work and public affairs, I took advantage of special occasions to sum up or draw upon my scientific studies. All were written in the unique environment for business-cycle research that my revered friend and teacher, Wesley Clair Mitchell, created nearly fifty years ago, at the National Bureau. All therefore bear the imprint of his thinking and that of my other colleagues—particularly Moses Abramovitz, Solomon Fabricant, Milton Friedman, Ruth Mack, Geoffrey Moore, Anna Schwartz, and Leo Wolman—as well as my own labors. I acknowledge with gratitude the debt of learning and fellowship I owe to each of them, and also to my devoted assistants across the years—Irving Forman, Jane Kennedy, Edward Kilberg, Joyce Rose, Sophie Sakowitz, Louise Smith, and Johanna Stern.

These resurrected essays are presented as they were originally published, except for a few minor stylistic changes and several deletions to avoid any mischievous crossing of the boundary line between economic diagnosis and policy prescription. Mrs. Joan Tron assumed full responsibility for all printing arrangements and Mrs. Rose helped with the proofs. I extend my thanks to them and also to the original publishers who generously consented to the reprinting.

April, 28, 1969   *Arthur F. Burns*

Foreword

The essays in this volume draw upon the research and thinking of an economist who has devoted his life to study of the nature and causes of prosperity and depression. The first essay, written originally for the new *International Encyclopedia of the Social Sciences,* captures the essence of the phenomenon of the business cycle as we now know it. The other essays illuminate that sketch, by illustrating more specifically many of its propositions and findings.

Arthur Burns has put his knowledge to the hard test of formulating business-cycle policies at the highest levels of responsibility in government. As Chairman of President Eisenhower's Council of Economic Advisers from 1953 to 1956, and as counselor to both the Executive and Legislative branches of the Federal Government since then, he has had to diagnose and to recommend. The essays in this book, therefore, represent a distillation of the factual information and insights that he brought with him to this task, as well as what he learned from it, and hence have many implications for policy. But they do not include Burns' many writings on the course he believed government should currently pursue. Thus the book seeks to diagnose, interpret, and report upon economic problems, but in keeping with the National Bureau's tradition it avoids recommending specific courses of action by government, business, trade unions, or any other social groups.

Indeed, the reader will observe, I believe, that the book is itself a tribute to the value and practicability of subjecting economic policies to scientific scrutiny. For it demonstrates that one intensely concerned with policy can also write objectively and dispassionately about the factors that have, over a long history, brought about inflation or depression, rapid growth or economic sluggishness. It is a tribute as well to the scientific and scholarly qualities of the author.

While the reader, therefore, will not find here a specific policy pronouncement on how to achieve rapid economic growth and a high level of employment without inflation, he will become better educated about the factors that need to be considered in shaping policy toward this goal. This in fact was the fundamental purpose of a grant made to the National Bureau by the Alfred P. Sloan Foundation in 1964, which has been drawn upon to finance the publication of this report.

It is a privilege to write the foreword to a book that goes so far to achieve this purpose.

Geoffrey H. Moore

Contents

Tables and Charts

The Business Cycle in a Changing World

ONE

The Nature and Causes of Business Cycles

ECONOMIC change is a law of life. Nowadays, we commonly associate economic instability with business booms and recessions, and we have become accustomed to speaking of these vicissitudes in economic fortune as the "business cycle." However, economic instability has been man's lot through the ages, whether he has made his living by hunting and fishing, by cultivating crops, or by practicing the arts of commerce, industry, and finance. Economic history discloses endless variations of economic conditions. Even the meaning of "good times" keeps changing as the aspirations of people and their performance undergo changes. But relative to the standards of each age and place, some years are prosperous, others dull, still others depressed.

I. TYPES OF ECONOMIC MOVEMENT

The outstanding feature of modern industrial nations is the growth of their economies. Thus, the population of the United States has risen steadily, year in and year out. So too, with very

Originally published in *International Encyclopedia of the Social Sciences,* Vol. 2, pp. 226–245. Reprinted with permission of the publisher of the *Encyclopedia,* Sills (ed.), copyright (©) 1968 by Crowell Collier and Macmillan, Inc.

few exceptions, has the stock of housing, industrial plant, machinery, school buildings, highways, and other major forms of capital. The gross national product—that is, the total output of commodities and services—has fluctuated continually, but has done so along a rising secular trend. So also has output per capita, per worker, or per man-hour worked. In short, the American economy, viewed in the aggregate, has been basically characterized by growth of resources, growth of output, and growth of efficiency.

When we look beneath the surface of aggregate economic activity, we find some industries and communities growing rapidly, others growing only gradually, and still others declining. These divergent trends reflect a host of influences—among them, business innovations, population changes, shifts in consumer preferences, the discovery of new mines or oil fields, the exhaustion of old mines or timberlands, and changes in governmental policies. For example, the capital invested in American railroads and their volume of traffic increased rapidly during the nineteenth century, responding to the economic growth of the country and in turn stimulating it. But the railroads also grew at the expense of coaches, canals, and other waterways, which they gradually superseded by offering better service or charging a lower price. Years later the competitive trend was reversed, as new methods of transportation came into being—first, trolley lines, then buses, trucks, passenger automobiles, pipelines, airplanes, and improved waterways. These battled the railroads for traffic as vigorously as railroads in their youth had fought their commercial rivals. More recently, railroads have begun to retaliate through the use of radically new freight cars and other innovations. Such divergence of industrial trends is one of the expressions of economic progress.

Business cycles have been intimately connected with the

lopsided surges of development that mark economic progress. However, business cycles are not the only type of fluctuation to which economic life is subject. During certain hours of the day, most of us are at school or at work; during other hours we relax in whatever way suits our tastes or needs. This daily cycle in activity is so regular and dependable that we take it for granted. The same is true of the weekly cycle which brings its day or days of rest. Whatever difficulties or opportunities the daily and weekly cycles may have posed for our remote ancestors, our own lives and social institutions have become adjusted to their repetitive course. We know that shops will be closed at certain hours and on certain days, and we plan our shopping accordingly. We know that the nation's production will decline abruptly when factory workers put down their tools in the late afternoon, but we also know that their jobs do not cease on that account and that they will take up their tools again the next morning or when the weekend is over. In view of the extreme brevity and regularity of these cyclical movements, we pay no attention to them in judging whether business is improving or worsening.

Much the same is true of the seasonal fluctuations that run their course within the period of a year. Partly because of vagaries of the weather or the calendar, partly because of changes in business practice, the annual cycle is less regular than the daily or weekly cycle. Nevertheless, we expect business in general to be more brisk in the spring than in the summer or winter, and we ordinarily find it so. We expect department store sales to reach a peak during the Easter shopping season and a still higher peak before Christmas, and so we find it. We expect unemployment to be at its highest in February and at its lowest in October, and so it usually is. Workers in seasonal trades may not cherish the fluctuation to which they are subject, but they can reasonably count on returning to their jobs when the dull season ends and can plan their lives accordingly. In view of the substantial regularity of seasonal fluctuations, businessmen as well as economists usually put them out of sight when they seek to determine whether a particular branch of trade—or the economy as a whole—is expanding or contracting.

Business cycles differ in vital respects from these daily, weekly, and annual cycles. First, the recurring sequence of changes that constitutes a business cycle—expansion, downturn, contraction, and upturn—is not periodic. In other words, the phases of business cycles repeat themselves, but their duration varies considerably and so too does their intensity and scope. Second, since business cycles last from about two to ten years, they are considerably longer than the other cycles. Third, business cycles have a more powerful tendency to synchronize industrial, commerical, and financial processes than do the shorter cycles. Thus, the daily and weekly cycles in total production have no counterpart in inventories, bank loans, or interest rates, while seasonal fluctuations vary widely from one business activity to another. Fourth, although custom has left its imprint on the daily and annual cycles, they are part of the natural environment of man. Business cycles, on the other hand, are a product of culture. They are found only in modern nations where economic activities are organized mainly through business enterprises and where individuals enjoy considerable freedom in producing, pricing, trading, and saving or investing.

When economic plans and decisions are made independently by millions of business firms and households, some imbalance is frequently bound to occur between output and sales, or between output and the stock of equipment, or between inventories and outstanding orders, or between costs of production and prices. This much can be reasonably anticipated by everyone. However, the locus of the imbalance, its timing and magnitude, and the adjustments to which it leads can rarely, if ever, be foreseen with precision. In short, the business cycle lacks the brevity, the simplicity, the regularity, and dependability, or the predictability of its cousins. For all these reasons, although the business cycle is often the vehicle of progress, it also spells instability for society. When the economy starts on a downward course, no one can be sure how many months the recession will last, whether it will degenerate into a depession, how many business firms will go bankrupt, how far prices will decline, and—most important of all from a human standpoint—how many men and women will become unemployed. Although the United States and other countries are learning rapidly how to adapt to business cycles and to bring them under control, they remain troublesome.

Business cycles are not merely fluctuations in aggregate economic activity. They are also fluctuations that are widely diffused throughout the economy, and this fact distinguishes them from the convulsions of economic fortune that characterized earlier times as well as from the other short-term variations of our own age. Continuous and fairly pervasive fluctuations do not arise in a nation's economy until its activities of production, distribution, and consumption have become closely interwoven through division of labor, the making and spending of money incomes, a system of banking and credit, a mode of production relying extensively on fixed capital, and some ease in communication and transportation. Since these institutions emerged gradually in the Western world, the phenomenon of business cycles itself developed gradually and no precise date can be assigned for its first mature expression. It appears, however, that business cycles have existed in the United States, Great Britain, and France for nearly two hundred years, and that they have marked the economies of other modern nations practicing free enterprise since the latter part of the nineteenth century—if not longer. Earlier centuries, while free from business cycles, did not escape the ordeal of economic instability. This is evident from the hardships that frequently accompanied or followed bad harvests, epidemics, wars, earthquakes, monetary upheavals, high-handed acts of rulers, civil disorders, and similar fortuitous events.

In recent decades, the Soviet Union and other nations that organize economic activity through state enterprises and governmental edicts have also escaped business cycles; but they have not escaped economic fluctuations. Variations in harvests, political purges, wars, monetary revolutions, and misadventures, as well as successes of planning, have left their mark on the aggregate economic activity of these nations. Of course, episodic or erratic disturbances also powerfully influence the course of economic activity in the United States and in other developed nations that practice free enterprise, but they appear to do so by hastening or retarding, by strengthening or opposing, the economic processes that of themselves tend to generate cyclical movements. The ragged contours of most business cyles testify to the role of random disturbances, and so too does the strong individuality of successive business cycles.

Business cycles also need to be distinguished from specific cycles—that is, cycles in specific activities, such as mining coal or trading in securities, which have about the same order of duration as the business cycle but may or may not match its timing. Occasionally, specific cycles appear to be superimposed, so to speak, on longer cycles marked by their own rises and declines. Huge swings, lasting about ten to twenty-five years, have been common in building construction in various countries. Waves of this order of duration, but consisting of accelerations and retardations of growth rather than of actual rises and declines, also appear to have characterized aggregate economic activity in the United States. These Kuznets cycles, as they are often called, reflect variations in the intensity of successive business cycles. A distinction between major and minor cycles, such as Hansen makes, likewise involves a grouping of successive business cycles. On this view, the interval between the troughs of severe depressions is a major cycle, so that some major cycles may include only one business cycle while others include two or more. Long waves of about fifty years—usually called Kondratieff cycles—have also been alleged to characterize aggregate economic activity of Western nations. The existence of these waves, while suggested by price movements, has not yet been established.

The terms used by economists to describe the phases of business cycles are rich in diversity but are gradually becoming standardized. The "peak" of a business cycle marks the end of "expansion" and the beginning of "contraction." The "trough" marks the end of contraction and the beginning of expansion. Frequently, "prosperity" is used interchangeably with "expansion," although it is better practice to restrict terms such as "prosperity" or "boom" to the higher reaches of particular expansions when full employment is closely approximated. The term "recession" does double duty. It is widely used to refer to the transition from expansion to contraction, just as "recovery" or "revival" is used to refer to the transition from contraction to expansion. Contractions of varying intensity are also commonly distinguished by the terms "recession" and "depression"; the former refers to a moderate contraction of aggregate activity that lasts in the neighborhood of a year, while the latter refers to a severe contraction or to one which, while moderate, lasts distinctly longer than a year. The term "crisis" originally was used to denote the financial disturbances that frequently occurred during the transition from expansion to contraction, but later it came to be applied to any transition from expansion to contraction. Nowadays, the term "crisis" is usually reserved for a violent disruption of financial markets without regard to the stage of the business cycle in which such a disturbance occurs.

II. GROWTH OF KNOWLEDGE ABOUT BUSINESS CYCLES

In view of the complexity of business cycles and the innumerable differences between them, their essential features and causes have long been a matter of debate. The lack of full or precise economic statistics, which was especially serious before World War I, inevitably contributed to uncertainty about the actual course of business cycles and their causes. But as public concern about crises, inflation, depressions, and unemployment grew, economists have also pressed their investigation of this range of problems.

During much of the nineteenth century, interest was focused on commerical crises—that is, the sharp rise of money rates, scramble for liquidity, drop of prices, and spread of bankruptcies that frequently marked the culmination of a boom. With the emergence of the concept of a business cycle, various economists became concerned with the entire round of events that preceded and followed a crisis. The business cycle itself, however, was still viewed as centering, in the main, in activities of commerce and finance. Some economists traced its causes to natural forces, others to psychological factors, and still others to the workings of the monetary and banking system. Toward the end of the century, interest began to shift to phenomena of industry and employment, and more particularly to the great fluctuations that characterized the capital goods industries. This change of outlook reflected the growth of manufacturing, transportation, and public utility enterprises in modern nations, the relative decline of agriculture, and a growing realization that the transition from prosperity to recession could occur without a crisis or panic but not without a substantial increase of unemployment. In later decades, numerous explanations of the business cycle were developed that gave a large role to investment—usually to investment in fixed capital but sometimes to investment in inventories. Economists stressed different factors that had a bearing on the investment process—such as population growth, territorial expansion, stock of capital, the state of optimism, new technology, bunching of innovations, the rate of change in consumption, variation of interest rates, and changes of costs, prices, and profits. Or else they attributed primary significance to particular features of economic organization—such as industrial competition, uncertainty of demand, or the inequality of incomes. More frequently than not, the various theories differed mainly in their points of emphasis and therefore served to supplement one another.

The truly outstanding contributions to knowledge of business cycles were made by a small number of economists. Clément Juglar, 1819–1905, pioneered by demonstrating, in the course of a massive factual study of prices and finance, that crises were merely a passing phase of a recurring, wavelike fluctuation in business activity. Mikhail Tugan-Baranovskii, 1865–1919, was the first influential economist to see in the fluctuating rate of growth of the fixed capital of a country the main cause of its business cycles. Knut Wicksell, 1851–1926, clarified the cumulative processes of the business cycle by analyzing the consequences of a discrepancy between the rate of return on investment, which was liable to shift because of technological or other real changes in opportunity, and the market rate of interest. Albert Aftalion, 1874–1956, developed the implications for the business cycle of certain industrial facts—the long period required to bring new fixed capital into being, the long life of capital goods, and the capacity of minor changes in consumption to generate large changes in the net additions to the fixed capital required by business firms. Joseph A. Schumpeter, 1883–1950, viewed economic growth itself as a cyclical process and attributed the business cycle to the bunching of innovations, which forced difficult readjustments on old enterprises but in the end resulted in a more effective use of existing resources. Wesley Clair Mitchell, 1874–1948, carried factual investigation of business cycles far beyond earlier efforts, sharpened the concept of a self-generating cycle in a business system, and clarified the interrelations of costs, prices, and profits during a business cycle. John Maynard Keynes, 1883–1946, stressed the dynamic role of investment in altering the level of national income, formulated a consumption function which treats consumer spending as a passive response to national income, and with the aid of this function clarified the process whereby an increment of investment, besides adding directly to a nation's income, raises it indirectly by stimulating larger consumer spending. Through the contributions of these pioneers and of many other economists and economic statisticians, notably Warren M. Persons, Simon Kuznets, and Jan Tinbergen, significant advances have been made in recent decades in describing with some precision the major features of business cycles and also in understanding the processes whereby they are generated.

This paper presents in nontechnical language the main results of modern research on the nature and causes of business cycles. It should be borne in mind, however, that the concrete manifestations of the business cycle keep changing and that numerous aspects of business cycles are still obscure. These facts justify extensive new research. The investigations that economists have currently under way focus on speculative model building, econometric model building, historical studies of individual cycles, statistical studies of fluctuations in individual processes or in the economy at large, experiments with forecasting techniques, and studies of business-cycle policy. This variety of approaches sometimes leads to methodological controversies. But no serious student of business cycles any longer questions that empirical research must be guided by an analytic framework or that speculative theorizing must be tested by an appeal to experience.

III. CYCLICAL BEHAVIOR OF AGGREGATE ACTIVITY

The business cycle involves to some degree the entire system of business—the formation of firms and their disappearance, prices as well as output, the employment of labor and other resources, costs and profits, the flow of incomes to individuals and consumer spending, savings and investments, exports and imports, trading in securities as well as commodities, the extension and repayment of loans, the money supply and its turnover, and the fiscal operations of government. Since there is no unique way of combining all these activities, the business cycle cannot be fully depicted by any single measure. However, the behavior of the entire congeries of fluctuations is indicated reasonably well for recent decades by statistical series of fairly comprehensive economic coverage—such as industrial production, total or nonagricultural employment, the flow of personal income, bank clearings or debits, and the gross national product.

The picture of a typical business cycle which emerges from these statistical records and also from earlier historical descriptions is that of a sustained rise in aggregate economic activity followed by a sustained, but smaller and shorter, decline. Activity at the peak of a business cycle is not merely higher than at the immediately preceding and following troughs. With very rare exceptions, it is also higher than at the preceding peak and lower than at the following peak. Likewise, the trough of a business cycle is usually higher than its immediate predecessor. In view of these typical characteristics, a business cycle almost always includes a visible element of growth. It is not merely an oscillation. The expansion, which ultimately carries aggregate activity to new heights, is typically most rapid in its early stages—the more so when it follows a severe contraction than when it follows a mild one. Although the rate of advance usually tapers off as the expansion proceeds, at times it reaccelerates as an expansion draws to a close without, however, regaining its initial speed. During contractions the rate of decline is usually fastest in the middle stages.

Between 1854 and 1961 the average length of business cycles in the United States was forty-nine months, with the average expansion lasting thirty months and the average contraction nineteen. The duration of individual cycles varied considerably —from ten to eighty months for expansions, from seven to sixty-five months for contractions, and from seventeen to one hundred and one months for full cycles. In a sense, aggregate activity was "depressed" over longer intervals than the duration of contractions may suggest, since some time must elapse before recovery can restore activity to the level attained at the preceding cyclical peak. On the other hand, the level of activity in the months immediately following a peak is often only a little lower than at the peak. During the ten business cycles from 1919 to 1961, when expansions averaged thirty-five months and contractions fifteen, the increases of industrial production ranged from 18 to 93 per cent and averaged 38 per cent, while the declines ranged from seven to 66 per cent and averaged 26 per cent. Total output and employment, however, have fluctuated within decidedly narrower ranges. The reason is that they encompass, besides volatile activities like manufacturing and mining, relatively stable activities such as retailing, the service trades, and governmental work. Thus, during the business-cycle contraction of 1957–58, when industrial production declined 14.2 per cent, total real output fell only 4.6 per cent and employment in nonagricultural establishments 4.3 per cent (see Table 1.1 and Chart 1.1).

In other industrial countries the average duration of business cycles has been somewhat longer than in the United States. For example, between 1879 and 1932, fifteen business cycles ran their course in the United States, but only ten in Germany, and eleven in Great Britain and France. Typically, the amplitude of business cycles has also been smaller in other countries than in the United States. Although the business cycles of individual countries often synchronize, some divergence of economic fortune has always been present. In general, the minor cycles of individual nations have followed a relatively independent course, while the larger cyclical movements have tended to be of international scope.

IV. CYCLICAL BEHAVIOR OF INDIVIDUAL ACTIVITIES

Many, but by no means all, individual activities reflect the cyclical movements of comprehensive aggregates of economic activity. The fortunes of individual firms are often dominated by personal factors or conditions peculiar to their industry or locality. Activities like the production of wheat experience fluctuations that are heavily influenced by the weather and bear little relation in time to business cycles. Activities involving the

TABLE 1.1. A Partial Chronology of Business Cycles [a]

United States		Great Britain	
Peak	Trough	Peak	Trough
	1834	1792	1793
1836	1838	1796	1797
1839	1843	1802	1803
1845	1846	1806	1808
1847	1848	1810	1811
1853	Dec. 1854	1815	1816
June 1857	Dec. 1858	1818	1819
Oct. 1860	June 1861	1825	1826
Apr. 1865	Dec. 1867	1828	1829
June 1869	Dec. 1870	1831	1832
Oct. 1873	Mar. 1879	1836	1837
Mar. 1882	May 1885	1839	1842
Mar. 1887	Apr. 1888	1845	1848
July 1890	May 1891	1854	Dec. 1854
Jan. 1893	June 1894	Sept. 1857	Mar. 1858
Dec. 1895	June 1897	Sept. 1860	Dec. 1862
June 1899	Dec. 1900	Mar. 1866	Mar. 1868
Sept. 1902	Aug. 1904	Sept. 1872	June 1879
May 1907	June 1908	Dec. 1882	June 1886
Jan. 1910	Jan. 1912	Sept. 1890	Feb. 1895
Jan. 1913	Dec. 1914	June 1900	Sept. 1901
Aug. 1918	Mar. 1919	June 1903	Nov. 1904
Jan. 1920	July 1921	June 1907	Nov. 1908
May 1923	July 1924	Dec. 1912	Sept. 1914
Oct. 1926	Nov. 1927	Oct. 1918	Apr. 1919
Aug. 1929	Mar. 1933	Mar. 1920	June 1921
May 1937	June 1938	Nov. 1924	July 1926
Feb. 1945	Oct. 1945	Mar. 1927	Sept. 1928
Nov. 1948	Oct. 1949	July 1929	Aug. 1932
July 1953	Aug. 1954	Sept. 1937	Sept. 1938
July 1957	Apr. 1958		
May 1960	Feb. 1961		

SOURCE: Based on studies of the National Bureau of Economic Research.

[a] The dates given are subject to revision. Work on the extension of the chronologies for Great Britain, Germany, and France is under way.

Germany				France			
Peak		Trough		Peak		Trough	
			1866				1840
	1869		1870		1847		1849
	1872	Feb.	1879		1853		1854
Jan.	1882	Aug.	1886		1857		1858
Jan.	1890	Feb.	1895		1864	Dec.	1865
Mar.	1900	Mar.	1902	Nov.	1867	Oct.	1868
Aug.	1903	Feb.	1905	Aug.	1870	Feb.	1872
July	1907	Dec.	1908	Sept.	1873	Aug.	1876
Apr.	1913	Aug.	1914	Apr.	1878	Sept.	1879
June	1918	June	1919	Dec.	1881	Aug.	1887
May	1922	Nov.	1923	Jan.	1891	Jan.	1895
Mar.	1925	Mar.	1926	Mar.	1900	Sept.	1902
Apr.	1929	Aug.	1932	May	1903	Oct.	1904
				July	1907	Feb.	1909
				June	1913	Aug.	1914
				June	1918	Apr.	1919
				Sept.	1920	July	1921
				Oct.	1924	June	1925
				Oct.	1926	June	1927
				Mar.	1930	July	1932
				July	1933	Apr.	1935
				June	1937	Aug.	1938

CHART 1.1. Production, Prices, and Employment in the United States, 1919–65 [a]

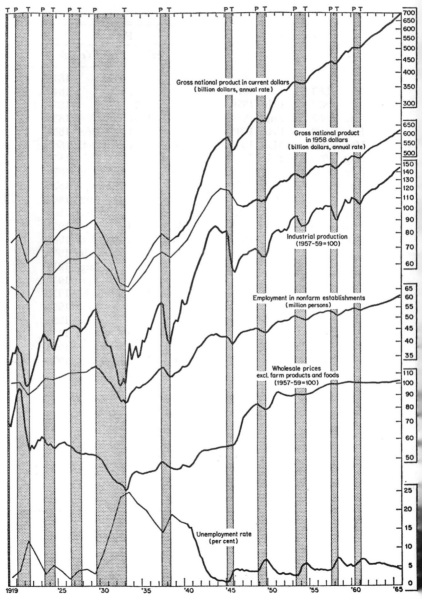

[a] T indicates trough; P indicates peak; shaded areas represent business-cycle contractions; unshaded areas represent expansions. Data are quarterly, except for the following, which are annual: GNP in current dollars, 1919–38; GNP in 1958 dollars, 1919–46; employment, 1919–28; unemployment rate, 1919–39.

production of new products, like radio tubes in the 1920's or transistors more recently, may defy business-cycle contractions during the early and rapidly growing stage of their history. Some financial magnitudes, like the money supply, decline during severe contractions but merely experience a reduced rate of growth during ordinary contractions. Others, like commercial bank investments or the cash balances of corporations, tend to move contracyclically. Even activities that generally move with the business cycle sometimes skip a cycle, or undergo an extra fluctuation of their own, or move especially early or late during recessions or recoveries. In short, some economic activities are free from cyclical fluctuations over extended periods or are subject to an independent rhythm, while even the numerous activities that tend to keep in step with the business cycle have specific cycles whose turning points are scattered.

This diversity of movement in various branches of the economy means that expansion in some activities is always accompanied by contraction in others. We find, for example, that expansions in individual branches of production run side by side with individual contractions, whether business as a whole is depressed or prosperous. The turns of the specific cycles are not, however, distributed at random through time. On the contrary, they come in clusters, so that at a time when the troughs in production are bunched the peaks are few, and vice versa. But when the number of troughs in a given month exceeds the peaks, the number of expanding activities must also be larger the following month. Hence, the bunching of cyclical turns results, so to speak, in protracted periods when a majority of individual branches of production experience expansion, followed by protracted periods when a majority experience contraction. Empirically, the periods when expansions preponderate are virtually coterminous with the upward phases of the cycle in aggregate production; that is to say, aggregate production expands when individual expansions dominate. Moreover, when the expanding activities constitute a large majority, the amplitude of the cyclical rise in total production is apt to be larger than when the majority is small. To put this relationship another way, when the cyclical rise of total production is especially large, the industrial scope of expansion also tends to be especially broad. The scope of individual contractions, while usually less extensive than that of expansions, is similarly correlated with cyclical declines in aggregate production. All these relations in the sphere of production hold, and in the same way, between individual branches of employment and total employment, between individual branches of expenditure and total expenditure, and, indeed, between individual business processes and business as a whole.

The shift from a widening to a narrowing scope of expansions usually takes place gradually and follows a cyclical course. Rising activities are only a bare majority at the beginning of a business-cycle expansion. Their number swells as aggregate activity increases, though expansion reaches its widest scope not when aggregate activity is at a peak but perhaps six months or a year earlier. In the neighborhood of the peak, crosscurrents are the outstanding feature of the economic situation. Once the economy turns down, the number of expanding activities becomes smaller and smaller, but the scope of contraction does not widen indefinitely. Perhaps six months or a year before aggregate activity reaches a trough, the proportion of contracting activities is already at a maximum. Thereafter, the majority of contracting activities dwindles, while the minority of expanding activities keeps growing and before long becomes the ruling majority. About the time when that happens, the tide of aggregate activity begins rising again. A continual transformation of the economic system thus occurs beneath the surface phenomena of aggregate expansion and contraction.

The degree of clustering and the precise sequence of the cyclical turns of individual branches of production or employment vary from one business-cycle turn to the next. New and rapidly growing industries tend to move down late at downturns and to move up early at upturns. Activity in the machinery trades tends to move somewhat late at both upturns and downturns. Apart from these tendencies, the sequence within any cluster of cyclical upturns in individual branches of industry usually bears little resemblance to the sequence within the next cluster of either downturns or upturns.

Rather strong repetitive tendencies emerge, however, when production and employment are viewed in relation to other economic processes. Activities preparatory to investment expenditure—such as the formation of new firms, appropriations for capital expenditure by corporations, issuance of building permits, contracts for residential building, orders for machinery and equipment, contracts for commercial and industrial construction, additions to private debt, and new equity issues—typically begin declining while total production, employment, the flow of incomes, and the average level of wholesale prices are still rising. Similarly, these visible preparations for investment typically recover several months before production, employment, incomes, and wholesale prices end their cyclical decline. Cyclical fluctuations in profit margins, in the proportion of corporations achieving rising profits, and in prices of common stocks also tend to lead the tides of aggregate activity, and so too—although less consistently—do the fluctuations of total corporate profits. Other activities that tend to move up early in recoveries and to move down early in recessions are investment in inventories of materials, spot prices of industrial raw materials, and certain marginal adjustments of the work force, such as the average length of the work week and the rate of new hirings.

On the other hand, many economic processes or activities tend to lag in the course of business cycles. Outstanding among these are labor costs per unit of output, interest rates charged by banks on business loans, mortgage yields, retail prices, business expenditures on new plant and equipment, the installation of new industrial facilities, and aggregate business inventories. Of course, the cyclical turns in these lagging processes tend to precede opposite turns in aggregate activity.

The internal composition of the economy keeps changing in the course of a business cycle but not only on account of differences in cyclical timing. Just as individual activities do not rise or fall in perfect unison, so also they do not rise or fall by any uniform percentage during a business cycle. Some economic magnitudes—for example, retail sales and bank interest rates on business loans—move within a range that is narrow relative to their level. Others—especially business profits, capital gains or losses, and orders for investment goods—have enormous fluctuations. These and many other differences of cyclical amplitude are a recurring feature of business cycles. The turmoil that goes on within aggregate economic activity during a business cycle is, therefore, in no small part systematic.

In a typical business cycle, aggregate production fluctuates over a wider range than do aggregate sales. Moreover, sales by manufacturers fluctuate more widely than sales by wholesalers, while the latter fluctuate more than sales by retailers. The production of durable goods—both those destined for producers and those destined for consumers—fluctuates more widely than that of nondurables. Industrial production usually fluctuates more than the level of industrial prices at wholesale, which in turn fluctuates more than the level of retail prices or of wage rates. The cyclical fluctuation in the number of man-hours worked is larger than the fluctuation in the number employed, and the latter is larger in commodity-producing industries than in the service trades. Wage disbursements fluctuate within a wider range than salary payments or the flow of property income to individuals but within a much narrower range than profits. Corporate profits also fluctuate much more widely than dividend payments or total personal income. Consumer expenditures fluctuate still less than personal income, while personal savings fluctuate more than personal income but less than corporate savings. Cyclical amplitudes are larger in private investment expenditure as a whole than in consumer expenditure and they are also larger in consumer spending on durable goods than on nondurables or services. Again, amplitudes are typically larger in construction contracts than in the volume of construction executed, larger in business orders for machinery and equipment than in their production or shipments, larger in additions to inventories by business firms than in gross or net additions to their fixed capital, and larger in additions to inventories of the firms manufacturing durable goods than of those manufacturing nondurables. Finally, new security issues fluctuate more widely than trading on the stock exchanges, stock prices more than commodity or bond prices, short-term interest rates more than bond yields, open market interest rates more than customer rates, extensions of consumer installment credit more than repayments, imports more than exports, governmental revenues more than expenditures, and so through the gamut of processes that make up the economy.

Since disparities of cyclical amplitude and timing, such as those just noted, tend to be repeated in successive business cycles, the proportions that critical economic factors bear to one another tend to change in a systematic manner during a business cyle. For example, investment expenditure fluctuates much more widely relative to its size than does consumer spending; hence the ratio of investment to the gross national product tends to move with the business cycle, while the ratio of consumer spending to gross national product traces out an inverse movement. The amplitude of cycles is larger in total production than in sales; hence, inventory investment passes through a cycle of accumulation and liquidation that closely matches or even leads the cycle in aggregate activity, while the movement of total inventories lags both in recoveries and recessions. Government expenditures usually fluctuate within a smaller range or bear a much looser relation to the business cycle than do revenues; hence, the budgetary surplus, taken in an algebraic sense, tends to move with the business cycle. One more illustration will have to suffice. The rate of increase of the labor force varies little between expansions and contractions of aggregate activity; employment, on the other hand, moves strongly and synchronously with the tides in activity but typically rises more slowly than the labor force both at the beginning and toward the very end of expansion. Unemployment, therefore, typically turns up before aggregate activity starts receding and turns down only after economic recovery is already under way.

The empirical features of business cycles will be further elucidated in later pages. The point to note now is that our generalizations are largely based on intensive studies of the business cycles that have occurred in the Unites States during recent decades, although considerable confirmation has also been provided by studies of other countries—notably, Great Britain, Canada, Italy, and Japan. It is also well to keep in mind, first, that the generalizations emphasize the repetitive features of the economic changes that take place during business cycles; second, that they merely express strong tendencies toward repetition—not invariant rules of behavior. Diversity and individuality are no less characteristic of business cycles than the family resemblance among them, and this fact inevitably complicates the task of understanding the nature and causes of business cycles. Fortunately, there is less uncertainty about the broad processes that typically generate business cycles than about the specific causes of this or that cyclical episode.

V. THE CUMULATIVE PROCESS OF EXPANSION

The continual transformation of the economy during a business cycle, which we have just reviewed, indicates that once the forces of recovery have taken hold, they will cumulate in strength. In other words, the expansion will spread out over the economic system, gather momentum, and for a time become a self-reinforcing process.

The proximate impulse to expansion may come from an increase of spending by business firms, consumers, or the government, or it may originate outside the domestic economy. The source or sources of the expansive impulse will be considered later. For the moment, let us assume merely that the economy is jarred out of its depressed level by an appreciable rise in the volume of newly initiated construction. A chain of familiar consequences will then be set in motion. Contractors will hire additional labor, disburse larger sums in wages, place larger orders for materials, supplies, and equipment with dealers or manufacturers, and finance at least a part of their rising outlays from new bank loans. The employment of labor on construction sites will at first increase only a little but after a few weeks or months—as the sequence of technical operations permits—more rapidly. Sales by retail shops and service establishments that cater to consumers will follow suit; for most construction workers will soon spend all or part of their larger income, and some will even feel encouraged to buy on the installment plan. The impact of the additional spending by contractors and their workmen will be spotty and uneven, but the effects will gradually spread out. Although some dealers or manufacturers will be content to meet the enlarged demand by drawing down their inventories, others will want to maintain inventories at their current level, and still others will seek to expand them in order better to accommodate a rising volume of sales. Here and there, therefore, not only will production of services and of goods made to specification be stimulated but also of staples that are normally carried in stock.

In response to larger construction spending, the rough balance between expanding and contracting enterprises that had previously ruled in the economy will thus be tipped, albeit irregularly, toward expansion. As firms revise their production schedules upward, they also will often increase their purchases from other firms, give fuller work to their present employees, perhaps recall some former employees or hire new ones, but in any event disburse larger sums in wages. Thus, each expanding center of production will stimulate activity elsewhere, including lending by the banks, in ever-widening circles. The spread of expansion from these centers will serve to check or counteract spirals of contraction that meanwhile are being generated at other points. With the scope of the expansion gradually becoming wider, retailers will be more prone to place orders with their suppliers in quantities that exceed their current sales, wholesalers and manufacturers will behave similarly, working hours will lengthen here and there, the work force will grow in an increasing number of firms and in the aggregate, and so too will income disbursements and sales to consumers.

We have supposed thus far that the higher volume of newly initiated construction will merely be maintained. In fact, construction work will tend to grow and so too will the activity of those making all sorts of machinery and equipment. Business firms, viewed in the mass, will still be operating well below capacity; but some firms—and their number is now increasing —will be operating at or close to full capacity. Moreover, as production rises, the profits of these firms, and indeed of business generally, will tend to improve. For a time, service enterprises—shops, theaters, buses, airlines, etc.—can handle more customers without adding appreciably, if at all, to the aggregate hours worked by their employees. That is much less likely to happen in manufacturing and other commodity-producing establishments. However, since these enterprises also rely heavily on overhead types of labor, their labor requirements per unit of output will tend to fall as output expands, thus reinforcing increases of productivity stemming from improvements of organization or technology. Experience shows that the swiftest advances of output per man-hour typically occur in the early stages of a business-cycle expansion and that they then usually outweigh such increases as may occur in wage rates. The result is that unit labor costs of production tend to decline rather sharply, at least for a few months. Depreciation charges per unit of output will also be falling. Meanwhile, such increases as occur in other cost items are as yet apt to be quite moderate, and they can frequently be offset by advancing selling prices. Hence, an increasing number of firms will find that their profit margins are rising handsomely and, since their volume of business is also growing, that their total profits are rising still more. With business profits and consumer incomes improving on a wide front, with shortages of capacity looming more frequently, with delivery periods lengthening, and with interest rates, machinery and equipment prices, and construction costs still relatively favorable, it is only natural that contracts and orders for investment goods should rise briskly. Investment expenditures will follow suit, though with an irregular lag and diminished amplitude.

Moreover, as the expansion spreads, it generates in more

people a feeling of confidence about the economic future—a mood that may gradually change from optimism to exuberance. As people become more optimistic, they respond more strongly to such increases of sales, prices, or profits as keep occurring. In other words, a given increase of sales, prices, or profits evokes a larger business response. An advance of prices, whether in commodity markets, business salesrooms, or on the stock exchange, is now more apt to encourage expectations that prices will go still higher. Increases of sales, improvements of profits, and delays of deliveries are similarly projected. In this sort of environment, dishoarding and borrowing become easier to rationalize and buying rises briskly all around. Many firms, fearing that they may not get all of the supplies they will soon need, begin bunching their orders more heavily and some actually order more than they expect to get. Not a few investors who had previously postponed action on attractive projects because the time did not seem right, now decide to go ahead. The new spirit of enterprise fosters more new projects that are related loosely, if at all, to the specific shortages of facilities that keep arising. More business firms brush up their long-range plans for expansion or modernization. More promoters push projects to exploit new products or techniques. More new firms are organized to share in the growing markets. More legislatures authorize improvements worthy of an era of prosperity. More families decide to buy a new automobile, to refurnish their home, or to build or buy a new house. Thus, the widening scope of expansion and the improved outlook that goes with it foster both investment and consumption, with advances of the one reinforcing the other in a cumulative process.

Even an adverse development, such as a strike in a major industry or a deliberate effort to reduce inventories of some major product, may now be taken in stride. At an early stage of the expansion, any such reversal of fortune could have sufficed to terminate it. Now, in view of the high level of business and consumer optimism and the large backlog of outstanding commitments for capital goods, a brief inventory adjustment is merely apt to bring a pause to the growth of aggregate economic activity; once this adjustment is completed the economy can resume its advance in spirited fashion.

VI. GATHERING FORCES OF RECESSION

And yet, as history so plainly teaches, a general expansion of economic activity sometimes lasts only a year and rarely lasts more than three or four years. Why does not the process of expansion continue indefinitely? And if the expansion must end, why is it not followed by a high plateau of economic activity instead of a decline? A partial answer to these questions can sometimes be found in disturbances that originate outside the mainstream of the domestic economy—such as political developments that threaten radical changes in property rights, or a drastic cut of military expenditures at the end of a war, or a major crisis abroad. Developments of this nature are entirely capable of cutting short an expansion that otherwise would have continued. However, experience strongly suggests that even in the absence of serious external disturbances the course of aggregate activity will in time be reversed by restrictive forces that gradually but insistently come into play as a result of the expansion process itself.

First, as the expansion continues, the slack in the economy is taken up and reduced. Although improvements of technology and new installations keep adding to the capacity of the nation's workshops, production generally rises still faster; hence, idle or excess capacity diminishes in a growing majority of the nation's businesses. Although the nation's labor force keeps growing, jobs increase faster; hence, unemployment declines. Although the reserves of the banking system may be expanding, bank loans and investments generate deposits at a faster rate; hence, the ratio of reserves to deposits keeps falling. Although producers of metals and other materials and supplies respond to the brisk demand by raising production schedules, they are frequently unable to move quickly enough; hence, deliveries stretch out or become less dependable. The pecuniary expression of the mounting shortages is a general rise of prices —of labor, credit, raw materials, intermediate products, and finished goods; but that is not all. The shortages are real and their physical expression is a narrower scope of the expansion itself. Rising sales by a particular firm or industry still release forces of physical expansion elsewhere, but their effects are blunted since more and more businessmen must now contend with bottlenecks. Once labor is in short supply in a community, an increase of employment by one firm must often result in some reduction of employment elsewhere in the same community. Once this or that material is in short supply, some firms must get along with less than they need or wait longer for deliveries. Once the banking system stops expanding credit or materially reduces its rate of expansion, any new loans to some firms will affect adversely the ability of other firms to get the credit they need. Instances of this sort multiply as the economy moves toward full employment. At some point, therefore, the scope of the expansion stops widening and begins to narrow. Although aggregate activity is still growing, it can no longer maintain its initial rapid pace.

Second, the advance of prosperity tends to raise unit costs of production and therefore threatens profit margins—unless selling prices rise sufficiently. Taking the business system as a whole, much the largest item in costs and one which businessmen watch with the greatest care is labor—more precisely, the cost of labor per unit of output. This cost depends, first, on the hourly wage of labor and, second, on output per man-hour. Both tend to rise as the expansion progresses, but at unequal rates. The price of labor moves sluggishly in the early part of the expansion, but advances of wages tend to become more frequent and larger as competition for labor increases and trade unions take advantage of improved market conditions. Increasing resort to overtime work at premium rates of pay accentuates the rise in the average price of labor, and so too does the faster upgrading of workers. On the other hand, output per man-hour, which improved sharply early in the expansion, tends to increase more gradually as the expansion lengthens, and it may also decline before the expansion is over. To be sure, improvements in organization and technology continue to be made at a thousand points at this as at every stage of the business cycle. However, their effectiveness in raising productivity is offset by developments that increasingly grow out of prosperity—such as a decline in the average quality of newly hired labor, fatigue of both workers and their managers, restlessness among workers and rapid turnover of labor, the need to put some obsolete plants or equipment back into use, the need to operate some highly efficient plants beyond their optimum capacity, and the need or wish to add liberally—once substantial increases of business have occurred—to indirect or overhead types of labor. Thus, as the expansion of aggregate activity continues, increases of productivity tend to diminish or even vanish, while the price of labor not only rises but tends to rise faster than productivity. The result is that unit labor costs of production tend to move up persistently.

Third, the increases of construction costs, equipment prices, and interest rates that are generated by the expansion process gradually become of more serious concern to the investing community. After all, a rise in long-term interest rates tends to reduce the value of existing capital goods at the very time that it raises the carrying charges on new investments. Higher costs of new capital goods likewise serve to raise fixed charges. For a time, optimistic expectations concerning the earnings stream from new investment projects overpower the restraining influence of higher costs of capital goods or of higher interest rates, but they will not do so indefinitely. A firm that expects to earn 20 per cent annually from a new project can overlook a modest rise of construction costs or interest rates, especially when it plans to finance the investment from retained earnings or depreciation reserves. Not all investors, however, are in such a fortunate position. Homebuilders, in particular, are sensitive to a rise of construction and financing costs, partly because their activities are largely financed by borrowing and partly because interest charges are a very considerable fraction of the total cost of operating a dwelling. Experience shows that contracts for residential construction typically turn down before commitments for any other major category of investment. Business orders for machinery and equipment, as well as contracts for new factories, commercial buildings, and public utility plants still keep rising for a time. These types of investment are more responsive to prospective demand than to conditions of supply; but as the expansion of economic activity becomes more intense, they too begin to feel the pressure of rising costs. In deciding to invest in a particular project, a business firm may have given little heed to recent increases in costs. That decision, however, must still be followed by another, namely, whether to get the project under way now or later. Investors know that they will have the new plant or equipment on their hands for a long time and that their annual carrying charges will depend on the cost of the new capital goods, if not also on the rate of interest. They have got along thus far without the desired investment, and they will have to manage in any event without it for some months or years. If, therefore, they expect costs to be appreciably lower a year or so from now, they may well bide their time. Such postponements in placing orders and contracts become more frequent even as business decisions to invest continue to accumulate.

The rise in construction, equipment, and financing costs during an expansion impinges so broadly on the investing class that it would eventually check the investment boom even if prosperity were diffused uniformly over the economic community. However, this is not the case, and the uneven spread of profits is still another major development that impedes the continuance of expansion. At every stage of the business cycle there are bound to be some firms whose profits are declining or whose losses are increasing. But these firms are not a steady fraction of the business population, and there are cogent reasons for expecting their numbers to increase as the expansion of aggregate activity stretches out. To protect profit margins, selling prices must rise sufficiently over the entire range of business enterprise to offset higher unit costs of production. Since business conditions are good, many firms can and do raise prices that much or more. But there are always some firms that find it hard to advance selling prices, and their number tends to grow at an advanced stage of the expansion. In some industries, sales have recently been pushed with such vigor that the markets for their products are approaching saturation at existing prices. In other industries, exaggerated notions concerning the volume of sales that could be made at a good profit have led to overstocking or overbuilding, so that prices come under pressure. Errors of this type occur at all times, but they are likely to be bunched when enthusiasm has infected a large and widening circle of businessmen. In still other cases, business custom, long-term contracts, or governmental regulation make it difficult or inexpedient to raise selling prices. Of course, firms that cannot advance selling prices will try all the harder to resist increases in costs, but such efforts meet with limited success at a time of extensive shortages. With the rise in unit costs of production continuing across the business front, more and more firms therefore find that their profit margins are becoming narrower, thus offsetting the influence on profits of rising sales or reinforcing the influence of declining sales—instances of which now become more numerous. We thus find in experience, as we should expect, that after a business expansion has run for some time, the proportion of firms enjoying rising profits begins to shrink, although profits of business in the aggregate still continue to advance.

These developments—the narrowing scope of expansion as full employment is approached, the rise of unit labor costs, the rise of financing costs, the rising cost of new capital goods, the spread of these cost increases across the economy, and the shrinkage in the proportion of business firms experiencing rising profits—tend gradually to undermine the expansion of investment. Prominent among the first to reduce investment commitments are the firms whose fortunes are waning. Their curtailments spread doubt among businessmen whose profits are still rising, many of whom have also become concerned about prospective profits or have come to feel that construction and financing costs will recede before long from the abnormal level to which they have been pushed by prosperity. These attitudes and responses are likely to be reflected in some weakening of stock exchange prices, which in turn will stir fresh doubts. With investment commitments declining, but actual expenditures still rising, backlogs of unfilled orders for capital goods and of uncompleted contracts for business construction must sooner or later turn down. Meanwhile, uncompleted contracts for residential construction have, in all probability, already been declining for some time. The decline in these several backlogs induces reductions in orders for raw materials and parts, and the reduced pressure on suppliers in turn serves to stabilize, if not lower, prices. Since many of the consumer trades can now also count on faster deliveries, the orders placed with their suppliers are likely to turn down as well. These changes reinforce efforts to adjust inventories that have already been induced at numerous points by the narrower scope of expansion and the reduced rate of growth of aggregate activity. For all these reasons, while inventories on hand still keep rising, investment in inventories begins declining. In view of the smaller backlogs, business expenditures on fixed capital will themselves gradually move to a lower level a little later. Public expenditures may still rise, but they are unlikely to do so on a sufficient scale to offset the declines of private investment. The growth of consumer spending, therefore, is retarded, if it does not actually stop. As these adjustments proceed, the balance between expanding and contracting economic activities tips steadily toward contraction. The need for overtime is much reduced, unemployment begins to rise, aggregate production soon turns down—in short, a business recession gets under way.

VII. THE PROCESS OF CONTRACTION

The course of a typical recession is well known. A decline of production is accompanied by a reduction in the number of jobs, besides a reduced work week for many. The flow of incomes to individuals, therefore, tends to decline, and consumer spending—at least for expensive durable goods—follows suit. Retailers and wholesalers are now more apt to place orders for merchandise that are below the level of their respective sales. Many manufacturers, in their turn, also attempt to reduce their inventories. Taking the economy as a whole, the broad result of these efforts is that production declines more than sales, and that inventory investment not only declines but is soon succeeded by liquidation. Meanwhile, quoted prices of many commodities, especially of raw materials, tend to soften, and discounts or concessions from list prices become more numerous and larger. Wage rates, however, are generally maintained and actually rise here and there. Even when they decline somewhat, unit costs of production still tend to rise, perhaps sharply, because it takes time before overhead costs, including the employment of indirect types of labor, can be adjusted to the lower volume of business. Many firms that are already experiencing lower profit margins therefore find that they must put up with still lower margins, while others first begin to feel the profit squeeze. With sales more often than not also declining, an increasing majority of businesses now experience falling profits, bankruptcies become more frequent, business profits in the aggregate—which probably began shrinking before sales did—decline further, and stock exchange prices extend their fall as well. In view of these developments, many businessmen and consumers, even if they are not actually poorer, become more concerned about the future. New business commitments for investment in fixed capital therefore tend to become less numerous, and—unless forces of recovery soon come into play—investment expenditures of this type as well as outlays on consumer durables will extend their decline, which is as yet modest, and reinforce the contraction process.

As a decline in one sector reacts on another, the economy may begin spiraling downward on a scale that outruns the magnitudes that we ordinarily associate with recession. The likelihood that a depression will develop depends on numerous factors—among them, the scale of speculation during the preceding phase of prosperity, the extent to which credit was permitted to grow, whether or not the quality of credit suffered significant deterioration, whether any major markets became temporarily saturated, how much excess capacity had been created before the recession started, whether and in what degree the balance of international payments has become adverse, the organization of the financial system and its ability to withstand shocks, the shape of political developments, and the aptness and scale of monetary actions and other governmental efforts, if any, to stem the economic decline. If the onset of the contraction is marked by a financial crisis or if one develops somewhat later, there is a substantial probability that the decline of aggregate activity will prove severe and perhaps abnormally long as well. For when businessmen and their bankers begin to scramble for liquidity, both trade credit and bank credit will decline and so too will the money supply; commodity prices at wholesale and retail will slump and wage rates decline, while interest rates for a time rise sharply; confidence will become impaired and many investment projects will be abandoned instead of merely being postponed; business losses and bankruptcies will multiply; more workers will earn less or become totally unemployed; and, since spells of unemployment also lengthen, more and more families will deplete their savings and be forced to reduce their spending drastically. Even if the shift from expansion to contraction is made gradually, untoward disturbances originating outside the economy may still strike with great force and transform a mild contraction into a depression.

VIII. FORCES OF PROGRESS AND RECOVERY

Normally, however, a contraction in aggregate activity does not lead to depression. A contraction is not a mirror image of expansion, as it might well be if the business cycle were merely an oscillation. A contraction does not usually cumulate and feed on itself in the manner of an expansion. Normally, many progressive developments continue, and some even become stronger, during the contraction phase of the business cycle; in other words, the forces making for contraction are powerfully counteracted by forces of growth that limit the degree to which it can cumulate.

What are these forces of growth? First, businessmen and consumers in a modern nation are accustomed to seeking and to expecting economic improvement. This optimistic state of mind generally continues during a contraction, provided its dimensions remain moderate. Investment opportunities, connected with new technology or market strategy, always keep arising in the minds of imaginative and resourceful men. Not a few of these opportunities are acted on promptly in spite of the recession. Second, most people are extremely reluctant to give up the standard of living that they have managed to attain, and in any event they cannot quickly readjust family expenditures. Hence, consumer spending is well maintained in the face of declines of income that are judged to be temporary. Third, the pitch of both interfirm and interindustry competition becomes more intense during a recession. Unlike investment commitments, which are at their highest level before aggregate activity turns down, the bunching of installations of new plant and equipment is likely to be heaviest when the recession is well under way. The newer facilities typically serve new products or permit lower costs of production of old products. Many progressive enterprises are therefore able to extend their markets even when business as a whole is falling off. Firms that suffer from shifts of demand or from an outworn technology may have managed to limp along or even do reasonably well when activity was brisk. Now, finding that competitors are penetrating their markets on a scale that threatens survival, the hard-pressed firms are more likely to move with energy to modernize their plant, acquire new equipment, improve their products, try out new marketing strategies, and eliminate waste. Meanwhile, vigorous businesses whose plants are operating at or close to optimum capacity do not stand still. Not a few of them anticipate a large expansion of sales when the dull season is over, and therefore undertake additions or improvements to their plant and equipment. Fourth, a nation's resources normally continue to grow even during a recession. Since the population is still growing, the stabilizing force of consumption is reinforced. Since the number of business firms is still increasing, the formation of new businesses contributes, although at a reduced rate, to the demand for capital goods. Since the stock of housing, consumer durables, and industrial facilities is still expanding, a large market is assured for repairs, improvements, and replacements, although there is undoubtedly some postponing of this type of expenditure. Fifth, public efforts to promote economic growth and the general welfare are customary in a well-governed nation. These efforts may not always be wise or geared closely to the business cycle, but neither are they confined to times of prosperity. On the contrary, they are more likely to come during recessions —especially in recent times when full employment has become an increasingly firm objective of the public policy of nations.

The progressive forces that operate during recessions serve as a brake on the cumulative process of contraction. True, aggregate activity falls below the level reached at the peak of prosperity. The decline, however, is usually of moderate proportions. Not only that, but sales decline much less in the aggregate than production and the level of sales soon becomes higher than that of production. For a while, the liquidation of inventories proceeds at an increasing rate, but this cannot continue. To handle the volume of business on hand, especially if sales stabilize or decline very gradually, manufacturers and distributors must soon slow down, if not halt, the decline of their inventories. Taking the economic system as a whole, once inventory disinvestment declines more rapidly than the decline of sales, production must begin rising. Of course, a recovery of production will be preceded by an increase of orders, and an early upturn of orders is precisely what occurs when dealers and manufacturers take steps to slow down appreciably the decline of their inventories.

While business firms keep bringing inventories into better alignment with their sales, other developments that grow out of the recession also favor an early recovery. Since the reserves of commercial banks tend to pile up again, reserve ratios improve. Hence, interest rates decline and credit becomes more readily available. The effects of easy credit are likely to be felt most promptly by smaller businesses and the home-building industry, but they tend to ramify as banks put their reserves to use. When the demand for loans is still deficient, banks seek out customers energetically. At the same time, they augment their investments in bonds, thereby strengthening the bond market and stimulating a renewed interest in preferred stocks and gilt-edged common stocks. Meanwhile, numerous readjustments in the nation's workshops serve to lower unit costs of production. In view of the decline of aggregate demand, wage rates often stop rising and sometimes decline a little, overtime operations become less frequent, not a few of the less efficient enterprises go out of business, production is increasingly concentrated in the most modern plants and on the best equipment, many of the less efficient workers are let go, the ranks of the overhead types of labor are thinned here and there, and workers generally become more attentive to their duties. These changes reinforce the improvements of organization and technology which always occur in a progressive economy and which are often speeded up during a recession, in response to the keener competition that develops at such a time. Of course, the beneficial changes in the costs of production of individual businesses are frequently offset or nullified by declining selling prices. However, once the adjustments of inventories have made good headway, commodity prices tend to stabilize. Hence, more and more firms are apt to find that their profit margins begin improving. With the prospect of profits brightening, interest rates declining, and costs of capital goods lower, some of the numerous investment projects that had previously been postponed are now revived and they supplement the new crop of active projects. As these developments become stronger, the decline of investment commitments ceases, new firms are established in larger numbers, orders and contracts for investment goods turn up, inventory disinvestment continues to ebb, and a recovery of aggregate production and employment soon gets under way.

Thus, corrective forces released by the recession combine with the more persistent forces of growth to bring the contraction of aggregate activity to a halt. Typically, the process works fairly speedily and the contraction is over in about a year or a year and a half. However, as previously noted, a contraction sometimes develops into a spiraling depression. When that happens, declining investment in fixed capital supplants inventory disinvestment as the principal drag on the economy. Worse still, the stubborn human trait of optimism begins to give way, so that a mere readjustment of inventories may bring only an abortive recovery. Once many men begin to lose faith in themselves or in the institutions of their society, full recovery may need to wait on substantial innovations or an actual reduction in the stock of fixed capital, unless powerful external influences come into play—such as a reorganization of the monetary system, massive governmental expenditures, or a sudden increase of exports on account of foreign developments. Fortunately, no industrial country has suffered a spiraling depression since World War II, and the likelihood of such a development—as will be noted later—has been greatly reduced.

IX.   DIFFERENCES AMONG BUSINESS CYCLES

The preceding sketch of the nature and causes of business cycles has stressed typical behavior. Yet no business cycle of actual experience corresponds precisely to our sketch, and some cycles bear only a faint resemblance to it. What history discloses is a succession of business cycles that differ considerably in length, in the intensity of their phases, in the industrial and financial developments that gain prominence during their course, and in their geographic scope. In American experience, for example, while expansions have normally run longer than contractions, there is no peacetime expansion on record before 1960 that lasted as long as the decline from 1873 to 1879. Industrial production has typically fluctuated over a wider range than industrial prices, but the opposite is true of several business cycles associated with wars. Interest rates have commonly risen during expansions of aggregate activity, but they continued to decline during almost the entire expansion from 1933 to 1937. Broad indexes of wholesale prices have generally declined during contractions of activity, but they failed to do so during the recession of 1890–91 or 1957–58. Contracts and orders for investment goods have typically moved up before total production or employment in the recovery process, but they did not do so at the upturns of 1914 or 1933. Declining stock prices have frequently signaled the approach of a recession, but the stock market crash of 1929 came after aggregate activity had already turned down. Some economic declines, such as those of 1887–88 and 1926–27, were merely pauses in the growth of the domestic economy. Others, such as the depression of 1920–21, attained international scope, while the depression of the 1930's became a world-wide upheaval of catastrophic proportions.

In view of these and countless other variations among business cycles, the causes of any particular cycle are always in some degree peculiar to it. One prolific source of cyclical variation in the United States, as elsewhere, is found in the behavior of money, foreign trade, and the balance of payments. For example, good harvests in 1879, when crops abroad were poor, stimulated large exports of grain at favorable prices, thereby improving farmers' incomes, enlarging the business of shippers, inducing an inflow of gold, and otherwise speeding economic recovery. In 1891 and 1892, fear that political agitation for free silver would result in abandonment of the gold standard led to domestic hoarding of gold, to massive gold shipments abroad, and finally to a financial crisis in the spring of 1893. The expansion of 1891–93, therefore, developed nothing like the vigor suggested by our account of the cumulative process of expansion. The outbreak of war in Europe in 1914 soon caused a sharp upsurge in American exports, thereby checking a contraction in aggregate activity that otherwise might have dragged on. To cite one more illustration, the expansion of 1958–60 proved incomplete, in large part because of the restrictive monetary and fiscal policies that were undertaken by the government to curb inflationary pressures and to prevent further deterioration in the balance of international payments.

Business-cycle movements often spread from one country to another and sometimes engulf almost the whole world economy. Foreign trade, commodity prices, stock prices, and interest rates play a vital role in this process of transmission, both directly and through their influence on business psychology. The economies of most commercial nations are far more closely tied to the course of foreign trade and investment than is the economy of the United States. In view of the large role of foreign trade in small countries like the Netherlands or Norway, conditions abroad can have a decisive influence on domestic prosperity. Even in a larger country like Great Britain, an improvement of exports has not infrequently been the immediate cause of economic recovery. However, as the economic activity of a nation expands, its imports also tend to rise, partly because of a larger need for foreign raw materials and partly because of larger purchases abroad of equipment and consumer products. Meanwhile, since domestic markets keep improving, some firms find it more profitable or more convenient to cultivate home trade than to push exports. If, in response to the upswing of activity, domestic costs and prices advance more rapidly than prices charged by foreign enterprises, exports will probably suffer and monetary reserves—whether of gold or foreign currencies—will tend to diminish. A restriction of credit often follows, because under a regime of stable exchange rates the state of a country's balance of payments and the size of its monetary reserves and borrowing facilities may leave little room for an independent financial policy. This pattern of developments has become familiar to the nations of western Europe and to Japan.

Many nations of Latin America, Asia, and Africa derive their foreign exchange mainly from the export of one or at most a few raw materials, supplemented by investments made in these countries by foreigners or, perhaps, by gifts from abroad. But the prices of internationally traded raw materials tend to fluctuate widely, in part because of variations in the state of demand in the industrial countries. These price fluctuations often have a critical bearing on the ability of the raw material producing nations to acquire from abroad the capital goods and supplies needed to develop their economies.

Not only are the economies of different nations tied together, but as various theories of long waves or major cycles have sought to suggest, no business-cycle movement can be understood solely in terms of what happened during that phase or the one just preceding it. Thus, the American contractions of 1923–24 and 1926–27 were merely minor interruptions of a great onrush of economic activity from 1921 to 1929. The period began with a rapid increase of production, was followed by a stretch of slower growth, and ended on a note of reacceleration. Financial activities followed a different and more hectic course. Emerging as an international creditor after the war, the United States played its new role with exuberance. Through 1924 the volume of foreign loans was substantial, yet the loans were on the whole of sound quality—as attested by later experience. The next few years witnessed a further expansion of foreign loans and a sharp deterioration of their quality. The speculative craze expressed itself also in other financial areas, notably in the real estate market and superlatively in the stock market. Consumer credit shared in the general upsurge and made possible a huge expansion in the output of durable consumer goods during the 1920's, not only absolutely but also relative to total output, thus adding a new hazard to economic stability. The financial situation was also made vulnerable by the great pyramiding of international credits that developed under the gold exchange standard. Governmental policies in the United States after 1929, which brought on tax increases and—worse still—tolerated the destruction of a third of the nation's money supply, cannot escape a very large part of the responsibility for the Great

Depression; but neither financial developments abroad nor the course of policy, private and public, in the decade prior to the depression can go blameless.

X. PROGRESS TOWARD ECONOMIC STABILITY

Besides such differences among business cycles as we have noted, which largely reflect episodic influences, there are other differences of a more persistent kind. Just as the business cycle itself emerged gradually in the course of economic evolution, so many of its features have undergone changes as the economy has continued to evolve.

The structure of a nation's economy and its institutions inevitably leave their stamp on the character of its cyclical fluctuations. Thus, after the introduction of the Federal Reserve System, the fluctuations of short-term interest rates in the United States became narrower, while the lag of long-term interest rates during recoveries and recessions became shorter and of late has virtually vanished. With the growth of trade unions and increasing resort to long-term labor contracts, wage rates have become less responsive to cyclical contractions of activity. More important still, the precise relations among the movements of production, employment, and personal income have kept changing as the structure of the American economy and its institutions have evolved. During the early decades of the nineteenth century, when agriculture was the dominant occupation, occasional declines in the nation's total volume of production, whether large or small, had little effect on the number of jobs and sometimes had slight influence even on the flow of money incomes. Later, as wage jobs gained rapidly in importance, the movements of employment and personal income fell into step with production. In recent times, however,

numerous changes in the structure of the American economy
have served powerfully to reduce the impact of a cyclical decline of production on the lives and fortunes of individuals.

Important among these changes is the vast expansion of
government, the greatly increased role of the income tax in
public revenues, the shift of income tax collection to a pay-as-
you-go basis, the rapid growth of unemployment insurance
and other programs of social security, the growing frequency
and scale of private pensions, the spread of business corporations, and their increasing pursuit of stable dividend policies.
As a result of these and related developments, the movement
of personal income is no longer closely linked to the fluctuations of production. For example, in the course of the recession
of 1957–58, the physical volume of industrial production fell
14 per cent and of total production nearly 5 per cent. In the
early decades of this century, aggregate personal income
would have responded decisively to such a decline in production. This time government receipts and expenditures offset the
drop in the flow of income from production, first, because
much less was collected in taxes from corporations and individuals, second, because the amount of unemployment insurance and other social security payments rose. Corporations in
turn reacted to the decline in profits by reducing their savings
rather than the flow of dividends or pensions to individuals. In
the end, the aggregate of personal incomes, whether before or
after taxes, declined less than 1 per cent, and in the case of
after-tax incomes even this decline was over before the recession ended.

Major structural changes have also occurred in the sphere of
employment. Manufacturing, mining, construction, and freight
transportation are the cyclically volatile industries; but their
relative importance as providers of jobs has been gradually declining in recent decades, while that of the more stable service

industries has been increasing. In addition, the proportion of people who work as managers, engineers, scientists, accountants, secretaries, salesmen, or in kindred "white-collar" occupations has been steadily rising. Much of this type of employment is of an overhead character and therefore less responsive to the business cycle than are the jobs of machine operators, craftsmen, truck drivers, laborers, and others in the "blue-collar" category. It appears, therefore, that changes in the structure of the labor force have of late been loosening the links which, over a considerable part of economic history, tied the short-run movements of total employment in the United States rather firmly to the movements of production. We can no longer suppose, moreover, when employment falls during a recession, that there will be a corresponding decline in the number of people receiving an income. On the contrary, as a result of the widening sweep of social security programs, the number of income recipients actually increased during each recession of the postwar period.

These developments have left an imprint on the behavior of consumer spending in recent business cycles. First, consumers have maintained their spending at a high level even after business activity had been declining for some months, so that the cumulative process of contraction has been curbed. Second, retail trade has tended to turn up before production or employment, instead of lagging during the recovery stage as it did in earlier times. Thus, consumer spending has emerged as one of the active factors in arresting recession and hastening recovery. Of course, if the fluctuations of production had been larger in the postwar period, the impact of recessions on the lives of working people would have been greater. On the other hand, the more stable behavior of personal income and consumption has itself been a major reason why recent contractions of activity have been brief and of only moderate intensity.

Many other factors have contributed to this result. The need to overhaul the financial system became clear during the 1930's and led to numerous reforms, among them the development of the long-term amortized mortgage, the regulation of stock exchanges, the insurance of mortgages, the creation of a secondary market for mortgages, the insurance of savings and loan accounts, and—most important of all—the insurance of bank deposits. These financial reforms have served to prevent crises or the propagation of fear. Even more basic has been the change in political attitudes that emerged during the 1930's and which the Congress later articulated in the Employment Act of 1946. It is now generally agreed that mass unemployment is intolerable under modern conditions and that the federal government has a continuing responsibility to promote a high and rising level of employment and production. In recent times, therefore, the business cycle has no longer run a free course, and this fact has figured prominently in the plans of businessmen as well as consumers. The general expectation of the postwar period has been that the government would move with some vigor to check any recession that developed, and that its monetary, fiscal, and regulatory actions would contribute to that objective. By and large, this confidence has been justified by events. Not only has monetary policy in the main been shaped with a view to promoting stable prosperity, but fiscal policy—which previously had been handicapped by the convention of annually balanced budgets—has lately also been guided by the state of the economy. Business firms too have been paying closer attention to the business cycle. There is evidence, in particular, that inventories are being better managed and that this is helping to moderate the cyclical swings in production. On the other hand, governmental policies have often served to intensify inflationary expectations or pressures, and this has become a recurring problem.

The nations of western Europe have also experienced structural changes in the postwar period that, on balance, have worked in a stabilizing direction. White-collar occupations have gained in importance, and so too have systems of social security and of tax collection on a pay-as-you-go basis. Some countries, especially Sweden, achieved notable success with contracyclical policies well before the United States. Of late, all of western Europe has been striving energetically and ingeniously to promote economic expansion and full employment, and these efforts have been attended by great success. Even before World War II, the business cycle was a milder type of fluctuation in western Europe than in the United States, and the difference has persisted in the postwar period. Indeed, the main problem facing European nations in recent years has not been unemployment but rather the difficulties caused by inflation and balance-of-payments disequilibria. Japan has also been struggling with this problem.

It would, nevertheless, be premature to conclude that the older hazards of the business cycle belong to the past. True, the business cycle has become milder as a result of a favorable conjuncture of structural changes and of both better and wider understanding of the requirements of business-cycle policy. Certainly, there is increasing recognition of the desirability of preventing recessions, rather than merely acting to moderate them once they occur. However, the forces that tend to generate cyclical movements have not vanished in western Europe or Japan any more than in the United States. It is possible that in the future a "recession" will mean merely a reduced rate of growth of aggregate activity instead of an actual and sustained decline, but there is as yet insufficient ground for believing that economic developments will generally conform to this model in the near future. Hence, the wise course for economists is to continue basic research on the nature and causes of business cycles, to remain watchful of developments that seem likely to bring on a slump in activity, and to extend the search for acceptable pathways to prosperity without inflation.

BIBLIOGRAPHY

ABRAMOVITZ, MOSES 1950 *Inventories and Business Cycles, With Special Reference to Manufacturers' Inventories.* New York: National Bureau of Economic Research.

AFTALION, ALBERT 1913 *Les crises périodiques de surproduction.* 2 vols. Paris: Rivière. Volume 1: *Les variations périodiques des prix et des revenus: Les théories dominantes.* Volume 2: *Les mouvements périodiques de la production: Essai d'une théorie.*

AMERICAN ECONOMIC ASSOCIATION 1944 *Readings in Business Cycle Theory.* Edited by Gottfried Haberler et al. Philadelphia: Blakiston. Includes an article by Kondratieff. A bibliography appears on pages 443–487.

AMERICAN ECONOMIC ASSOCIATION 1965 *Readings in Business Cycles.* Edited by Robert A. Gordon and Lawrence R. Klein. Homewood, Ill.: Irwin.

BURNS, ARTHUR F. 1954 *The Frontiers of Economic Knowledge: Essays.* Published for the National Bureau of Economic Research. Princeton Univ. Press.

BURNS, ARTHUR F.; and MITCHELL, WESLEY C. 1946 *Measuring Business Cycles.* New York: National Bureau of Economic Research.

CLARK, JOHN J.; and COHEN, MORRIS (editors) 1963 *Business Fluctuations, Growth and Economic Stabilization: A Reader.* New York: Random House. A bibliography appears on pages 623–669.

FRIEDMAN, MILTON; and SCHWARTZ, ANNA J. 1963 *A Monetary History of the United States: 1867–1960.* National Bureau of Economic Research, Studies in Business Cycles, No. 12. Princeton Univ. Press.

HABERLER, GOTTFRIED (1937) 1958 *Prosperity and Depression: A Theoretical Analysis of Cyclical Movements.* 4th ed., rev. & enl. Harvard Economic Studies, Vol. 105. Cambridge, Mass.: Harvard Univ. Press; London: Allen & Unwin.

HANSEN, ALVIN H.   (1951) 1964   *Business Cycles and National Income.* Enl. ed. New York: Norton. A bibliography appears on pages 699–710.

HICKS, JOHN R.   (1950) 1956   *A Contribution to the Theory of the Trade Cycle.* Oxford: Clarendon.

JOHNS HOPKINS UNIVERSITY, DEPARTMENT OF POLITICAL ECONOMY 1957   Business Fluctuations. *Economic Library Selections,* Series 2, No. 4.

JUGLAR, CLÉMENT   (1862) 1889   *Des crises commerciales et de leur retour périodique en France, en Angleterre et aux États-Unis.* 2d ed. Paris: Guillaumin. Partially translated as *A Brief History of Panics and Their Periodical Occurrence in the United States;* published by Putnam in 1916.

KEYNES, JOHN MAYNARD   1936   *The General Theory of Employment, Interest and Money.* London: Macmillan. A paperback edition was published in 1965 by Harcourt.

KUZNETS, SIMON   1961   *Capital in the American Economy: Its Formation and Financing.* National Bureau of Economic Research, Studies in Capital Formation and Financing, No. 9. Princeton Univ. Press. See especially pages 316–388.

MITCHELL, WESLEY C.   1913   *Business Cycles.* Berkeley: Univ. of California Press. Part 3 was reprinted by the University of California Press in 1959 as *Business Cycles and Their Causes.*

MITCHELL, WESLEY C.   1927   *Business Cycles: The Problem and Its Setting.* New York: National Bureau of Economic Research.

MOORE, GEOFFREY H. (editor)   1961   *Business Cycle Indicators.* 2 vols. National Bureau of Economic Research, Studies in Business Cycles, No. 10. Princeton Univ. Press. See Volume 1, pages 736–744, for a list of business-cycle reports by the National Bureau of Economic Research, which has led for many years in this field of study.

PERSONS, WARREN M.   1919   Indices of Business Conditions. *Review of Economics and Statistics,* 1:5–107.

PIGOU, ARTHUR C.   (1927) 1929   *Industrial Fluctuations.* 2d ed. London: Macmillan.

ROBERTSON, DENNIS H.   (1915) 1948   *A Study of Industrial Fluctuations.* London School of Economics and Political Science Series of Reprints of Scarce Works on Political Economy, No. 8. London: Aldwych.

SCHUMPETER, JOSEPH A. 1939 *Business Cycles: A Theoretical, Historical, and Statistical Analysis of the Capitalist Process.* 2 vols. New York and London: McGraw-Hill. An abridged version was published in 1964.

THORP, WILLARD L. 1926 *Business Annals.* New York: National Bureau of Economic Research.

TINBERGEN, JAN 1938–1939 *Statistical Testing of Business-Cycle Theories.* 2 vols. Geneva: League of Nations, Economic Intelligence Service. Volume 1: *A Method and Its Application to Investment Activity.* Volume 2: *Business Cycles in the United States of America: 1919–1932.*

TUGAN-BARANOVSKII, MIKHAIL I. (1894) 1913 *Les crises industrielles en Angleterre.* 2d ed. Paris: Giard & Brière. First published as *Promyshlennye krizisy v sovremennoi Anglii, ikh prichiny i vliianie na narodnuiu zhizn'.*

UNIVERSITIES–NATIONAL BUREAU COMMITTEE FOR ECONOMIC RESEARCH 1956 *Policies to Combat Depression.* Princeton Univ. Press. A report of the National Bureau of Economic Research, Special Conference Series, No. 7.

WICKSELL, KNUT (1898) 1936 *Interest and Prices: A Study of the Causes Regulating the Value of Money.* London: Macmillan. First published as *Geldzins und Güterpreise.*

TWO

New Facts on Business Cycles

I. THE NEED FOR SCIENTIFIC WORK

DESPITE the relatively good business conditions of
recent years, the business cycle continues to haunt the thinking
of the American people. The reason is not only a wish to oblit-
erate the human miseries and material wastes of recurring
depressions. The reason is also political necessity. The old
Marxist dogma that capitalism is doomed to collapse on the
rocks of economic crisis has become a weapon of propaganda,
used adroitly and energetically to confuse the uninformed and
to stir discontent the world over. Our government and other
democracies have met the challenge by building a variety of
defenses against depression. How well the defenses have been
built, no one yet knows. The business decline which started in
the fall of 1948 has fortunately been checked, and some credit
for this achievement can be assigned to governmental policy.
But it is easy to exaggerate the influence of government on the
course of events. An outstanding feature of the business situation during 1949 was the high and rising activity in the auto-

Originally published in *Thirtieth Annual Report of the National Bureau
of Economic Research* (May 1950), pp. 3–31. Reprinted here from *Business Cycle Indicators*, G. H. Moore (ed.), Princeton University Press,
1961, Vol. I.

mobile and housing industries, which continued to feel the stimulus of war-induced shortages. Had these industries faced "normal" markets, it seems fairly certain that the contraction in business would have gone deeper. For the present, obituaries on the business cycle are romantic expressions of human impatience, not records of solid achievement. They serve neither the nation nor economics, and may prove seriously harmful if they lead to any relaxation of the scientific work on business fluctuations now going forward in universities and other research centers.

The National Bureau's research on business cycles began nearly thirty years ago. Our first publication on national income was already concerned with its fluctuations, and later studies have added materially to a growing body of knowledge about business cycles. But only a relatively small part of the results reached by the Bureau's investigation has as yet been published. Scientific work flourishes best when investigators are free to permit their researches to mature, and this inevitably means a modest and highly uneven rate of publication. The current year, however, is one of plenty. Among the works on business cycles soon to be published is Wesley Mitchell's unfinished book *What Happens during Business Cycles,* which is remarkably complete as far as it goes. The list includes also Moses Abramovitz' scholarly volume *Inventories and Business Cycles* and three substantial Occasional Papers: *Behavior of Wage Rates during Business Cycles* by Daniel Creamer, *Cyclical Diversities in the Fortunes of Industrial Corporations* by Thor Hultgren, and *Statistical Indicators of Cyclical Revivals and Recessions* by Geoffrey H. Moore.

I feel prompted by this upsurge of publications to give some account of the National Bureau's work on business cycles. I cannot attempt to summarize either the research in process or the completed studies. Instead, I shall describe a few facts developed by our investigation that may prove of some help to economists and men of affairs facing the hard task of appraising an uncertain future. What I shall say is based largely on American experience before World War II—a period to which all students must turn when they seek to form a considered judgment of how our business economy functions under peacetime conditions.

II. DISPERSION OF SPECIFIC CYCLES

Economic activities generally move in cycles—that is, wavelike fluctuations lasting from about two to ten years. "Specific cycles" of this character appear in prices as well as output, in markets for securities as well as commodities, in the spending of incomes as well as saving, in the flow of goods to consumers as well as business enterprises. Of the hundreds of time series analyzed by the National Bureau, all but about 3 per cent have continuously undergone cyclical movements. The occasional exceptions include steady series like railroad commutation traffic, extremely volatile series like net gold movements between the United States and Great Britain, and series of "list" prices that sometimes remain unchanged for a decade or longer and then rise or fall by a vertical step.

These exceptional series are excluded from Chart 2.1; also all annual series, and such of the monthly or quarterly reports as cover merely a small part of the period between the two wars. Otherwise, the chart includes virtually all the American series that we have analyzed. They encompass a wide range of activities—producing commodities, merchandising, employment, disbursing incomes, commodity pricing, wages, interest rates, security transactions, inventory holdings, and the behavior of the banking system. Most series summarize some activity in the nation at large—for example, production of coal or sales by department stores—but a considerable number are of narrower geographic scope. The precise list varies somewhat from one stretch of the interwar period to another; in most years the total number runs between six and seven hundred.

The chart sets forth the distribution, month by month, of the cyclical turns of this large and varied collection of time series. If anyone is so naive as to believe that most economic activities reach like turns on the same or almost the same month, this

CHART 2.1. Distribution of Turning Points of Specific Cycles in a Sample of over 600 Economic Time Series, 1919–39

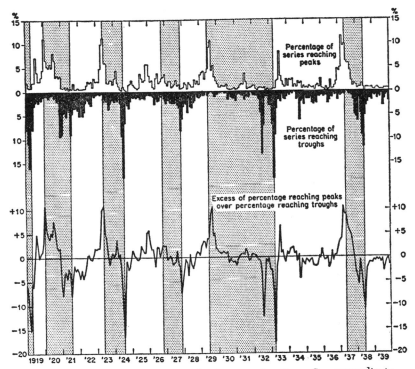

NOTE: Shaded areas represent business contractions. See appendix to this chapter.

chart should disabuse him. What it shows is wide dispersion of cyclical peaks and troughs. Practically every month some series attain peaks while others reach troughs. The occasional gaps on the chart, it may be justly supposed, would be closed if our collection of time series were still more comprehensive.

From the wide dispersion of the specific turning points, a simple but important implication may at once be drawn. If in a given month or quarter some activities are at a peak, they must have been undergoing cyclical expansion in immediately preceding months. If in the same month or quarter other activities are at a trough, they must have been undergoing cyclical contraction in immediately preceding months. Since in each month or quarter some activities attain cyclical peaks while others drop to troughs, it follows that expansions have run side by side with contractions all the time. This persistent feature of economic change is brought out vividly by Chart 2.2, which is simply an arithmetical transformation of the frequencies of peaks and troughs displayed on the preceding chart. Curve A shows the percentage of series undergoing expansion each month from 1919 to 1939, and curve B shows the excess of the percentage expanding over the percentage contracting. The percentages in curve A fluctuate over a wide range but never reach 100 or 0.

This picture of the diffusion of cyclical movements over our economic system would be very different if the cycles in individual activities followed the same temporal course. In that event curve A would be a step-line, with ordinates of 100 for a stretch of months or years, succeeded by values of 0 for another stretch, then values of 100 again, and so on. With everything rising and falling in unison, there would be little need to fuss with specific factors in business, and one might center attention exclusively on aggregate activity. But business cycles— that is, the cycles in aggregate activity encountered in histori-

CHART 2.2. Percentage of Series Undergoing Cyclical Expansion and Their Cumulative, 1919–39, Based on Sample of over 600 Economic Time Series

A Percentage of series undergoing cyclical expansion
B Excess of percentage of series undergoing cyclical expansion over percentage undergoing contraction
C Cumulative of B

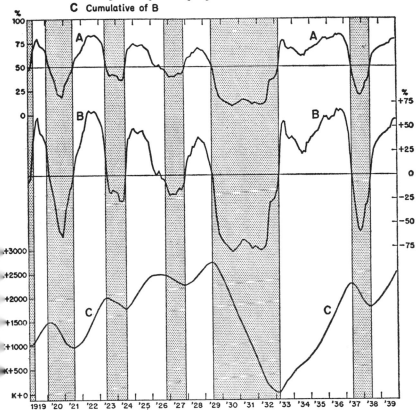

NOTE: Shaded areas represent business contractions. Origin of vertical scale of C is arbitrary, since K is any constant. See appendix to this chapter.

cal experience—are of a very different character. They are marked by expansions and contractions that are only partially diffused through the economy, and it is therefore of the utmost importance to obtain as clear a notion as we can of how the specific cycles of different activities are tied together.[1]

III. THE BUSINESS CYCLE AS A CONSENSUS OF SPECIFIC CYCLES

We have already taken one step in this direction by registering, month by month, the frequency with which specific peaks and troughs are reached, and then combining the frequencies so as to show the percentage of series expanding each month. Let us now carry this process of combination a step further. Assume that a series rises or falls each month by one unit. If, therefore, aggregate activity encompassed 100 items, of which eighty rose in a given month and twenty fell, the total rise during the month would be sixty units. If next month eighty-five rose and fifteen fell, the total rise would be seventy units. By starting with a base figure and cumulating the net percentage of rising series—that is, the excess of the proportion rising over the proportion falling—we should get a schematic picture of the movements in aggregate activity itself. Curve C in Chart 2.2 has been constructed on this principle. It traces out five remarkably clear cycles, which idealize the fluctuations in several familiar indicators of aggregate economic activity—industrial production, factory employment, and

---

[1] For further analysis along the lines of this and the next section, see the following publications by the National Bureau: A. F. Burns and W. C. Mitchell, *Measuring Business Cycles*, Chapter 4, section II; *Twenty-sixth Annual Report*, pp. 22–24; Mitchell's *What Happens during Business Cycles: A Progress Report*, Chapter 5; and especially Geoffrey Moore's *Statistical Indicators of Cyclical Revivals and Recessions* (Occasional Paper 31).

railroad car loadings—plotted on the next chart. Not only that, but the chronology of turning points in curve C is nearly identical with the chronology of business cycles previously determined by the National Bureau.

Curve C is, of course, no better than its antecedents. It shows the net effect of the temporal distribution of the cyclical turns in our sample of series, and it shows nothing else. It is a highly artificial aggregate which abstracts from every other feature of its components. That is why its cycles are so clear and smooth, in contrast to the jagged fluctuation of most economic time series. It is significant, nevertheless, that this simple construct has enabled us to reproduce rather faithfully the familiar movements of recent business cycle history. For if "business cycles" can be built up, so to speak, from a mere knowledge of turning points of individual activities, the path to a scientific understanding of business cycles may be considerably shortened by concentrating on the timing relations among specific cycles.

We have seen in Chart 2.1 that the turning points of specific cycles are so widely scattered that expansions in some activities always accompany contractions in others. But the turning points are not distributed at random through time. If they were, sustained fluctuations such as have occurred in aggregate activity would be highly unlikely. The turns of the specific cycles come in clusters which have, as a rule, definite points of concentration. When the peaks are bunched the troughs are few, and vice versa. The bunching is brought out best in Chart 2.1 by the excess each month of peaks over troughs, which—except for occasional stray items—is continuously of the same sign for numerous months. But the proportion of advancing series must decline when peaks exceed troughs, and rise when troughs exceed peaks. Hence the bunching of cyclical turns is reflected in protracted periods when a majority of series undergo expansion, followed by protracted periods when a majority undergo contraction.

Charts 2.2 and 2.3 add the vital fact that each period in which expansion has been dominant matches closely the upward phase of aggregate economic activity, and each period in which contraction has been dominant matches closely the downward phase; in other words, the succession in time of expanding and contracting majorities is much the same as the succession of expansions and contractions of business cycles. Hence, as Wesley Mitchell observes in his book, "business cycles consist not only of roughly synchronous expansions in many activities, followed by roughly synchronous contractions . . . ; they consist also of numerous contractions while expansion is dominant, and numerous expansions while contraction is dominant." And just as the succession of a majority of individual expansions by a majority of individual contractions, or vice versa, has been accomplished in periods lasting from about two to eight years during the interwar era, so the cycles in aggregate activity have had this order of duration.

The substitution of one of these majorities for the other takes place gradually, and indeed follows a definite cyclical course as Chart 2.2 demonstrates. Rising series are only a thin majority at the beginning of a business cycle expansion. Their number swells as aggregate activity increases, though expansion reaches its widest scope not when aggregate activity is at a peak, but perhaps six months or a year earlier. In the neighborhood of the peak, crosscurrents are the outstanding feature of the business situation. Once the economy is on the downgrade, the number of expanding activities becomes smaller and smaller, though the scope of expansion does not shrink indefinitely. Perhaps six months or a year before the aggregate reaches a trough, the proportion of contracting activities is already at a maximum; thereafter the majority of contracting ac-

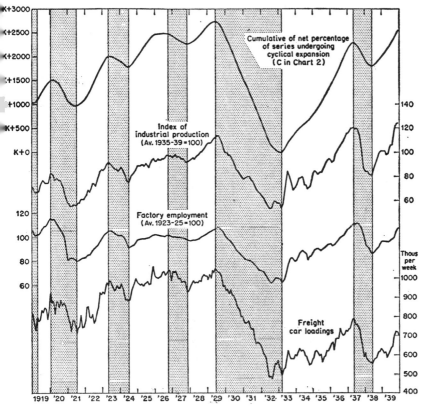

NOTE: Shaded areas represent business contractions. Origin of vertical scale of top curve is arbitrary, since K is any constant. Top curve is a simple aggregate of specific cycles, as explained in the appendix to this chapter.

tivities dwindles, while the minority of expanding activities becomes ever stronger and before long becomes the ruling majority.

Thus a continual transformation of the economic system occurs beneath the surface phenomena of aggregate expansion and contraction. A business cycle expansion does not mean that nearly everything within the economy is moving upward, nor does a business cycle contraction mean that nearly everything is shrinking. There are two cycles in economic activity, not one. First, there is the cycle of sustained expansions and contractions in the aggregate itself. Second, there is the cycle in the distribution of expansions and contractions within the aggregate. The first cycle is "seen" since we are accustomed to following comprehensive records of business conditions. The second cycle is "unseen" since few of us subject the components of comprehensive aggregates to close examination. An "unseen" cycle in the relative distribution of expansions and contractions of specific activities corresponds to each "seen" cycle of their aggregate. But whereas the proportion of expanding activities moves in the same direction as the aggregate in the early stages of a business cycle expansion or contraction, it moves in the opposite direction in later stages. The proportion of expanding activities is already declining months before aggregate activity reaches a peak, and is already rising months before the aggregate reaches its trough.

Further evidence on these basic propositions is supplied by Charts 2.4 and 2.5. The first of these charts compares two fairly homogeneous groups of series—production and employment—with our all-inclusive sample. The next chart comes from Geoffrey Moore's Occasional Paper 31, cited above. It is based on a mass of series selected on account of their rather regular conformity to business cycles. Like Chart 2.1, it includes widely different activities, but spans more than half a century

CHART 2.4. Percentage of Series Undergoing Cyclical Expansion, Three Groups of Series, 1919–39

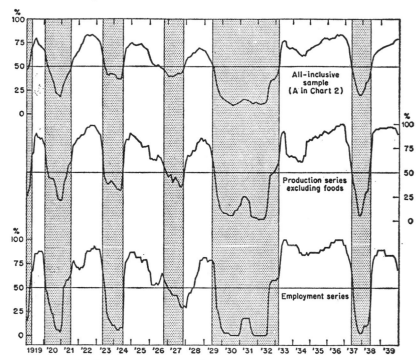

NOTE: Shaded areas represent business contractions. See appendix to this chapter.

instead of a mere two decades. It appears from these exhibits that the features of business cycles I have emphasized—the variety of cyclical movements in individual activities, their tendency toward a consensus, and an inner cycle in the distribution of expanding and contracting activities within the external cycle of aggregate activity proper—cannot be ascribed to any special characteristics of the interwar period or to the heterogeneity of our full sample of series or the fuzziness of

CHART 2.5. Percentage of Series Undergoing Cyclical Expansion, Moore's Sample of Well-Conforming Series, 1885–1939

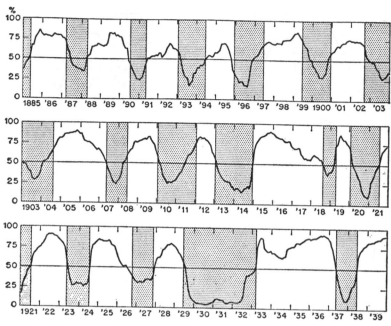

NOTE: Shaded areas represent business contractions. See appendix to this chapter.

their aggregate, but must be reckoned as underlying properties of over-all aggregates of economic activity however defined.

IV. WHY BUSINESS FLUCTUATIONS SPREAD UNEVENLY

Before presenting more statistical results, it may be well to pause and consider the reasonableness of the picture of business cycles thus far developed. Let us suppose that economic activity, having recently moved at a depressed level, is jarred out of its routine by a moderate increase in "spending." The additional spending might be by business firms, governments, or consumers within the nation, or it might originate outside the domestic economy. For simplicity let it be assumed that domestic consumers, as a class, enlarge their spending, that they do so at a time when their income is unchanged, and that technological changes do not occur in the sequel. What, then, will be the likely consequences of this "autonomous" increase in spending?

It is plain that in the very short run the direct effects will dominate, and that they will depend upon the direction of the new outlay. If the spending is on railroad travel, theatrical performances, or the like, involving merely the use of some idle capacity, there will be an immediate increase in incomes, but both the number of men employed and their average workweek are likely to remain unchanged. If the spending is on personal services of barbers or lawyers, the number of man-hours worked is sure to increase at once and with it the national income, but not necessarily the number of men employed. If the spending is on imported commodities there will not be any immediate increase in domestic employment. So it may be also if the spending is on domestic commodities carried in stock; for dealers or manufacturers may not see fit or be unable to replenish their inventories. If the spending is on goods made to order employment is likely to rise, though that will not happen if the jobs generated in any short period by the new spending are insufficient to offset the decline in work on projects started in earlier periods. Even blinking this complication, it is useful to distinguish between additional spending on custom-made articles such as furniture, which may merely lengthen the workweek in existing shops, and increased spending on new dwellings, which is practically sure to augment the numbers employed.

The preceding remarks may be generalized. Whether the consuming public or some other group is responsible for the increase in spending, as long as we look merely at what happens in the very short run we should expect spotty reactions through the economy, not over-all expansion. The impact of the new spending will be uneven, perhaps only a small minority of firms benefiting from it. Each firm has its own peculiar heritage of circumstances—size and condition of plant, goods on hand, work in process, liquid assets, outstanding contracts, customers' good will, labor relations, managerial skills. Hence different enterprises will appraise differently whatever expansion in sales they experience; those making fairly similar appraisals will still respond differently, and those who happen to respond in much the same way will not always achieve similar results. Indeed, we could not even be confident that the total number of men and women at work will increase in the circumstances envisaged, unless two conditions are met: first, that the new "spending" is on goods made to specification in new "shops" set up for the purpose; second, that purchases of this type ceased their decline some months back and are now at a stable level.

New construction meets adequately the first condition, and if we suppose that the second is also met, we can speak more definitely of the outcome. Practically all construction projects are built to fresh specifications. Each requires a new site on which a temporary factory, so to speak, is set up and a work force assembled. Hence any increase in spending on construction is reasonably certain to add promptly to the number employed. Not only will employment increase, but in view of the long period required to carry out construction projects, the increase will be sustained for months, sometimes years. The work on a construction job is unevenly distributed over time, but for every type of project there is a characteristic pattern of labor input, which often rises until the job is about half completed and then declines. Hence a jump in the rate of starting new construction will lead to a gradual increase in employment on construction sites. In the case we have supposed, employment will grow at an increasing rate for several months, the precise period depending upon the size and character of the projects initiated, then rise at a diminishing rate until a level proportionate to the higher rate of ordering is attained.

In this sketch I have tacitly assumed that the higher rate of new construction "starts" is maintained over a period at least equaling that required to carry out a typical construction project—which nowadays is probably a little over a half year. As employment on construction sites expands over a period of this duration, there may at first be no increase in the production of building materials. Dealers or fabricators who consider their stocks excessive will permit them to go lower, and those who seek to augment their supplies may not be able to do so as readily in the case of one material as another. But if the rate of initiating construction is maintained at the new level, an increasing number of dealers will expand their purchases and more and more producers will expand their output. In the long run—which may need to be reckoned in years rather than months—orders, production, employment, shipments, inventories, and related business factors will be generally higher throughout the construction trades.

Few industries, and none of a magnitude comparable with construction, have its power to convert a discontinuous increase in spending—whether it returns promptly or only after a few months to the old level—into a sustained expansion of employment, which for a time is even accelerative. But whatever the industry, if a higher rate of sales is maintained long enough, employment will surely rise and so will the activities associated with it. For a while the effects will be spotty, but with the passage of time adjustments will be set in motion throughout the industry as well as in those on which it closely depends for its materials and supplies. And as the higher rate of spending generates new incomes, its effects will spread out in new channels having little in common with the original direction of the new spending. People will spend part or all of their larger incomes, and their additional outlay will be swollen by that of business firms seeking to add to inventories or "fixed" plant. In this cumulative process the banking system and the capital market will play a part; and once the movement has gathered strength, it may continue of its own momentum even if the original increase in spending, which might have been a governmental instead of a consumers' buying spurt, is no longer maintained. But it is not my purpose here to examine the actual process whereby a business cycle expansion cumulates.

My aim has been merely to suggest that there are economic reasons why crosscurrents are more prominent in some stages of the business cycle than at others. Factors peculiar to individual businesses and markets are always at work. The adoption of new technical processes, introduction of new products, opening up of new sources of supply, migration of people, shifts in demand, formation of new firms, disappearance of old ones, and the weather itself—these factors, whatever their precise role may be in generating or transmitting business changes, create crosscurrents in both good times and bad. Nevertheless, I have tried to set forth reasons for expecting the crosscurrents to be especially numerous at the beginning of a business cycle expansion. As expansion progresses, we should expect its scope to widen, as actually happens according to our statistical summary. But after some time, obstacles to further expansion are likely to multiply, though aggregate activity keeps climbing. Here and there banking facilities will be inadequate to finance further expansion. Here and there in the industrial process "bottlenecks" will emerge, and the increase in supplies slow down or vanish. Here and there prices will remain steady in the face of rising costs, and discourage programs for expansion. Here and there nearly everyone in the labor force will be at work, and the growth of some firms will be at least partly balanced by the decline of others in the neighborhood. Thus it is reasonable to expect what our charts so forcefully show, that with the passage of time the scope of a business cycle expansion will shrink though the expansion still continues.

V. TYPICAL SEQUENCES WITHIN A BUSINESS CYCLE

I need not stop to adapt these commonplaces to the phenomena of a business cycle contraction. For present purposes it is sufficient that the statistical finding on which I have dwelt is a meaningful and reasonable result, namely, that the proportion of economic activities undergoing expansion traces out a cyclical curve which precedes the movements of aggregate activity, whether it be rising or falling. In view of this finding two broad propositions may be set down. First, a business recession starts while aggregate activity is still expanding and a recovery starts while the aggregate is still contracting. Second, a recession or recovery spreads gradually over the economic system and in time reverses the tide of aggregate activity. These propositions naturally raise the question whether the transitional changes in business cycles have a stable economic character. For example, the decline in the proportion of advancing series toward the close of expansion might be produced by cyclical peaks in a random assortment of activities. On the other hand, it might be produced by substantially the same set of activities, cycle after cycle; in other words, the sequence of downturns in one cycle might be much like the sequence in any other. To grapple with this issue, the veil of anonymity clothing our time series must be lifted.

Chart 2.6 does this in part by segregating three highly important groups of series in our sample—those reporting orders for investment goods, industrial production, and income payments. The curves are constructed on the same principle as the cumulative in Chart 2.2 which, it will be recalled, is based solely on a specification of the cyclical turning points in individual series. But whereas the simple aggregate of that chart includes our full sample of series, the aggregates of Chart 2.6 are constructed from "homogeneous" subgroups. The curve marked "orders for investment goods" combines all series relating to construction contracts, building permits, equipment orders, and orders for materials such as are predominantly used in making investment goods. The curve for production includes all the production series in our full sample except foodstuffs. The curve for income payments includes all available series of this type, though it happens to be dominated by payrolls. Taken together, these three groups account for about a third of the series in the full sample.

The simple aggregates of the specific cycles in our several groups trace out movements that correspond closely to one another and to the cycles in business activity identified by the National Bureau. But the cyclical timing of the groups varies: as a rule the maxima and minima of investment orders lead the corresponding turns of production, which again lead the corresponding turns of income payments. Now, a maximum or minimum represents a point of balance between expanding and contracting series within a group. Hence the sequence of

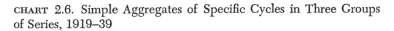

CHART 2.6. Simple Aggregates of Specific Cycles in Three Groups of Series, 1919–39

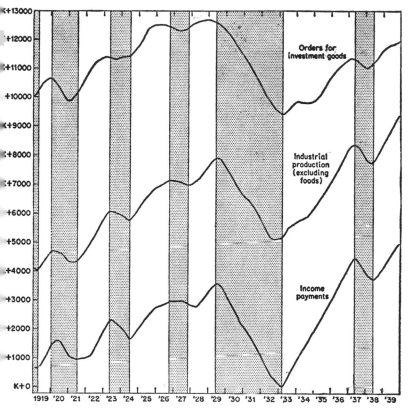

NOTE: Shaded areas represent business contractions. Origin of vertical scale of top curve is arbitrary, since K is any constant. See appendix to this chapter.

maxima means that at a downturn in aggregate activity the shift from a majority to a minority of expansions comes first in the group on investment orders, later in production, a little later still in income payments. At an upturn in aggregate activity there is a similar succession of shifts from a majority to a minority of contractions. These systematic sequences express a tendency of our several groups to occupy similar positions relative to one another within each cluster of turns surrounding a business cycle turn.

The results depicted in Chart 2.6 are restricted to investment decisions at the time they become effective, the physical volume of production, and the disbursement of incomes. This is only part of the evidence that a system exists in individual upturns at business revivals and in individual downturns at recessions. Speaking broadly, our studies indicate that new orders, construction contracts or permits, stock prices and transactions, security issues, business incorporations, and hours worked per week tend to lead the tide in aggregate activity; so do the liabilities of business failures on an inverted basis. On the other hand, production, employment, commodity prices, imports, and business profits tend to move with the tides in aggregate activity; while income payments, wages, interest rates, retail sales, and inventories are laggards.[2] These cyclical traits are not infrequently obscured or deflected by special circumstances, but when numerous time series and long periods are analyzed a tendency toward repetition in cyclical sequences comes clearly to the surface.

To gain more definite knowledge of cyclical sequences, it is well to concentrate on series of broad economic coverage. Table 2.1, which is adapted from Wesley Mitchell's analysis of "comprehensive" series in *What Happens during Business Cycles*, will serve my immediate purpose. Each series in the

[2] See the following publications by the National Bureau: Bulletin 69; A. F. Burns and W. C. Mitchell, *Measuring Business Cycles* (Chapters 4, 9–12); Occasional Papers 26, 31, and 32; Evans' *Business Incorporations in the United States, 1800–1943* (Chapter 9); and the studies by Mitchell, Abramovitz, and Creamer, previously mentioned. See also the earlier studies by W. M. Persons, especially his papers in *Review of Economic Statistics*, January and April 1919.

table has some right to the claim of being a "true" aggregate or average of its kind, in contrast to the artificial ones I have largely used hitherto. The table shows directions of movement during a typical business cycle—here divided into eight stages, four each for expansion and contraction. Of course, each stage covers several months, and the table is therefore insensitive to minor differences in timing, such as the short lag in income payments. Further, it hides many crosscurrents that would appear in less comprehensive series, and completely omits certain business factors of which we should take account— especially wage rates, inventories, banking, and governmental finance. But with all its faults, the table identifies actual time series and thus shows more concretely than have previous exhibits the typical round of developments that constitute a business cycle.

Let us then take our stand at the bottom of a depression and watch events as they unfold. Production characteristically rises in the first segment of expansion; so do employment and money income; and so do commodity prices, imports, domestic trade, security transactions. Indeed, every series moves upward except bond yields and bankruptcies. In the second stage the broad advance continues, though it is checked at one point— the bond market where trading begins to decline. Bond prices join bond sales in the next stage; in other words, long-term interest rates—which fell during the first half of expansion— begin to rise. In the final stretch of expansion, declines become fairly general in the financial sector. Share trading and stock prices move downward; the liabilities of business failures, which hitherto have been receding, move up again; security issues and construction contracts drop; the turnover of bank deposits slackens; and bank clearings in New York City, though not as yet in the interior, become smaller.

These adverse developments soon engulf the economic system as a whole, and the next stage of the business cycle is the

TABLE 2.1. Characteristic Direction and Amplitude of Twenty-Six "Comprehensive" Series During a Business Cycle

		Typical Direction of Movement			
		Expansion			
Series No.	Series	Trough to First Third	First to Middle Third	Middle to Last Third	Last Third to Peak
1.	Bond sales, NY Stock Exchange	+	−	−	−
2.	RR bond prices	+	+	−	−
3.	Commercial failures, liab., *inv.*	+	+	+	−
4.	Common stock prices	+	+	+	−
5.	Shares sold, NY Stock Exchange	+	+	+	−
6.	Corporate security issues	+	+	+	−
7.	Construction contracts, value	+	+	+	−
8.	Deposits activity	+	+	+	−
9.	Bank clearings, NYC	+	+	+	−
10.	Incorporations, no.	+	+	+	+
11.	Bank clearings, outside NYC	+	+	+	+
12.	Bank clearings, total	+	+	+	+
13.	Imports, value	+	+	+	+
14.	Industrial production, total	+	+	+	+
15.	Fuel & electricity production	+	+	+	+
16.	Pig iron production	+	+	+	+
17.	RR freight ton-miles	+	+	+	+
18.	Factory employment	+	+	+	+
19.	Factory payrolls	+	+	+	+
20.	Income payments, total	+	+	+	+
21.	Corporate profits	+	+	+	+
22.	Commercial failures, no., *inv.*	+	+	+	+
23.	Department store sales	+	+	+	+
24.	Wholesale trade sales, value	+	+	+	+
25.	Wholesale commodity prices	+	+	+	+
26.	RR bond yields	−	−	+	+

SOURCE: See appendix to this chapter.

a A plus denotes rise, a minus denotes fall. Series 3 and 22 are inverted here.

b Expressed as percentage of mean value during a cycle.

Contraction				No. of Business Cycles Covered	Per Cent of Conforming Movements During Span of Stages in Which Series Is Said To		Av. Amplitude [b] of Movements During Span of Stages in Which Series Is Said To	
Peak to First Third	First to Middle Third	Middle to Last Third	Last Third to Trough		Rise	Fall	Rise	Fall
—	—	+	+	14	86	79	35.0	14.7
—	+	+	+	19	65	74	7.4	3.8
—	—	+	+	14	86	93	74.5	57.8
—	—	—	+	16	94	82	26.8	20.2
—	—	—	+	16	94	88	40.6	36.2
—	—	—	+	8	100	75	46.9	46.1
—	—	—	+	7	86	75	43.2	30.4
—	—	—	+	16	94	88	14.3	16.7
—	—	—	+	18	100	89	30.8	26.6
—	—	—	+	19	84	80	26.9	10.2
—	—	—	+	14	100	79	25.5	12.8
—	—	—	+	14	100	86	29.2	20.4
—	—	—	+	16	94	75	26.1	18.9
—	—	—	—	5	100	100	35.2	32.5
—	—	—	—	5	100	100	25.5	14.6
—	—	—	—	16	100	100	54.2	44.9
—	—	—	—	6	100	88	27.8	25.1
—	—	—	—	6	100	100	21.8	22.8
—	—	—	—	5	100	100	36.3	39.9
—	—	—	—	4	100	50	22.6	17.6
—	—	—	—	4	100	100	168.8	174.6
—	—	—	—	16	75	88	22.3	26.1
—	—	—	—	4	100	75	17.6	9.1
—	—	—	—	3	100	100	17.7	19.1
—	—	—	—	11	82	91	8.7	8.9
+	—	—	—	19	74	65	3.7	6.2

first stage of contraction. Production, employment, commodity prices, personal incomes, business profits—indeed, practically all processes represented in the table—decline. Of course, the liabilities of business failures continue to rise, which merely attests the sweep of depression. Long-term interest rates also maintain their rise. But in the next stage the downward drift of bond prices ceases; that is, the rise in long-term interest rates is arrested. By the middle of contraction, bond sales join the upward movement of bond prices. More important still, the liabilities of business failures begin declining, which signifies that the liquidation of distressed business firms has passed its worst phase. These favorable developments are reinforced in the following stage. Share trading and prices revive; business incorporations, security issues, and construction contracts move upward; money begins to turn over more rapidly; even total money payments expand. Before long the expansion spreads to production, employment, prices, money incomes, and domestic trade. But this is already the initial stage of general expansion—the point at which our hurried observation of the business cycle started.

This recital of cyclical developments is rough and inadequate. Of course, it delineates characteristic movements during business cycles, not invariant sequences. That the description fits imperfectly individual business cycles is apparent from the conformity percentages in Table 2.1. Yet these percentages also suggest that the deviations from type are not so numerous as to destroy the value of our generalized sketch. And if this much can be accepted, an important conclusion immediately follows, notwithstanding the omissions of the table; namely, that the check to the dominant movement of business activity, whether it be expansion or contraction, is typically felt especially early in financial processes and activities preparatory to investment expenditure.

The sequences in the table express interrelated developments; they are not disconnected facts. Even my bleak description has not escaped causal overtones. An informed reader who makes the effort will not find it hard to forge explicit causal links. Take, for example, the early recovery of the bond market from depression. The explanation can partly be found in the behavior of commercial banks. With reserves growing, short-term interest rates declining, and "sound" loans difficult to arrange, the banks naturally seek to expand their holdings of bonds. Private investors attempt to do likewise, but at the expense of stocks since business profits are still declining rapidly. The broad result is a revaluation of security holdings: bond prices and trading move upward, while the stock market keeps going down. But high-grade preferred stocks are a fairly close substitute for gilt-edged bonds, and blue-chip common stocks for preferred stocks. As the yield on bonds diminishes, stocks of strong concerns become more attractive to alert investors. In time declining interest rates exert an upward pressure on stock prices generally, offsetting the influence of falling profits. And so one may continue to link the signs recorded in the table, and fill the blanks in our knowledge of how expansions and contractions cumulate. But if the links are to be of tolerable strength, they must be hammered out of materials beyond those in the table, among which some knowledge of what goes on within broad aggregates is essential.

VI. THE CYCLICAL BEHAVIOR OF PROFITS

Of this I shall give a large illustration. The operations of our business economy depend in a significant degree on the relation that unit costs, unit prices, and the physical volume of sales bear to one another. These three factors are summed up in profits—the driving force of business enterprise. According to

Table 2.1 corporate profits characteristically rise throughout the expansion and decline throughout the contraction of business cycles. That this is a tolerably faithful summary of recent experience is evident from Chart 2.7, which sets profits against

CHART 2.7.   Corporate Profits and Related Movements, 1920–38

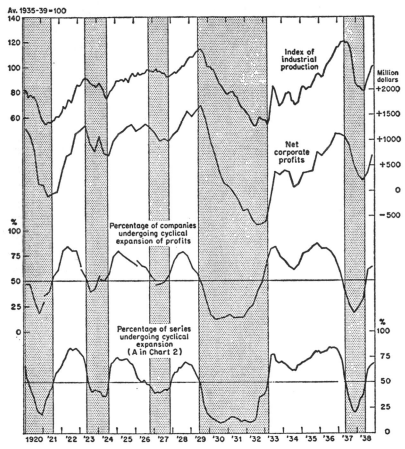

NOTE: Shaded areas represent business contractions. See appendix to this chapter.

industrial production and the National Bureau's chronology of business cycles since 1920. Reliable reports on quarterly profits are not available for earlier years, and we must be content with a span of observations hardly long enough for confident generalization. However, the evidence on profits seems reasonable in view of the behavior of production, just as the latter seems reasonable in view of the behavior of security issues and construction contracts. Thus, it appears at first blush that profits tend to favor the continuation of prosperity or depression practically until the end of the phase, and that forces capable of reversing the tides of business activity are ordinarily not to be found in profits as such. Reasoning along these lines will lead one to suppose that actual profits are an unsatisfactory gauge of prospective profits, and to seek this key to business movements elsewhere—in orders, sales, inventories, the price-wage ratio, the stock exchange, or other places.

These lines of investigation are worth pursuing. At the same time, much can be learned about changes in prospective profits from the distribution of actual profits. After all, business firms do not have a common pocketbook. As long as we reason from aggregates we assume that they behave as if they had one, and it is only common sense to stop and ask how much difference separate pocketbooks do make. The third curve from the top in Chart 2.7 supplies as good a statistical answer as now seems attainable. It is based on the cycles of profits in a sample of companies analyzed by Thor Hultgren. The curve shows that "at every stage of the business cycle the fortunes of some companies . . . ran counter to the main stream." [3] Not only that, but the proportion of firms experiencing an expansion of

[3] See Hultgren's *Cyclical Diversities in the Fortunes of Industrial Corporations*, Occasional Paper 32. Cf. J. Tinbergen, *Statistical Testing of Business-Cycle Theories: A Method and Its Application to Investment Activity*, Geneva, 1939, and L. Klein's note in *Thirtieth Annual Report of the National Bureau of Economic Research*, Part Three.

profits began to decline well before the peak in total profits or total economic activity, and to increase long before the trough. In other words, developments in the sphere of profits that actually foreshadow reversals in the direction of aggregate activity are obscured when we view profits in the aggregate.

Earlier in this report I noted that there are two cycles in economic activity, one "seen" and another "unseen," and that the "unseen" cycle in the distribution of individual activities throws its shadow ahead of the "seen" cycle in the aggregate. We now find two cycles in profits, the "unseen" cycle in the distribution of companies throwing its shadow ahead of the "seen" cycle for all corporations. Chart 2.7 demonstrates, moreover, that in the period covered the "unseen" cycles in profits and in general economic activity follow similar paths. The two curves are made from widely dissimilar and independent materials, but this fact merely corroborates our earlier conclusion that recession and recovery start well in advance of any reversal in the direction of aggregate activity. However, the casual links between the curves are as yet obscure; and while the available data will not permit exhaustive analysis, we should attempt to determine as well as may be whether the companies whose profits run counter to the dominant cyclical movement are in fact the foci of gathering recovery or recession.

Meanwhile, it may be observed that the behavior displayed on our chart accords with rational expectations. In the early stages of an expansion unit costs often decline as industrial facilities are improved or utilized more fully. But as prosperity cumulates, unit costs tend to mount for business firms generally; and since in many cases selling prices cannot be raised, profit margins here and there will narrow, thus offsetting the influence on profits of an increase in sales or reinforcing the effects of an occasional reduction in sales. The "squeeze" on profits becomes more widespread the longer the business expansion continues. In the first place, all firms do not have the same power to advance prices; some are prevented or limited by custom, trade marks, or governmental regulation. Secondly, errors pile up as mounting optimism warps the judgment of an increasing number of businessmen concerning the sales that can be made at profitable prices. Thus, after a business expansion has run for some time, the proportion of firms experiencing rising profits begins to shrink, although the profits of business in the aggregate continue to climb. Such development spreads doubt or financial pressure to firms whose profits are still rising, and in time moderates their investments in sympathy with that of the growing number of firms whose business fortune is waning. Of course, a check to investment from this source strengthens an emerging tendency to postpone investment projects until a time when, it is felt, construction costs and financing charges will recede from the abnormal level to which they have been pushed by prosperity.

Minor changes aside, these are some of the crucial developments generated by prosperity, as Mitchell originally analyzed the problem in his *Business Cycles,* published in 1913. A series of converse developments may be expected in depression. A great deal of evidence may now be cited in support of these expectations, though definite knowledge is not yet available of the scale on which investment projects are shelved in late expansion or resuscitated in late contraction, or of the links that tie firms with declining and rising profits into a system of cumulating responses.

One reason for emphasizing the role of profits in the business cycle is their extraordinarily wide fluctuation. Thus far I have abstracted from the cyclical amplitudes of different processes, which together with the variations in timing transform the internal composition of the economy during a business cycle. Of this fundamental feature of business cycles I can say little on the present occasion; but I at least wish to call attention to the wide differences among the amplitudes of the "comprehensive" series in Table 2.1, and to record the finding that in our economic system, taken as a whole, production fluctuates more widely than sales to final users. As a consequence of the latter, additions to inventories trace out cyclical movements that conform closely to the cycles in production, and account for a considerable part of the changes in it. These facts were first glimpsed by Simon Kuznets. Later Moses Abramovitz, besides making more refined and extensive measurements, developed their rich implications in his *Inventories and Business Cycles*.[4] More recently, Ruth Mack has brought fluctuations of shorter time span than business cycles within the orbit of the original generalization, and compiled evidence suggesting that inventory investment plays an even more important part in the variations of production that occur every few months than in those that extend over a business cycle.

VII. FORECASTING BUSINESS CYCLES

I have stressed in this report some of the repetitive features of business cycles established by the National Bureau's studies. Yet the very charts on which I have relied as my witnesses attest also variability in the duration of business cycles, in the relative length of their phases of expansion and contraction, their amplitude, their economic scope, the speed with which a sizable majority of expanding activities is converted into a minority or vice versa, the intervals separating the upturns or downturns of different activities, and even their sequence. As

[4] See Abramovitz' *Inventories and Business Cycles*, especially Chapters 1 and 21; also Bulletin 74, NBER, by Kuznets. Cf. Alvin H. Hansen, *Fiscal Policy and Business Cycles*, New York, 1941, Chapter 1–2.

everyone knows, the contraction of 1929–33 was exceptionally long and deep, as well as very widely diffused. The contraction of 1926–27, on the other hand, was mild though not exceptionally brief. Chart 2.6 gives some inkling of the dynamic impact of investment outlays for new plant and equipment during business revivals and recessions, but this branch of expenditure was not the active factor in lifting the nation out of depression in 1914 or 1933. In recent years monetary and fiscal management has left only faint traces of the cyclical pattern of long-term interest rates which ruled before the 1930's and which I have recorded in Table 2.1. The same table states that stock prices move early in revivals and recessions, but is silent on the occasional lapses from this tendency. None of the exhibits in this report shows agricultural production, a major industry dominated in the short run by the weather, or singles out exports which fluctuated in virtual independence of business cycles before World War I.

I take it as a matter of course that it is vital, both theoretically and practically, to recognize the changes in economic organization and the episodic and random factors that make each business cycle a unique configuration of events. Subtle understanding of economic change comes from a knowledge of history and large affairs, not from statistics or their processing alone—to which our disturbed age has turned so eagerly in its quest for certainty. If I have emphasized the repetitive elements in business cycles gleaned from statistical records, it is because a constructive contribution can come also from that direction. Findings such as I have reported add to the understanding of business cycles, and may even prove helpful in predicting reversals in the direction of total economic activity —or at least in identifying them as such promptly. That this hope is not entirely a pipe dream is indicated by Chart 2.8.

The chart shows artificially simple aggregates, struck on the

CHART 2.8. Simple Aggregates of Specific Cycles in Two Groups of Series Differentiated by Their Cyclical Timing, 1919–39

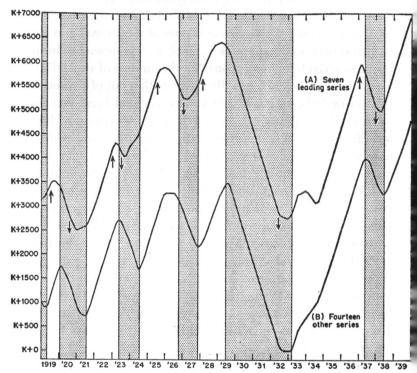

NOTE: Shaded areas represent business contractions. Origin of vertica scale is arbitrary, since K is any constant. See text for explanation o arrows, and appendix for other explanations.

plan previously described, of the specific cycles in two smal groups of series. Taken together, they are the twenty-one in dicators of cyclical revivals selected by the National Bureau ir 1937 on the basis of performance in past revivals.[5] After rank ing these twenty-one series according to their average timing at revivals through 1933, the top third were segregated from

[5] See *Statistical Indicators of Cyclical Revivals*, Bulletin 69.

the rest. Curve A includes this top third, which spans average leads from 7.8 to 4.2 months. Curve B covers the remaining two-thirds, the extreme series having an average lead of 3.6 months and an average lag of 1.8 months. In view of the method of selecting the two groups, curve A may be expected generally to lead curve B at recoveries. There is no technical reason, however, for a lead at recessions, or for that matter at the recovery of 1938. Nevertheless, curve A turns down and up in every instance before curve B; more important still, it does so before the turning points of general business activity expressed by our chronology of business cycles. If there were no genuine tendency toward stability of cyclical sequences, the probability of attaining such results would be slender.

Four forecasting principles are embodied in Chart 2.8, and they are more significant than their particular expression. First, since the cyclical timing of single processes cannot be implicitly trusted, a measure of protection against surprises of the individual case may be won by combining the indications of numerous series. Second, since there is a tendency toward repetition in cyclical sequences, economic series may be grouped into two or more classes according to their timing. Third, while the group with the longest leads is of keenest interest, groups that tend to move later serve the important function of confirming or refuting the indications offered by the vanguard. Fourth, since the "unseen" cycle in the distribution of cyclical expansions and contractions within an aggregate tends to throw its shadow before the movements of the aggregate, this propensity may be harnessed by the forecaster. How that practice would extend the lead of curve A over B is indicated by the upward and downward pointing arrows on the chart, which are placed respectively at the maxima and minima of the proportion of series in group A undergoing expansion.

These matters are being investigated further by Geoffrey Moore. Besides improving the selection of indicators made in 1937, he has devised a technique for grafting current monthly observations onto cyclical units such as I have combined in Chart 2.8 on empirical and in Chart 2.6 on economic considerations. His tentative results are presented in Occasional Paper 31 and should prove extremely helpful to the many economists who can master statistical devices without being mastered by them.

VIII. MILD AND SEVERE DEPRESSIONS

The fear of business cycles which rules economic thinking is a fear of severe depressions. The reasons for concern about the magnitude of emerging economic movements are compelling, and extend beyond the sphere of private activity or profit. Our society can readily make political as well as economic adjustments to a mild contraction such as that of 1926–27 or 1948–49, perhaps even to rapid but brief declines such as occurred in 1907–08 and 1937–38. The really serious threat to our way of life comes not from business contractions of this character, but from the long and deep depressions that devastate homes and industries—as in the 1870's, 1890's and the early 1930's. To glimpse economic catastrophe when it is imminent may prevent its occurrence: this is the challenge facing business cycle theory and policy. A preceding generation concentrated on the causes and cures of commercial crises; later interest shifted to business cycles, and more recently to fluctuations in employment. But the crucial problem of our times is the prevention of severe depressions, not of business or employment cycles. It is in this direction that research must move in the future, and the first and fundamental task is to determine why some business contractions are brief and mild while others reach disastrous proportions.

Some insight into this problem is afforded by the experience of the 1920's. Each of the successive cyclical waves during this decade carried further the belief in a "new era" of boundless prosperity. As speculative fever mounted, even the business declines that occurred were ignored or explained away. The boom in common stocks of that decade and its aftermath are notorious, but speculation was by no means confined to stocks. Ilse Mintz has recently added an important chapter on foreign bonds, and Raymond Saulnier has contributed another on urban mortgage lending.[6] Mrs. Mintz' study is concerned with American loans extended to or guaranteed by foreign governments from 1920 to 1930. After observing that "the 1920's were the defaultless era in foreign lending," she suggests that the quality of the loans progressively deteriorated during the decade. This was well concealed until severe depression brought a test of quality. "Only 6 per cent of the issues of 1920 defaulted in the 1930's while 63 per cent of those of 1928 suffered this fate; dividing the period into its earlier and its later half only 18 per cent of all issues from 1920 to 1924 became bad while the corresponding ratio for 1925 to 1929 is as high as 50 per cent." Saulnier's sample survey of urban mortgage loans by life insurance companies suggests a similar relaxation of credit standards during the late twenties. It shows, for example, that of the loans extinguished in 1935–39 the foreclosure rate was 40 per cent on such of the loans as were made during 1925–29, but only 32 per cent on those made in 1920–24 and 25 per cent on those made in 1930–34.

These new facts accord with an old hypothesis; namely, that developments during "prosperity"—which may cumulate over

[6] See *Deterioration in the Quality of Foreign Bonds Issued in the United States, 1920–1930*, by Ilse Mintz, NBER, New York, 1951; and *Urban Mortgage Lending by Life Insurance Companies*, by R. J. Saulnier, NBER, New York, 1950. See also an earlier study by George W. Edwards, *The Evolution of Finance Capitalism*, New York, 1938, pp. 231–232.

one or more expansions—shape the character of a depression.[7] But the results I have cited do not explain, for example, why the revival in the first half of 1931 proved abortive. That unfortunate episode cannot be understood without study of foreign conditions, the policies pursued by the Federal Reserve System, and other matters. I make these remarks merely to suggest that a host of developments during a business decline, largely unconnected with what happened during the preceding "prosperity," may convert what might have been a mild contraction into a severe one. This too is an old hypothesis, and of course it supplements rather than rivals the hypothesis that the sources of deep depression are imbedded in preceding prosperity.

Our past work on business cycles has laid an excellent foundation for comparative study of mild and severe cyclical movements. *Measuring Business Cycles* demonstrates a high and positive correlation between the amplitude and economic scope of business cycle phases. Abramovitz has found an inverse correlation between the length of a business cycle phase and the proportion of the change in gross national product that is accounted for by inventory accumulation or decumulation.[8] Geoffrey Moore has found qualitative differences in the movements of agricultural prices and production during mild and severe depressions.[9] In Occasional Paper 34 Daniel Creamer supplies important information on the behavior of wages during business cycles of varying intensity, and Milton Friedman is now investigating monetary changes during mild and vigorous cyclical movements. But we have only begun to exploit our vast collection of records which cover expansions and contractions of widely different length and depth in several coun-

[7] See, for example, *Measuring Business Cycles*, p. 460.

[8] See Abramovitz, *Inventories and Business Cycles*, Chapter 21.

[9] See his "Harvest Cycles," Ph.D. dissertation, Harvard University, 1947.

tries. Full investigation of the problem why some business declines remain mild while others reach catastrophic magnitude is a natural extension of our research program, and one for which we have long prepared. It will call for considerable new effort, and the merging of the skills of the historian, economic theorist, and statistician. If we can turn to it promptly and energetically, we may make a telling contribution to the economic knowledge our society so sorely needs.

APPENDIX

Only a relatively small fraction of the series summarized in this paper were used in deriving the National Bureau's chronology of business cycles. For the chronology, see Table 1.1. Concerning the methods used in dating specific and business cycles, see Burns and Mitchell, *Measuring Business Cycles*, Chapter 4.

Except when otherwise noted, all the series in the following charts are monthly.

CHART 2.1

The sample is an extension of Moore's sample of well-conforming series, briefly described in the note to Chart 2.5 in this appendix. The present sample includes series that conform poorly or slightly as well as those that conform well to business cycles. New series analyzed by the National Bureau since Moore's compilation was made (autumn 1948) are not included in Chart 2.1 or in any of the subgroups in later charts.

Except for the first year and a half of the period, the number of series in the comprehensive sample exceeds 600 every month. The average number is 656 for the twenty-one years 1919–39 and 665 for 1921–39. From 642 in January 1921, the number rises to more than 680 throughout 1922–28, after which it declines gradually to 635 in 1939.

The comparatively small number of series in the beginning of the period is due to the fact that many series in the National Bureau's collection begin in 1919, together with our practice of counting such series as additions to the sample only from the month of their first cyclical turn. A better practice would have been to introduce such series into the tabulations from the month of their first observation; and we have in fact adjusted this way the tabulations of the subgroups shown in later charts. These corrections proved to be so slight in the subgroups that we have not deemed it essential to make them in the full sample. After 1921 the effects produced by the corrections are not at all significant; they are not carried in the subgroups beyond 1922. A comparable inexactitude attends our practice of treating series that terminate during the period 1919–39 as if they ended in the month following their last observed cyclical turn; but the number of series affected thereby is negligible throughout the period.

To take account of the fact that some series characteristically behave invertedly (falling during business cycle expansions and rising during contractions), the peaks of such series are counted as troughs and the troughs as peaks. For a precise definition of inverted behavior, see *Measuring Business Cycles,* Chapter 5, Sec. I and X. Concerning duplications and weighting, see notes to Charts 2.4 and 2.6.

CHART 2.2

The basic data used are the same as in Chart 2.1. As noted, the sample changes somewhat during the period covered; but the meaning of curves A, B, and C may be conveyed most readily by assuming a fixed number of series.

Let t represent the number of series reaching troughs in a given month, let p represent the number reaching peaks, let e and c represent the number expanding and contracting respectively, and let subscripts identify the month. Then $e_n = e_{n-1} + t_{n-1} - p_{n-1}$. Thus curve A is essentially derived from the bottom curve in Chart 2.1.

Curve B, in principle, is defined as follows: $e_n - c_n = e_{n-1} - c_{n-1} + 2(t_{n-1} - p_{n-1})$. Of course, when e and c are percentages, $e_n - c_n = 2e_n - 100$.

Let $e_0 - c_0$ be 0; in other words, fix the origin where $e = c$. Also, let T_n stand for $(t_n - p_n)$. Then the ordinate of curve C in month n is defined, in principle, as follows: $K + (e_1 - c_1) + (e_2 - c_2) + \ldots + (e_n - c_n)$, where K is an unknown constant. The indicated sum equals $K + 2[nT_0 + (n-1)T_1 + (n-2)T_2 + \ldots + T_{n-1}]$; the expression in brackets is a cumulative of the cumulative of T.

The meaning of curve C may be grasped without going through the preceding steps. Take a monthly time series, mark off its specific cycles, and discard all information pertaining to it except the dates of its cyclical turns. Draw a straight line with a slope of unity from the date of the first trough to the date of the succeeding peak, connect this peak and the following trough by a straight line with a slope of unity and so on. Repeat these operations on every series in the group; that is, convert each series into a "triangular curve." The arithmetic sum of such converted series will be curve C. That is why it is briefly described in the text and in later charts as a "simple aggregate of specific cycles." That is why, also, the scale of the curve is expressed in an abstract unit. (Curve C is described on the chart as the cumulative of B, which is expressed in percentages. From the viewpoint of curve C the percentages serve merely the function of splicing segments based on varying numbers of series.)

Curve C has interesting properties. Assume that its shape is as follows: the curve is continuous, it moves in cycles, the tops and bottoms of the cycles are rounded (first derivative zero), and there is just one point of inflection between the peak and trough. Let the trough come at date a, the point of inflection at i, the peak at s. Then $e_a = c_a$; $e_s = c_s$; $e_n > c_n$ between a and s; e_n increases between a and i; e_n decreases between i and s; $t_n > p_n$ between a and i; $t_n < p_n$ between i and s; and $\Sigma t_n = \Sigma p_n$ between a and s.

CHART 2.3

The specific time series on this chart are so well known that brief identification will suffice.

1. Index of industrial production: Federal Reserve Board, 1943 revision
2. Index of factory employment: Bureau of Labor Statistics
3. Freight car loadings: Association of American Railroads, Car Service Division

The series are seasonally adjusted: (1) by the compiler, (2) by Federal Reserve Board, (3) by National Bureau.

CHART 2.4

The total number of series included in the production group during some part of the period 1919–39 is 115; the average number in any month is over 100, and in no month is the number less that 97.

The total number of series in the employment sample is forty-one; the average number in any month is forty, and the number is never less than thirty-eight.

Like the "all-inclusive" sample in Chart 2.1, both the production and the employment subsamples contain duplications. These arise chiefly because comprehensive series as well as some of their components are included. Another reason is that some processes are represented by different series, as when records are compiled by different investigators. We have also studied nonduplicating groups consisting of fifty-eight production and twenty-one employment series, and these give results that are almost indistinguishable from those yielded by the 115 production and 41 employment series, respectively. For the list of twenty-one employment series, see *Twenty-sixth Annual Report*, p. 24. Experiments with weighting, apart from those implicit in duplications, have not been made.

The subgroup samples are handled differently than the all-inclusive sample, in that peaks and troughs of "inverted series" are not interchanged, but are tabulated as they come.

See notes to Charts 2.1 and 2.2.

CHART 2.5

For a full description of how this sample of well-conforming series was selected, see Chapter 7 of *Business Cycle Indicators*, G. H. Moore (ed.).

The number of series in a particular month changes steadily from 75 in January 1885 to 233 in January 1919, through a maximum of 366 in June 1922, to 330 in December 1939. By quinquennial dates, in June, the numbers in (A) Moore's sample and (B) our "all-inclusive" sample in Chart 2.1 are as follows:

	A	B
1920	336	602
1925	360	686
1930	356	674
1935	340	648

For the treatment of "inverted series," see note to Chart 2.1.

CHART 2.6

The number of series included in the group of new orders for investment goods during some part of the period 1919–39 is seventy; the average number in any month is over sixty-five, and the number is never less than sixty-three.

The group on income payments consists predominantly of payroll series, the only exceptions being (1) dividend payments and (2) total income payments to individuals. There are thirty-three payroll series in all, some of which are aggregates that overlap other series included in the sample. The average number of series in the group on income payments in any month is thirty-five, and in no month is the number less than thirty-four. Analysis of a nonduplicating sample for this group yielded results very similar to those shown on the chart; cf. note to Chart 2.4.

For the group on industrial production (excluding foods), see note to Chart 2.4. See that note also for the treatment of inverted series. For other details or interpretations, see notes to Charts 2.1 and 2.2.

Not all of the cyclical turning points can be easily made out in this chart. They are as follows:

Cyclical Turn	Orders for Investment Goods	Industrial Production (Excluding Foods)	Income Payments
Trough	Jan. 1919 [a]	Mar. 1919 [b]	Mar. 1919 [b]
Peak	Dec. 1919	Feb. 1920	June 1920
Trough	Jan. 1921	Apr. 1921	July 1921
Peak	Mar. 1923	May 1923	June 1923
Trough	Sept. 1923	July 1924	July 1924
Peak	May 1926	Nov. 1926	July 1927
Trough	May 1927	Nov. 1927	Apr. 1928
Peak	Jan. 1929	July 1929	July 1929
Trough	Mar. 1933	Oct. 1932	Mar. 1933
Peak	Mar. 1937	May 1937	May 1937
Trough	Feb. 1938	May 1938	June 1938

[a] Or earlier. [b] Uncertain.

CHART 2.7

Industrial production: see note to Chart 2.3.

Net corporate profits: series is quarterly, seasonally adjusted, and comes from Harold Barger, *Outlay and Income in the United States, 1921–1938, National Bureau,* 1942, pp. 297–299.

Per cent of companies undergoing cyclical expansion of profits: series is quarterly and comes from Thor Hultgren, *Cyclical Diversities in the Fortunes of Industrial Corporations.* Breaks in the series are due to expansion of the sample of companies. In each segment the number of companies is constant, being as follows in successive intervals:

Period	No. of Companies	Period	No. of Companies
1920–21	17	1926–27	153
1921–23	31	1927–29	155
1923–24	71	1929–33	185
1924–26	101	1933–38	244

None of these profits series enters the "all-inclusive" sample of Chart 2.1. Further details on the composition and coverage of the profits sample will be found in the work cited.

CHART 2.8

The twenty-one series on which this chart is based are listed below. The first seven constitute the group with longest average leads at revivals; the remainder comprises the group with shorter average leads or with lags at revivals.

1. Dow-Jones index of industrial stock prices
2. Liabilities of business failures (inverted)
3. Inner tube production
4. Railway operating income
5. Paper production

6. Bank clearings outside NYC
7. Residential building contracts, floor space
8. Passenger car production
9. Steel ingot production
10. Industrial building contracts, floor space
11. Pig iron production
12. Index of wholesale prices, Bradstreet's and BLS
13. Ton-miles of freight hauled by railroads
14. Truck production
15. Index of industrial production, Federal Reserve Board
16. Average hours per week, manufacturing
17. Index of business activity, A.T. & T.
18. Index of production, Standard Statistics Co.
19. Factory employment, total
20. Department store sales
21. Factory employment, machinery

For sources and brief descriptions of the behavior of these series, see W. C. Mitchell and A. F. Burns, *Statistical Indicators of Cyclical Revivals*, Bulletin 69, NBER, May 28, 1938. Readers who consult that bulletin will discover, however, that the top seven series in the present listing are not the same as the top seven presented there, nor are the ranges of the average timing measures the same in the bulletin and the present paper. These discrepancies are the result of revisions of the analyses on which Bulletin 69 was based, and reflect either changes in the basic data or of the seasonal adjustments, or both. Though the ranking of series has been altered, the changes in average timing measures are slight.

For another analysis along the lines of Chart 2.8, see Chapters 7 and 20 of *Business Cycle Indicators*, Geoffrey H. Moore (ed.). The latter presents a method of utilizing current monthly observations in a framework similar to that based on specific cycle units but not requiring the prior identification of specific cycles.

See note to Chart 2.1 for the treatment of the inverted series, and note to Chart 2.2 for the interpretation of the curves.

TABLE 2.1

The rise in series 26 and the fall in series 2 might have been treated as extending through midcontraction. See *Measuring Business Cycles,* pp. 192–193, 195.

In series 2, 17, and 24, the number of expansions covered is greater by one than the number of full cycles. In series 4, 7, 10, 19, 21, and 26, the number of contractions covered is greater by one than the number of full cycles. In series 17, there are two additional contractions (they arise from a gap in the series).

Most series in this table are identified in the source cited. See *ibid.*, Appendix C, notes to Table 21, for series 1, 3, 4, 8, 9, 11–13, 17, 22, 25; notes to Chart 9, for series 6; notes to Chart 3, for series 14; and notes to Chart 8 and Tables 18–19, for series 19. Concerning series 2, 5, 16, 26, see *ibid.*, Chapter 6, note 7.

To identify series 7, 18, 20, see Appendix 1 of *Historical Statistics of the United States, 1789–1945* (a supplement to the *Statistical Abstract of the United States*).

Series 10: G. Heberton Evans, Jr., *Business Incorporations in the United States, 1800–1943,* National Bureau, 1948, pp. 80–81.

Series 15: Computed by National Bureau by compiling a weighted aggregate of seasonally adjusted production data for anthracite coal, bituminous coal, crude petroleum, and electric power. The weight for each is the average value of a unit of output during 1922–31, except that the unit value for electric power is net of the cost of fuel consumed and of current purchased.

Series 21: Barger, *op. cit.*, pp. 297–299.

Series 23: Dollar volume of sales adjusted for price changes. Seasonally adjusted dollar sales from *Federal Reserve Bulletin,* August 1936, p. 631, and subsequent issues. Deflating index supplied by Federal Reserve Bank of New York.

Series 24: Federal Reserve Board index; seasonally adjusted by compiler. *Federal Reserve Bulletin,* December 1927, pp. 26–27, and subsequent issues.

THREE

Progress Towards Economic Stability

THE AMERICAN people have of late been more conscious of the business cycle, more sensitive to every wrinkle of economic curves, more alert to the possible need for contra-cyclical action on the part of government, than ever before in our history. Minor changes of employment or of productivity or of the price level, which in an earlier generation would have gone unnoticed, are nowadays followed closely by laymen as well as experts. This sensitivity to the phenomena of recession and inflation is a symptom of an increased public awareness of both the need for and the attainability of economic progress. It is precisely because so much of current industrial and governmental practice can be better in the future that our meetings this year are focused on the broad problem of improving the performance of the American economy. However, as we go about the task of appraisal and criticism, it will be well to discipline our impatience for reform. In the measure that we avoid exaggerating our nation's failures or understating its successes, we shall make it easier for ourselves as well as for econ-

Presidential address delivered at the Seventy-Second Annual Meeting of the American Economic Association, Washington, D.C., December 28, 1959. Reprinted, by permission, from *American Economic Review,* March 1960.

omists in other countries to see current needs and developments in a just perspective.

It is a fact of the highest importance, I think, that although our economy continues to be swayed by the business cycle, its impact on the lives and fortunes of individuals has been substantially reduced in our generation. More than twenty-five years have elapsed since we last experienced a financial panic or a deep depression of production and employment. Over twenty years have elapsed since we last had a severe business recession. Between the end of the Second World War and the present, we have experienced four recessions, but each was a relatively mild setback. Since 1937 we have had five recessions, the longest of which lasted only thirteen months. There is no parallel for such a sequence of mild—or such a sequence of brief—contractions, at least during the past hundred years in our own country.

Nor is this all. The character of the business cycle itself appears to have changed, apart from the intensity of its overall movement. We usually think of the business cycle as a sustained advance of production, employment, incomes, consumption, and prices, followed by a sustained contraction, which in time gives way to a renewed advance of aggregate activity beyond the highest levels previously reached. We realize that changes in the price level occasionally outrun changes in production, that employment is apt to fluctuate less than production, and that consumption will fluctuate still less; but we nevertheless think of their movements as being roughly parallel. This concept of the business cycle has always been something of a simplification. For example, during the early decades of the nineteenth century, when agriculture dominated our national economy, occasional declines in the physical volume of production, whether large or small, had little effect on the number of jobs and sometimes had slight influence even on the flow of money incomes. As agriculture diminished in importance, the nation's production, employment, personal income, consumption, and price level fell more closely into step with one another and thus justified our thinking of them as moving in a rough parallelism. In recent years, however, and especially since the Second World War, the relations among these movements have become much looser.

The structure of an economy inevitably leaves its stamp on the character of its fluctuations. In our generation the structure of the American economy has changed profoundly, partly as a result of deliberate economic policies, partly as a result of unplanned developments. In considering problems of the future, we can proceed more surely by recognizing the changes in economic organization which already appear to have done much to blunt the impact of business cycles.

I

In the early decades of the nineteenth century the typical American worker operated his own farm or found scope for his energy on the family farm. Governmental activities were very limited. What there was of industry and commerce was largely conducted through small firms run by capitalist-employers. Corporations were rare and virtually confined to banking and transportation. As the population grew and capital became more abundant, individual enterprise expanded vigorously but corporate enterprise expanded still more. An increasing part of the nation's business therefore came under the rule of corporations. By 1929, the output of corporate businesses was already almost twice as large as the output of individual proprietorships and partnerships. The gap has widened appreciably since then. Corporate profits have therefore tended to increase faster than the incomes earned by proprietors, who still remain very numerous in farming, retail trade, and the professions. Fifty years ago the total income of proprietors was perhaps two and a half times as large as the combined sum of corporate profits and the compensation of corporate officers. By 1957 this corporate aggregate exceeded by a fourth the income of all proprietors and by two-thirds the income of proprietors outside of farming.

The great growth of corporations in recent decades has occurred preponderantly in industries where the firm must operate on a large scale to be efficient and therefore must assemble capital from many sources. But a corporation whose stock is held publicly and widely has a life of its own, apart from that of its owners, and will rarely distribute profits at the same rate as they are being earned. While profits normally respond quickly and sharply to a change in sales and production, the behavior of dividends is tempered by business judgment. In practice, dividends tend to move sluggishly and over a much narrower range than profits. Corporations have therefore come to function increasingly as a buffer between the fluctuations of production and the flow of income to individuals. In earlier times the lag of dividends was largely a result of the time-consuming character of corporate procedures. More recently, the advantages of a stable dividend—especially its bearing on a firm's financial reputation—have gained increasing recognition from business managers. Meanwhile, modern trends of taxation have stimulated corporations to rely more heavily on retained profits and less on new stock issues for their equity funds, and this development in turn has facilitated the pursuit of stable dividend policies. Thus the evolution of corporate practice, as well as the growth of corporate enterprise itself, has served to reduce the influence of a cyclical decline of production and profits on the flow of income to individuals.

The expansion and the means of financing of governmental

enterprise, especially since the 1930's, have had a similar effect. The increasing complexity of modern life, a larger concept of the proper function of government, and the mounting requirements of national defense have resulted in sharp increases of governmental spending. Fifty years ago the combined expenditure of federal, state, and local governments was about 7 per cent of the dollar volume of the nation's total output. Governmental expenditures rose to 10 per cent of total output in 1929 and to 26 per cent in 1957. This huge expansion of governmental enterprise naturally led to increases in tax rates and to an energetic search for new sources of revenue. In time, taxes came to be imposed on estates, gifts, employment, sales, and—most important of all—on the incomes of both corporations and individuals. Fifty years ago customs duties still yielded about half of the total revenue of the federal government, and none of our governmental units as yet collected any tax on incomes. Twenty years later, personal and corporate income taxes were already the mainstay of federal finance. Subsequently, the activities of the federal government increased much faster than local activities and taxes followed suit. By 1957 the income tax accounted for nearly 70 per cent of federal revenue, 8 per cent of state and local revenue, and a little over half of the combined revenue of our various governmental units.

This dominance of the income tax in current governmental finance, together with the recent shift of tax collection toward a pay-as-you-go basis, has measurably enlarged the government's participation in the shifting fortunes of the private economy. During the nineteenth century, taxes were not only a much smaller factor in the economy, but such short-run elasticity as there was in tax revenues derived almost entirely from customs duties. Hence, when production fell off and private incomes diminished, the accompanying change in governmental revenues was usually small. In recent years, however, governmental revenues have become very sensitive to fluctuations of business conditions. When corporate profits decline by, say, a billion dollars, the federal government will collect under existing law about a half billion less from corporations. When individual incomes decline by a billion, the federal government may be expected to collect about $150 million less from individuals. State income taxes accentuate these effects. In short, when a recession occurs, our current tax system requires the government to reduce rather promptly and substantially the amount of money that it withdraws from the private economy for its own use. The result is that the income from production which corporations and individuals have at their disposal declines much less than does the national income.

Moreover, the operations of government are now so organized that the flow of personal income from production is bolstered during a recession by increased payments of unemployment insurance benefits. Unemployment insurance was established on a national basis in 1935, and the protection of workers against the hazards of unemployment has increased since then. Not all employees are as yet covered by unemployment insurance and the benefits, besides, are often inadequate to provide for essentials. Nevertheless, there has been a gradual improvement in the ability of families to get along decently even when the main breadwinner is temporarily unemployed. At present, over 80 per cent of those who work for a wage or salary are covered by unemployment insurance, in contrast to 70 per cent in 1940. The period over which benefits can be paid to an unemployed worker has become longer and the typical weekly benefit has risen in greater proportion than the cost of living. Furthermore, arrangements have recently been concluded in several major industries whereby benefits to the unemployed are supplemented from private sources.

Other parts of the vast system of social security that we have devised since the 1930's have also served to support the flow of personal income at times when business activity is declining. Payments made to retired workers kept increasing during each recession of the postwar period. The reason is partly that workers handicapped by old age or physical disability experience greater difficulty at such times in keeping their jobs or finding new ones and therefore apply for pensions in somewhat larger numbers. Another factor has been the intermittent liberalization of statutory benefits. But the most important reason for the steady increase of old-age pensions is the maturing of the social security system. In 1940, only 7 per cent of people of age sixty-five and over were eligible for benefits from the old-age insurance trust fund, in contrast to 23 per cent in 1948 and 69 per cent in 1958. The trend of other public pension programs and the various public assistance programs has also been upward. Between 1929 and 1957 the social security and related benefits paid out by our various governmental units rose from 1 per cent of total personal income to 6 per cent. In 1933, with the economy at a catastrophically low level, these benefit payments were merely $548 million larger than in 1929. On the other hand, in 1958—when business activity was only slightly depressed—they were $4.4 billion above the level of 1957. Even these figures understate the difference between current conditions and those of a quarter century ago, for they leave out of account the private pensions which are beginning to supplement public pensions on a significant scale.

As a result of these several major developments in our national life, the movement of aggregate personal income is no longer closely linked to the movement of aggregate production. During the postwar period we have had several brief but sizable setbacks in production. For example, in the course of the recession of 1957–58, the physical output of factories and mines fell 14 per cent, the physical output of commodities and services in the aggregate fell 5.4 per cent, and the dollar volume of total output fell 4.3 per cent. In earlier times personal incomes would have responded decisively to such a decline in production. This time the government absorbed a substantial part of the drop in the dollar volume of production by putting up with a sharp decline of its revenues despite the need to raise expenditures. Corporations absorbed another part of the decline by maintaining dividends while their undistributed profits slumped. In the end, the aggregate of personal incomes, after taxes, declined less than 1 per cent and the decline was over before the recession ended.

Although the details have varied from one case to the next, a marked divergence between the movements of personal income and production has occurred in each of the postwar recessions. Indeed, during 1953–54 the total income at the disposal of individuals defied the recession by continuing to increase. This unique achievement was due to the tax reduction that became effective soon after the onset of recession as well as to the structural changes that have reduced the dependence of personal income on the short-run movements of production.

II

When we turn from personal income to employment, we find that the imprint of the business cycle is still strong. During each recession since 1948, unemployment reached a level which, while decidedly low in comparison with the experience of the thirties, was sufficient to cause serious concern. But although the fluctuations of employment have continued to synchronize closely with the movements of production, the relation between the two has been changing in ways which favor greater stability of employment in the future.

As the industrialization of our economy proceeded during the nineteenth century, an increasing part of the population became exposed to the hazards of the business cycle. Manufacturing, mining, construction, freight transportation—these are the strategic industries of a developing economy and they are also the industries in which both production and jobs have been notoriously unstable. Shortly after the Civil War, the employees attached to this cyclical group of industries already constituted 23 per cent of the labor force. Employees of industries that have remained relatively free from cyclical unemployment—that is, agriculture, merchandising, public utilities, financial enterprises, the personal service trades, and the government—accounted for another 32 per cent. The self-employed in farming, business, and the professions, whose jobs are especially steady, made up the rest or 45 per cent of the work force. This was the situation in 1869. Fifty years later, the proportion of workers engaged in farming, whether as operators or hired hands, had shrunk drastically, and this shrinkage was offset only in part by the relative gain of other stable sources of employment. Consequently, the proportion of employees in the cyclical industries kept rising, decade after decade, and reached 36 per cent in 1919.

Clearly, the broad effect of economic evolution until about 1920 was to increase the concentration of jobs in the cyclically volatile industries, and this was a major force tending to intensify declines of employment during business contractions. Since then, the continued progress of technology, the very factor which originally was mainly responsible for the concentration in the cyclical industries, has served to arrest this tendency. The upward trend of production in manufacturing and the other highly cyclical industries has remained rapid in recent decades. However, advances of technology have come so swiftly in these industries as well as in agriculture that an increasing part of the nation's labor could turn to the multitude of tasks in which the effectiveness of human effort improves only slowly, where it improves at all. Thus the employees of "service" industries constituted 24 per cent of the labor force in 1919, but as much as 44 per cent in 1957. The proportion of self-employed workers in business and the professions, which was 9.4 per cent in the earlier year, became 10.6 per cent in the later year. True, these gains in types of employment that are relatively stable during business cycles were largely canceled by the countervailing trend in agriculture. Nevertheless, the proportion of employees attached to the cyclically volatile industries has not risen since 1919. Or to express this entire development in another way, the proportion of workers having rather steady jobs, either because they work for themselves or because they are employed in industries that are relatively free from the influence of business cycles, kept declining from the beginning of our industrial revolution until about 1920, and since then has moved slightly but irregularly upward.

Thus, the changing structure of industry, which previously had exercised a powerful destabilizing influence on employment and output, particularly the former, has ceased to do so. The new stabilizing tendency is as yet weak, but it is being gradually reinforced by the spread of "white-collar" occupations throughout the range of industry. For many years now, the proportion of people who work as managers, engineers, scientists, draftsmen, accountants, clerks, secretaries, salesmen, or in kindred occupations has been increasing. The white-collar group, which constituted only 28 per cent of the labor force outside of agriculture in 1900, rose to 38 per cent in 1940 and to 44 per cent in 1957. Workers of this category are commonly said to hold a "position" rather than a "job" and to be paid a "salary" rather than a "wage." Hence, they are often sheltered by a professional code which frowns upon frequent firing and hiring. Moreover, much of this type of employment is by its nature of an overhead character and therefore less responsive to the business cycle than are the jobs of machine operators, craftsmen, assembly-line workers, truck drivers, laborers, and others in the "blue-collar" category. For example, during the recession of 1957–58, the number of "production workers" employed in manufacturing, who approximate the blue-collar group, declined 12 per cent, while the employment of "nonproduction workers," who approximate the white-collar group, declined only 3 per cent. This sort of difference has been characteristic of recessions generally, not only the most recent episode, and on a smaller scale it has also been characteristic of industry generally, not only of manufacturing.

It appears, therefore, that changes in the occupational structure of the labor force, if not also in the industrial structure, have been tending of late to loosen the links which, over a considerable part of our economic history, tied the short-run movement of total employment rather firmly to the cyclical movement of total production, and especially to the cyclical movement of its most unstable parts—that is, the activities of manufacturing, mining, construction, and freight transportation. This stabilizing tendency promises well for the future, although up to the present it has not left a mark on records of aggregate employment that is comparable with the imprint that the stabilizing influences we discussed previously have left on personal income. In the postwar period, as over a longer past, the number of men and women at work, and even more the aggregate of hours worked by them, has continued to move in fairly close sympathy with the fluctuations of production.

We can no longer justifiably suppose, however, when employment falls two million during a recession, as it did between July 1957 and July 1958, that the number of people who receive an income has declined by any such figure. In fact, the number of workers drawing unemployment insurance under the several regular plans rose about 1.3 million during these twelve months, while the number of retired workers on public pensions rose another million. Hence, it may be conservatively estimated that the number of income recipients increased over 300 thousand despite the recession. In the other postwar recessions our experience was fairly similar. In other words, as a result of some of the structural changes on which I dwelt earlier, the size of the income-receiving population has grown steadily and escaped cyclical fluctuations entirely.[1]

III

Turning next to consumer spending, we must try once again to see recent developments in historical perspective. The fact that stands out is that the impact of business cycles on consumption has recently diminished, while the effects of consumption on the business cycle have become more decisive.

In the classical business cycle, as we came to know it in this country, once business investment began declining appreciably, a reduction of consumer spending soon followed. Sometimes the expansion of investment culminated because the firms of one or more key industries, finding that their markets were growing less rapidly than had been anticipated, made an

---

[1] This upward trend would appear steeper than I have suggested if recipients of property income and of public assistance were included in the count. In the present context, however, it has seemed best to restrict the income-receiving population to the working class, or more precisely, to members of the labor force or those recently in the labor force who receive an income as a matter of right and on some regular basis.

effort to bring their productive capacity or inventories into better adjustment with sales. Sometimes the expansion culminated because the belief grew that construction and financing costs had been pushed to unduly high levels by the advance of prosperity. Sometimes it culminated for all these or still other reasons. But whatever the cause or causes of the decline in investment, it made its influence felt over an increasing area of the economy. For a while consumer spending was maintained at a peak level or even kept rising. But since businessmen were now buying on a smaller scale from one another, more and more workers lost their jobs or their overtime pay, financial embarrassments and business failures became more frequent, and uncertainty about the business outlook spread to parts of the economy in which sales and profits were still flourishing. If some consumers reacted to these developments by curtailing their spending in the interest of caution, others did so as a matter of necessity. Before long, these curtailments proved sufficient to bring on some decline in the aggregate spending of consumers. The impulses for reducing business investments therefore quickened and the entire round of events was repeated, with both investment and consumption declining in a cumulative process.

As the contraction continued, it tried men's patience, yet in time worked its own cure. Driven by hard necessity, business firms moved with energy to reduce costs and increase efficiency. Consumers whose incomes were declining often saved less or dissaved in order not to disrupt their customary living standards. Hence, even if sales and prices were still falling, profit margins improved here and there. In the meantime, bank credit became more readily available, costs of building and terms of borrowing became more favorable, the bond market revived, business failures diminished, and the investment plans of innovators and others began expanding again.

When recovery finally came, it was likely to be led by a reduced rate of disinvestment in inventories or by a new rush to make investments in fixed capital. At this stage of the business cycle, consumer spending was at its very lowest level, if not still declining.

Many of these features of earlier business cycles have carried over to the present. However, the behavior of consumers in the postwar recessions has departed from the traditional pattern in two respects. In the first place, consumers maintained their spending at a high level even after business activity had been declining for some months, so that the tendency of recessions to cumulate was severely checked. During the recession of 1945 consumer spending actually kept increasing. In each of the later recessions it fell somewhat; but the decline at no time exceeded one per cent and lasted only a quarter or two. In the second place, instead of lagging at the recovery stage of the business cycle, as it had in earlier times, consumer spending turned upward before production or employment resumed its expansion. This shift in cyclical behavior appears clearly in department store sales, which have been recorded on a substantially uniform basis for several decades and are widely accepted as a tolerably good indicator of consumer spending. In the recoveries of 1921, 1924, and 1927, and 1938, these sales lagged by intervals ranging from two to four months. In 1933 their upturn came at the same time as in production and employment. It thus appears that, during the 1920's and 1930's, consumer spending in no instance led the economy out of a slump. In the postwar period, on the other hand, department store sales have led successive recoveries by intervals stretching from two to five months. Of course, department store sales cover only a small fraction of consumer expenditure, and correction for price changes would alter their historical record somewhat. But the main features of the cyclical behavior of dollar sales by department stores are broadly confirmed by other evidence on consumer spending, which is extensive for recent years. We may therefore conclude with considerable assurance that consumer spending has played a more dynamic role in recent times. Not only have consumers managed their spending during recessions so that the cumulative process of deflation has been curbed, but consumer spending has emerged as one of the active factors in arresting recession and hastening recovery.

This new role of the consumer in the business cycle reflects some of the developments of the postwar period that we considered earlier, particularly the greatly enhanced stability in the flow of personal income, the steady expansion in the number of income recipients, and the relative increase in the number of steady jobs. It reflects also the improvements of financial organization and other structural changes which have strengthened the confidence of people, whether acting as consumers or investors, in their own and the nation's economic future. Whatever may have been true of the past, it can no longer be held that consumers are passive creatures who lack the power or the habit of initiating changes in economic activities. There is no harm in thinking of consumer spending as being largely "determined" by past and current incomes, provided we also recognize that the level of current incomes is itself shaped to a significant degree by the willingness of people to work hard to earn what they need to live as they feel they should. The evidence of rising expectations and increased initiative on the part of consumers is all around us. It appears directly in the rapidly rising proportion of women in the labor force, in the sizable and increasing proportion of men who hold down more than one job, in the slackening of the long-term decline of the average workweek in manufacturing despite the increased power of trade unions, as well as indirectly in the improvement of living standards and the great upsurge of population. Indeed, the expansive forces on the side of consumption have been so powerful that we must not be misled by the cyclical responses of consumer spending, small though they were, to which I referred earlier. There are no continuous records of inventories in the hands of consumers; but if such statistics were available, we would almost certainly find that consumption proper, in contrast to consumer spending, did not decline at all during any of the postwar recessions.

In view of these developments in the realm of the consumer, it is evident that the force of any cyclical decline of production has in recent years been reduced or broken as its influence spread through the economy. Production has remained unstable, but the structure of our economy has changed in ways which have limited the effects of recessions on the lives of individuals—on the numbers who receive an income, the aggregate of personal incomes, consumer spending, actual consumption, and to some degree even the numbers employed. It is, therefore, hardly an exaggeration to assert that a good part of the personal security which in an earlier age derived from living on farms and in closely knit family units, after having been disrupted by the onrush of industrialization and urbanization, has of late been restored through the new institutions that have developed in both the private and public branches of our economy.

IV

In concentrating, as I have thus far, on the changes of economic organization which have lately served to reduce the impact of business cycles on the lives of individuals, I have provisionally taken the cyclical movement of production for granted. Of course, if the fluctuations of production had been larger, the impact on people would have been greater. On the other hand, the stabilized tendency of personal income and consumption has itself been a major reason why recent recessions of production have been brief and of only moderate intensity. Many other factors have contributed to this development. Among them are the deliberate efforts made in our generation to control the business cycle, of which I have as yet said little.

In earlier generations there was a tendency for the focus of business thinking to shift from the pursuit of profits to the maintenance of financial solvency whenever confidence in the continuance of prosperity began to wane. At such times experienced businessmen were prone to reason that it would shortly become more difficult to collect from their customers or to raise funds by borrowing, while they in turn were being pressed by their creditors. Under the circumstances it seemed only prudent to conserve cash on hand, if not also to reduce inventories or accounts receivable. Such efforts by some led to similar efforts by others, in a widening circle. As pressure on commodity markets, security markets, and on the banking system mounted, the decline of business activity was speeded and the readjustment of interest rates, particularly on the longer maturities, was delayed. More often than not the scramble for liquidity ran its course without reaching crisis proportions. Sometimes, however, as in 1873, 1893, and 1907, events took a sinister turn. Financial pressures then became so acute that doubts arose about the ability of banks to meet their outstanding obligations and, as people rushed to convert their deposits into currency, even the soundest banks were forced to restrict the outflow of cash. With the nation's system for making monetary payments disrupted, panic ruled for a time over the economy and production inevitably slumped badly.

It was this dramatic phase of the business cycle that first at-tracted wide notice and stimulated students of public affairs to seek ways and means of improving our financial organization. The Federal Reserve Act, which became law under the shadow of the crisis of 1907, required the pooling of bank reserves and established facilities for temporary borrowing by banks. The hope that this financial reform would ease the transition from the expanding to the contracting phase of business cycles has been amply justified by experience. But the Federal Reserve System could not prevent the cumulation of financial trouble during business expansions. Nor could it prevent runs on banks or massive bank failures, as the Great Depression demonstrated. The need to overhaul and strengthen the financial system became increasingly clear during the thirties and led to numerous reforms, among them the insurance of mortgages, the creation of a secondary market for mortgages, the insurance of savings and loan accounts, and—most important of all—the insurance of bank deposits. These financial reforms have served powerfully to limit the propagation of fear, which in the past had been a major factor in intensifying slumps of production.

But more basic than the financial innovations or any other specific measures of policy has been the change in economic and political attitudes which took root during the thirties. The economic theory that depressions promote industrial efficiency and economic progress lost adherents as evidence accumulated of the wreckage caused by unemployment and business failures. The political belief that it was best to leave business storms to blow themselves out lost its grip on men's minds as the depression stretched out. In increasing numbers citizens in all walks of life came around to the view that mass unemployment was intolerable under modern conditions and that the federal government has a continuing responsibility to foster competitive enterprise, to prevent or moderate general economic declines, and to promote a high and rising level of employment and production. This new philosophy of intervention was articulated by the Congress in the Employment Act of 1946, which solemnly expressed what had by then become a national consensus.

In recent times, therefore, the business cycle has no longer run a free course and this fact has figured prominently in the plans of businessmen as well as consumers. During the 1930's, when the objectives of social reform and economic recovery were sometimes badly confused, many investors suspected that contracyclical policies would result in narrowing the scope of private enterprise and reducing the profitability of investment. These fears diminished after the war as the government showed more understanding of the need to foster a mood of confidence so that enterprise, innovation, and investment may flourish. In investing circles, as elsewhere, the general expectation of the postwar period has been that the government would move with some vigor to check any recession that developed, that its actions would by and large contribute to this objective, and that they would do so in a manner that is broadly consistent with our national traditions. This expectation gradually became stronger and it has played a significant role in extending the horizons of business thinking about the markets and opportunities of the future. The upsurge of population, the eagerness of consumers to live better, the resurgence of Western Europe, the revolutionary discoveries of science, and the steady flow of new products, new materials, and new processes have added impetus to the willingness of investors to expend huge sums of capital on research and on the improvement and expansion of industrial plant and equipment. Some of these influences have also been effective in augmenting public investment. The fundamental trend of investment has therefore been decidedly upward. The private part of investment has continued to move cyclically; but it is now a smaller fraction of total national output and it has displayed a capacity to rebound energetically from the setbacks that come during recessions.

The specific measures adopted by the government in dealing with the recessions of the postwar period have varied from one case to the next. In all of them, monetary, fiscal, and house-keeping policies played some part, with agricultural price-support programs assuming special prominence in one reces-sion, tax reductions in another, and increases of public expen-diture in still another. Taking a long view, the most nearly consistent part of contracyclical policy has been in the mone-tary sphere. Since the early 1920's, when the Federal Reserve authorities first learned how to influence credit conditions through open-market operations, long-term interest rates have tended to move down as soon as the cyclical peak of economic activity was reached, in contrast to the long lags that were characteristic of earlier times. Since 1948 the decline of long-term interest rates in the early stages of a recession has also become more rapid. This change in the cyclical behavior of capital markets reflects the increased vigor and effectiveness of recent monetary policies. Inasmuch as optimism, as a rule, is still widespread during the initial stages of an economic de-cline, a substantial easing of credit, provided it comes early enough, can appreciably hasten economic recovery. This influ-ence is exerted only in part through lower interest rates. Of greater consequence is the fact that credit becomes more readily available, that the money supply is increased or kept from falling, that the liquidity of financial assets is improved, and that financial markets are generally stimulated. The effects of easier credit are apt to be felt most promptly by smaller businesses and the homebuilding industry, but they tend to work their way through the entire economy. There can be little doubt that the rather prompt easing of credit conditions, which occurred during recent setbacks of production, was of some significance in keeping their duration so short. Business firms have also been paying closer attention to the business cycle, and not a few of them have even tried to do something about it. These efforts have been expressed in a variety of ways—through the adoption of long-range capital budgets, closer control of inventories, and more energetic selling or some relaxation of credit standards in times of recession. I do not know enough to assess either the extent or the success of some of these business policies. Surely, business investment in fixed capital has remained a highly volatile activity—a fact that is sometimes overlooked by concentrating attention on years instead of months and on actual expenditures instead of new commitments. There is, however, strong evidence that the businessmen of our generation manage inventories better than did their predecessors. The inventory-sales ratio of manufacturing firms has lately averaged about a fourth less than during the 1920's, despite the increased importance of the durable goods sector where inventories are especially heavy. The trend of the inventory-sales ratio has also moved down substantially in the case of distributive firms. This success in economizing on inventories has tended to reduce the fluctuations of inventory investment relative to the scale of business operations and this in turn has helped to moderate the cyclical swings in production. Not only that, but it appears that the cyclical downturns of both inventories and inventory investment have tended to come at an earlier stage of the business cycle in the postwar period than they did previously, so that any imbalance between inventories and sales could be corrected sooner. Since consumer outlays—and often also other expenditures—were well maintained during the recent recessions of production, the rising phase of inventory disinvestment ceased rather early and this naturally favored a fairly prompt recovery of production.

Thus, numerous changes in the structure of our economy have combined to stimulate over-all expansion during the postwar period and to keep within moderate limits the cyclical declines that occurred in production. Indeed, there are cogent grounds for believing that these declines were even more moderate than our familiar statistical records suggest. The line of division between production for sale and production for direct use does not stand still in a dynamic economy. In the early decades of the industrial revolution an increasing part of our production was, in effect, transferred from the home to the shop and factory. This trend has continued in the preparation of foods, but in other activities it appears on balance to have been reversed. The great expansion of home ownership, the invention of all sorts of mechanical contrivances for the home, longer vacations, the general eagerness for improvement, if not also the income tax, have stimulated many people to do more and more things for themselves. Consumers have become equipped to an increasing degree with the capital goods they need for transportation, for the refrigeration of food, for the laundering of clothes, as well as for entertainment and instruction. They have also been doing, on an increasing scale, much of the carpentry, painting, plumbing, and landscaping around their homes. Such activities of production are less subject to the business cycle than the commercial activities which enter statistical reports. Yet these domestic activities have undoubtedly been expanding rapidly, and perhaps expanding even more during the declining than during the rising phase of the business cycle. Hence, it is entirely probable that the cyclical swings of production have of late been smaller, while the average rate of growth of production has been higher, than is commonly supposed.

V

It is in the nature of an economic vocabulary to change slowly, when it changes at all. We keep speaking of the price system, the business cycle, capitalism, socialism, communism, and sometimes we even refer to the "inherent instability" of capitalism or of communism; but the reality that these terms and phrases are intended to denote or sum up does not remain fixed. I have tried to show how a conjuncture of structural changes in our economy has served to modify the business cycle of our times. Some of these changes were planned while others were unplanned. Some resulted from efforts to control the business cycle while others originated in policies aimed at different ends. Some arose from private and others from public activities. Some are of very recent origin and others of long standing. The net result has been that the intensity of cyclical swings of production has become smaller. The links that previously tied together the cyclical movements of production, employment, personal income, and consumption have become looser. And, as everyone knows, the once familiar parallelism of the short-term movements in the physical volume of total production, on the one hand, and the average level of wholesale or consumer prices, on the other, has become somewhat elusive.

To be sure, special factors of an episodic character played their part in recent business cycles, as they always have. For example, a pent-up demand for civilian goods was highly significant in checking the recession of 1945. The tax reduction legislated in April 1948 helped to moderate the recession which began towards the end of that year. The tax cuts announced soon after business activity began receding in 1953 merely required executive acquiescence in legislation that had been passed before any recession was in sight. Again, the sputniks spurred the government's response to the recession of 1957–58. Special circumstances such as these undoubtedly weakened the forces of economic contraction at certain times; but they also strengthened them at other times. In particular, governmental purchases from private firms have not infrequently been an unsettling influence rather than a stabilizing force. We need only recall the drop of federal expenditure on commodities and services from an annual rate of $91 billion in the early months of 1945 to $16 billion two years later, or the fall from $59 billion to $44 billion soon after the Korean hostilities came to a close. The ability of our economy to adjust to such major disturbances without experiencing a severe or protracted slump testifies not only to our good luck; it testifies also to the stabilizing power of the structural changes that I have emphasized.

It seems reasonable to expect that the structural changes in our economy, which have recently served to moderate and humanize the business cycle, will continue to do so. The growth of corporations is not likely to be checked, nor is the tendency to pay fairly stable dividends likely to be modified. The scale of governmental activities will remain very extensive, and so it would be even if the communist threat to our national security were somehow banished. Our methods of taxation might change materially, but the income tax will remain a major source of governmental revenue. Governmental expenditures might fluctuate sharply, but they are not likely to decline during a recession merely because governmental revenues are then declining. The social security system is more likely to grow than to remain stationary or contract. Private pension arrangements will multiply and so also may private supplements to unemployment insurance. Our population will continue to grow. The restlessness and eagerness of consumers to live better is likely to remain a dynamic force. Research and development activities will continue to enlarge opportunities for investment. Governmental efforts to promote a high and expanding level of economic activity are not likely to weaken. Private businesses will continue to seek ways to economize on inventories and otherwise minimize the risk of cyclical fluctuations in their operations. Employment in agriculture is already so low that its further decline can no longer offset future gains of the service industries on the scale experienced in the past. The spread of white-collar occupations throughout the range of industry will continue and may even accelerate. For all these reasons, the business cycle is unlikely to be as disturbing or troublesome to our children as it once was to us or our fathers.

This is surely a reasonable expectation as we look to the future. Yet, it is well to remember that projections of human experience remain descriptions of a limited past no matter how alluringly they are expressed in language of the future. A lesson of history, which keeps resounding through the ages, is that the most reasonable of expectations sometimes lead nations astray. If my analysis is sound, it supports the judgment that the recessions or depressions of the future are likely to be appreciably milder on the average than they were before the 1940's. It supports no more than this. In view of the inherent variability of business cycles and our still somewhat haphazard ways of dealing with them, there can be no assurance that episodic factors will not make a future recession both longer and deeper than any we experienced in the postwar period.

Nor can there be any assurance that the conjuncture of structural changes on which I have dwelt will not be succeeded by another which will prove less favorable to economic stability. For example, although the stabilizing influence of the rising trend of white-collar employment in manufacturing has been more than sufficient to offset the cyclically intensifying influence of a greater concentration of employment in the durable goods sector, the balance of forces might be tipped the other way in the future. This could happen all the more readily if, as white-collar work continues to grow, the need to cut costs during a recession should make this type of employment less stable than it has been. Again, our exports in recent decades have tended to intensify the business cycle somewhat, and this factor may become of larger significance. Also, it still remains to be seen whether the rising trend of prices—to say nothing of the rapidly growing consumer and mortgage debt—may not serve to complicate future recessions.

A generation ago many economists, having become persuaded that our economy had reached maturity, spoke grimly of a future of secular stagnation. Parts of their analysis were faulty and their predictions have proved wrong; yet their warning helped to mobilize thought and energy to avert the danger of chronic unemployment. Of late, many economists have been speaking just as persuasively, though not always as grimly, of a future of secular inflation. The warning is timely. During the postwar recessions the average level of prices in wholesale and consumer markets has declined little or not at all. The advances in prices that customarily occur during periods of business expansion have therefore become cumulative. It is true that in the last few years the federal government has made some progress in dealing with inflation. Nevertheless, wages and prices rose appreciably even during the recent recession, the general public has been speculating on a larger scale in common stocks, long-term interest rates have risen very sharply since mid-1958, and the yield on stocks relative to bonds has become abnormally low. All these appear to be symptoms of a continuation of inflationary expectations or pressures.

Such developments have often led to economic trouble. They could do so again even if our balance of payments on international account remained favorable. That, however, has not been the case for some time. The "dollar shortage" which influenced much of our economic thinking and practice during the past generation seems to have ended. The economies of many areas of the Free World, especially of Western Europe and Japan, have lately been rebuilt and their competitive power has been restored. This reestablishment of competitive and monetary links between our country and others may cause us some inconvenience, but it is basically a promising development for the future. It should stimulate our economic growth as well as contribute to the economic progress and political stability of other nations of the Free World. Our financial policies, however, will gradually need to be adjusted to the changed international environment. Although our gold stocks are still abundant and the dollar is still the strongest currency in the world, we can no longer conduct our economic affairs without being mindful of gold, or of the short-term balances that foreign governments and citizens have accumulated here, or of the levels of labor costs, interest rates, and prices in our country relative to those in other nations. Unless the deficit in our balance of payments is soon brought under better control, our nation's ability to pursue contracyclical policies during a business recession may be seriously hampered.

We are living in extraordinarily creative but also deeply troubled times. One of the triumphs of this generation is the progress that our nation has made in reducing economic instability. In the years ahead, no matter what we do as a people, our economy will continue to undergo changes, many of which were neither planned nor anticipated. However, the course of events, both domestic and international, will also depend—and to a large degree—on our resourcefulness and courage in deliberately modifying the structure of our economy so as to strengthen the forces of growth and yet restrain instability.

Great opportunities as well as difficult problems face our nation. Monopoly power, which is still being freely exercised despite all the exhortation of recent years, can be curbed by moving toward price and wage controls or, as many economists still hope, by regenerating competition. Higher protective tariffs, import quotas, and "Buy American" schemes can be embraced or, as many economists hope, avoided. A tax structure that inhibits private investment and directs people's energy into activities that contribute little to the nation's economic strength can be retained or reformed. Costly farm surpluses can be further encouraged by government or discontinued. The problems posed by the slums and the inefficient transportation of many of our cities can be neglected or attacked with some zeal. The inadequacy of our unemployment insurance system can be ignored until the next recession or corrected while there is opportunity for a judicious overhauling. In general, our governmental authorities can deal with recessions by trusting to improvisations of public spending, which often will not become effective until economic recovery is already under way, or by providing in advance of any recession for fairly prompt and automatic adjustment of income tax rates to a temporarily lower level of economic activity. The coordination of governmental policies, which may make the difference between success and failure in promoting our national objectives, can be left largely to accidents of personal force and ingenuity or it can be made systematic through an economic policy board under the chairmanship of the President. These and other choices will have to be made by the people of the United States; and economists—far more than any other group—will in the end help to make them.

FOUR

Dealing with Recession and Inflation

THE PRESSURE for economic improvement, which is now being felt everywhere in the world, has been a dominant force throughout our nation's history. The typical American worker has not been content with a good income or a decent standard of living. He has striven to improve his skills, to increase his income, and to raise the standard of living of his family. The typical business manager has not been content to run an efficient enterprise. He has striven to equip it with the most modern contrivances, to improve its products or services, and to expand sales. The typical investor has not been content with a modest return on a safe investment. He has willingly risked capital to create economic opportunity—by exploring new processes, experimenting with new products, building new facilities, and developing new markets. Our economy has grown rapidly because we had faith in ourselves, because we have developed institutions that encourage enterprise and reward efficiency, and because we have believed in progress sufficiently to put enough aside from our current income to expand the productive plant and build the knowledge

Millar Lecture at Fordham University, October 15, 1957. Reprinted, by permission of the publisher, from *Prosperity Without Inflation*, Fordham University Press, New York, 1957, pp. 23–42.

that would be needed by a venturesome and growing population.

Americans today preponderantly believe in economic progress through free and competitive enterprise, just as our fathers did. But we have also come to believe that progress need not proceed as fitfully as in the past. Between 1854 and 1954 our economy experienced twenty-four full waves of expansion followed by contraction. Most of these setbacks to economic growth were brief and mild. However, some were severe, as in 1857–58 and 1907–08, and others were protracted as well as severe, as in the 1870's, the 1890's, and the 1930's. Whenever an economic depression developed, people generously shared what they had with their less fortunate neighbors. Private welfare agencies supplemented these personal efforts by distributing provisions to the needy, and local governments occasionally provided work relief. Such measures, however, failed to reach many needing assistance. Sometimes they added to the feeling of degradation produced by unemployment itself; and they did nothing to prevent the occurrence of economic slumps. They could not long satisfy the requirements of a society which, in the process of undergoing rapid industrialization, was also learning how to express its aspirations for a better life through the ballot boxes of democracy.

I

The concept of governmental responsibility for moderating economic fluctuations developed gradually and in response to hard experience. At the beginning of the century, public officials were already searching for ways of dealing with the most dramatic phase of the business cycle—that is, the prevention of financial crises such as had occurred in 1893 and in 1907. The violent movements of the price level between 1914 and 1921 stimulated the authorities of our newly organized Federal Reserve System to concern themselves during the twenties with the moderation of price fluctuations, in the hope that the business cycle itself might to some degree be tamed in the process. After the stock market crash of 1929, business activity kept declining for many months, unemployment reached proportions hitherto unexperienced, and general discontent mounted. Extensive governmental measures to stimulate recovery of employment, production, and prices became unavoidable. They were put in motion, first under the Hoover Administration, later—and on a broader scale—by the Roosevelt Administration.

Unemployment finally vanished during World War II, but the memory of its ravages during the thirties remained vivid. As the war approached a close, great apprehension was felt that mass unemployment might return once millions of men were released by the armed forces and by the civilian establishments then engaged in producing war goods. To register the nation's determination that this must not happen, the Congress passed with an overwhelming vote of the members of both our major parties the Employment Act of 1946, which solemnly declared that the federal government has a continuing responsibility to use all practicable means to foster free competitive enterprise, to prevent or moderate economic fluctuations, and to promote maximum employment, production, and purchasing power.

The Employment Act reflects a revolutionary change in economic and political thought. Only a generation ago, men concerned with economic affairs typically held the view that it was best to allow storms of business depression to blow themselves out. They knew, of course, that unemployment and business failures at times increased sharply. They deplored such developments, and therefore persistently argued for monetary stability and the prevention of booms. But once a business recession got under way, they were inclined to oppose any large governmental efforts to check the economic decline. In response to such proposals, they often took the position that economic adversity stimulated people to practice thrift and industry, that it served to redirect or weed out inefficient workmen and inefficient enterprises, and that economic progress was furthered in the process. Let the government raise enough taxes to cover its expenditures, let the banks maintain pressure on business firms to liquidate excessive inventories and avoid hazardous undertakings, let the financially weak firms take down their shingles and put up their shutters, let the general public practice greater frugality—incredible though it may now seem, these were the measures for curing a business depression that were widely and effectively advanced a mere twenty or thirty years ago.

The Great Depression of the thirties and the international troubles of later years forced most of us to reexamine our economic ideas. From personal observation or experience we have learned that self-reliant workers as well as the shiftless lose their jobs when business activity falls off appreciably, and that at such a time well-managed enterprises often follow the inefficient into bankruptcy. We have learned that in the course of a depression many men lose faith in themselves, and that some lose faith even in our economic and political institutions. We have learned that economic progress is a powerful weapon in the ideological struggle that of late has been stirring men's minds in distant lands, and that the continuance of prosperity is our best answer to the Marxist prophecy of crisis and collapse of free economies. We have come to recognize that in an age of international turmoil such as ours, federal tax revenues, expenditures, and debt transactions are bound to be very large, and that it therefore is unrealistic to suppose that the government any longer either can or should be a neutral factor in the economy.

Although our ability to limit recessions and prevent depressions has not yet been fully tested, we have made considerable progress in understanding economic fluctuations and we have learned to profit from the mistakes of the past. No government nowadays would tolerate the destruction of one-third of the nation's money supply during a period of depressed economic activity and prices. Yet that is precisely what happened between the fall of 1929 and the spring of 1933. No monetary authority is likely to repeat in the near future the blunder of the Federal Reserve System in the autumn of 1931 when, in the face of widespread economic fear and trouble, a tightening of credit was allowed to occur. Nor has the ineffectiveness of the liberalizing actions that followed in early 1932 escaped the attention of experienced observers. It is not enough to increase the availability and reduce the cost of credit during the declining phase of a business cycle. If such action is to be effective, it must come when the level of business and consumer confidence is high. This condition is much more likely to prevail in the early than in the advanced stage of a business contraction, particularly if the government pursues policies that otherwise encourage individual enterprise.

If prosperity is to flourish, people must have confidence in their own economic future and that of their country. This basic truth was temporarily lost sight of during the 1930's in the process of grafting new economic ideas and practices onto the old. In the five years from 1932 to 1936, unemployment at its lowest was nine million or 17 per cent of the labor force; at its highest it was thirteen million or 25 per cent of the labor force. The existence of such vast unemployment did not, however, deter the federal government from imposing new tax burdens.

Exemptions under the individual income tax were lowered from $3,500 to $2,500 for married persons. The minimum rate of the tax was raised from 1.5 to 4 per cent, and the maximum rate from 25 to 79 per cent. The exemption of dividends from the normal tax was repealed. The tax rate on capital gains of high income recipients was increased. The basic tax rate on corporate profits was raised from 12 to 15 per cent, besides the levying of a capital stock tax. An undistributed profits tax was imposed, with a maximum rate of 27 per cent. The exemption under the estate tax was sharply reduced, while the maximum rate of the tax was raised from 20 to 70 per cent. A new gift tax was enacted, with a maximum rate of 52½ per cent. A wide variety of new excise taxes was imposed—on automobiles and parts, cameras, phonograph records, sporting goods, furs, jewelry, radios, refrigerators, gasoline, electrical energy, telephone and telegraph messages, and toilet preparations. For a time, even candy, chewing gum, and soft drinks carried excises, as did checks drawn on bank accounts.

The Revenue Act of 1932 imposed the heaviest of these increases of taxation, but later legislation added new burdens in quick succession—in 1934, 1935, and again in 1936. People were unprepared for tax measures of such severity. The new taxes encroached on the spending power of both consumers and business firms at a time when production and employment were seriously depressed. Worse still, they spread fear that the tax system was becoming an instrument for redistributing incomes, if not also for punishing success. Greatly increased federal spending and borrowing, which accompanied the new and higher taxes, stirred further doubt in the minds of many businessmen and investors about the country's economic future. In the prevailing atmosphere of uncertainty, much of the constructive legislation of the time—as in the case of banking, the stock market, housing, public utilities, and social security—was poorly understood and likewise viewed with suspicion. Innovation and investment therefore languished. The effectiveness of the government's extensive recovery program was reduced. Although economic conditions on the whole improved, business remained sluggish and the unemployed still numbered over eight million as late as 1940.

From the storm and stress of the 1930's our economy has been able, however, to draw new strength in more recent years. The insurance of bank deposits and of savings and loan accounts, the long-term amortizable and insured mortgage, unemployment insurance, and tax revenues that respond sensitively to changes in the national income—all these automatic devices for curbing the rapidity with which a recession cumulates are an inheritance from that decade. More important still is the emergence of an attitude of mind which refuses to accept passively the antics of the business cycle or ways of dealing with recession that have been tried and found wanting.

The present generation looks to the government for leadership in reducing economic instability; and the basis for this confidence has been improving. To be sure, if the business or consuming public chooses to speculate widely in inventories, a general curtailment of production is bound to follow sooner or later. Or if plant expansion proceeds with great rapidity in many lines of activity at the same time, a temporary condition of overcapacity may easily develop and require correction. Nor are these the only developments that can cause general economic activity to contract. The essential objective, however, is not to prevent all contractions, but rather to maintain an environment that curbs excesses from which recessions often spring and to keep such recessions as do occur from degenerating into severe depressions. Recent history indicates that our public policies can be shaped so as to powerfully promote this broad objective.

II

In contrast to earlier generations, which stressed developments in financial and commodity markets, the modern tendency is to think of business recessions largely in terms of unemployment. Of course, not all of the unemployment that exists in our dynamic society is a grave social evil or problem. Some unemployment reflects the fluctuations of the seasons or the frictions of the labor market, where the search of enterprising men and women for better work opportunities is always important. This minimum of unemployment is practically irreducible over any short period, although not in the long run. No good measure of it is available, but in recent years economists have commonly taken it to be something like 4 per cent of our labor force. In other words, a condition of practically full employment is believed to exist when the unemployment rate is about 4 per cent or smaller. In our latest encounter with recession, however, the government did not allow this crude yardstick or any other convention to get in the way of prompt counter-cyclical action.

When economic clouds began to gather in the late spring of 1953, the government was alert to the possible danger of depression. A sizable accumulation of inventories by retailers and wholesalers was one of the first visible signs of impending trouble. A decline in the length of the work week in manufacturing was another. By mid-year it became clear that the build-up of stocks had been involuntary. Retail sales were sluggish, business expenditures on inventories began declining, and these developments were soon aggravated by the drop of military spending which followed the cessation of hostilities in

Korea. The efforts of businessmen to adjust inventories to current sales led to some reduction in output, and so too did the decline of governmental expenditure, particularly for defense outlays. In consequence, employment fell off appreciably in manufacturing industries, and to some degree in other parts of the economy. But the depression that many feared or expected did not develop.

In its new role of responsibility for the maintenance of the nations's prosperity, the federal government deliberately took speedy and massive actions to build confidence and pave the way for renewed economic growth. In May 1953, the Federal Reserve System moved to ease credit conditions by embarking on extensive purchases of securities in the open market. In late June and early July, a bolder step was taken, namely, the reserve requirements of member banks were reduced. This shift to a policy of credit ease was made before economic activity, viewed in the aggregate, had begun declining. In September, the Secretary of the Treasury removed any doubt about early tax cuts by announcing that the Administration would relinquish the excess profits tax and accept a reduction of the personal income tax, both of which were scheduled by earlier legislation for the end of the year. This unequivocal declaration of tax policy, like the earlier moves in the credit sphere, was made when the reported rate of unemployment was less than 2½ per cent. By January 1954, when the President submitted his Economic Report to the Congress, economic activity had already been receding for six months. The latest figure of unemployment then stood at 3 per cent. New and revised statistics which showed more serious deterioration were not as yet available. But, anticipating some extension of the economic decline, the Economic Report counseled the Congress that it "makes a vital difference whether an unemployment rate of 3 per cent is reached by rising up to that figure or declining to it," and that "prudence as well as zeal for economic improvement require that public policy contribute both to the immediate strength of the economy and to its long-term growth."

The President therefore recommended a broad program of legislation. High on the list were tax proposals which, besides correcting various personal inequities, would serve to stimulate business enterprise—through liberalized depreciation allowances on new investments, through fuller treatment of research and development outlays as current expenses, through partial tax credits to recipients of dividends for the income taxes already paid by corporations, and through the extension of the carryback of losses in reckoning income for tax purposes. These reforms of the tax structure were intended to supplement the removal of the corporate excess profits tax and the reduction of the personal income tax averaging about 10 per cent for most taxpayers, which had just become effective. The President also requested legislation to expand the scope and raise the benefits provided by the old-age and unemployment insurance systems, to extend and liberalize credit facilities for home ownership, to foster more energetically the clearance of slums and the rehabilitation of blighted neighborhoods, and to improve the nation's highways. Over the next few months the Congress largely adopted the President's recommendations. It also added a sizable cut in excise levies which, even after allowing for an increase of 1.3 billion dollars in social security contributions, brought the various tax reductions for individuals and businesses that became effective in 1954 to the huge figure of 6.1 billion dollars on a full-year basis.

These major steps to create an atmosphere favorable to the resumption of economic growth were reinforced by other actions, largely of an administrative character. The Federal Reserve authorities lowered the discount rate early in 1954 and later again reduced the reserve requirements of member banks. Governmental aid was projected for some hard-pressed industries—notably, to shipbuilding through a new construction program, and to zinc and lead mining through a revised stockpiling program. Some effort was made to assist hard-pressed localities by channeling government contracts to them and by boosting the allowable rate of accelerated amortization on such industrial investments in these areas as served to strengthen the nation's defense base. The ordinary housekeeping activities of government were managed with an eye to the immediate needs of the economy. For example, the Veterans Administration speeded up the processing of loan guaranty applications, the Federal Housing Administration did likewise with applications for loan insurance, the Department of Agriculture expedited arrangements to stimulate private construction of grain elevators, the Internal Revenue Service made advance payments to taxpayers who had been overassessed prior to final determination of the overassessment, the Bureau of Public Roads lost no time in implementing its expanded financial authority, and so on from one governmental bureau to another. Beyond these housekeeping steps, the Administration sought to check the decline in governmental spending, which in the case of the Defense Department had gone considerably further in the first half of 1954 than had been either planned or anticipated. A modest rescheduling of expenditure within the total set for fiscal year 1955 was adopted, with a view to raising somewhat the government's planned spending for the first six months of the year and thus reinforcing the processes of economic recovery which, while already visible on numerous fronts, were as yet of uncertain strength.

These actions to curb the decline of economic activity did not express the unfolding of any master plan in which all details had been worked out in advance and every contingency provided for. Not only is this sort of thing practically impossible, but any determined attempt to realize it could invite disaster. No two recessions ever run the same course; unforeseen developments are bound to occur; and measures that work well in one situation may work badly in another. A wise government will therefore seek to maintain flexibility in its approach and be prepared to do more in one direction and less in another, besides trying new measures. It will not entrust the nation's fate to a categorical economic forecast or to a rigid economic program.

There are, however, major principles suggested by experience that can usefully guide governmental efforts to check a recession. The first principle is that when the economy shows signs of faltering, prompt countermoves are required. Even mild measures on the part of government can be effective in the early stages of an economic decline. On the other hand, if action is withheld until a recession has gathered momentum, strong and costly measures may prove insufficient. Second, efforts to check a recession have to be coordinated, so that the steps taken by different agencies of our far-flung government may reinforce one another. Third, as far as possible every item of legislation or administrative action, whether it be of short- or long-range character, should encourage consumers and business firms to look with hope and confidence to their own and their country's economic future. Fourth, the actions taken should be on a sufficient scale to give reasonable promise of checking the recession, yet not so powerful as to stimulate extensive speculation or other excesses that may create trouble later. Fifth, while monetary, fiscal, and general housekeeping measures must to some degree go together, they need to be spaced so as to give the private economy a reasonable opportunity to carry out necessary adjustments and to muster its latent strength. Sixth, and by way of partial corollary from the three preceding principles, the emphasis at the start of a recession should ordinarily be on the easing of credit conditions, later on tax reductions for both individuals and businesses, still later on rescheduling of federal expenditure within totals set by long-term considerations, and—only as a last resort—on large public works programs. Of course, advance planning is essential, if public works expenditures are to be accelerated when they may be urgently needed to bolster the economy and if they are to be concentrated, as they should be, on projects that can be completed in relatively short periods and that will serve to support rather than to restrict the opportunities for private enterprise. Seventh, since no two recessions are alike and since they occur under different circumstances in a nation's life, the policies of government must be sensitively adjusted to the individual case. Thus, international factors and considerations of national security may at times justify giving early and preponderant emphasis to expansion of governmental expenditure.

These are the broad principles that guided governmental thought and policies during the recession of 1953–54 and imparted a certain unity and strength to the government's individual actions. That, of course, does not mean that all the measures taken proved fruitful. For example, the program for aiding depressed localities accomplished little beyond demonstrating a need for stronger or at least different measures. Again, the rescheduling of expenditures for the fiscal year 1955 was delayed in execution and became effective when it was no longer needed. But the program as a whole worked out reasonably well. A crash program such as many urged at the time was avoided. Governmental enterprises were kept from multiplying. Yet the contraction in economic activity never reached serious proportions and lasted only a year. At its lowest point, employment in nonagricultural establishments was only 3½ per cent below the preceding peak. Personal income declined still less, while disposable income—that is, personal income after taxes—defied the recession by actually increasing.

Natural forces of economic recovery, the continuance of prosperity abroad, and the safeguards provided by earlier legislation—all had a part in this outcome and in the great economic advance that followed. But the government also played its part. It did not leave the fate of the economy to the automatic stabilizers or to good fortune. It intervened actively and its measures proved effective—in large part because they were disciplined by general principles which had roots in experience and therefore commanded wide assent both within and outside the government.

III

We began to make progress as a people in solving the problem of depression only after we became sufficiently aroused to seek workable solutions. In recent years, many citizens have come to feel that we have been preoccupied with the need to prevent the miseries of depression, when in fact that matter was already being handled fairly well, while we have slighted the injustice and hardships that flow from inflation, when in fact these have been multiplying for a generation. Concern over inflation has been increasing. It has not yet become articulate enough to wring from the Congress a declaration of policy that would have a moral force such as the Employment Act exercises with regard to unemployment. On the other hand, any return to the pegging of yields on government securities, which contributed materially to the sharp rise in the general price level during the years immediately after the war, has today become almost unthinkable. With increased understanding of the need to curb inflation, the classical remedies for inflation—credit restraints and a balanced budget—are again in good repute and have of late been diligently applied. These are considerable advances. They have surely helped to keep the rise of the consumer price level since 1954 within moderate bounds. But just as surely they have not sufficed to stop inflation.

The application of credit restraints began early in the new expansion. Government officials knew that the measures that had been taken during 1953 and 1954 to build confidence, particularly the actions taken with regard to credit and taxes, carried the risk of exciting overconfidence and subsequent reaction. Already in the closing months of 1954 the sharp rise of stock prices and the financial methods used by builders to push sales of new homes caused some concern. Signs of speculation multiplied during the early months of 1955 as expansion of both credit and economic activity proceeded rapidly and on a widening front. Therefore, starting in January 1955, the government adopted one measure after another with a view to checking economic exuberance.

Although the demand for bank loans was abnormally high, the Federal Reserve authorities reduced their holdings of government securities, as they usually do in the early months of the year. Commercial banks therefore found it necessary to sell government securities or borrow at the Federal Reserve Banks to maintain their lending. The Federal Reserve authorities also raised stock margin requirements and the discount rate. The Treasury decided to tap the long-term capital market and put out a substantial issue of forty-year bonds. The Federal Housing Administration and the Veterans Administration reduced the maximum maturity and raised the minimum down payment on governmentally underwritten mortgages. Both agencies also put an end to the occasional but highly dubious practice of including the closing costs on the purchase of a home in the face value of underwritten mortgages. The Federal Home Loan Bank Board imposed limits on lending by the

Home Loan Banks to savings and loan associations. Government officials warned lenders that their progressively more liberal terms for financing instalment sales of automobiles were fraught with danger; and, to emphasize the government's concern, the several bank supervisory authorities added a section on consumer credit to their regular examination forms. These and related actions to restrain credit expansion were all taken by the late summer of 1955. In the meantime, the clamor to reduce taxes was successfully resisted, and the fiscal year 1955 ended with federal expenditures 3.2 billion dollars below fiscal 1954 on an administrative basis and 1.4 billion below on a cash basis.

Thus, as this recital indicates, the government moved rather promptly to curb the inflationary forces that gathered during 1955. Moreover, the effort to restrain general credit expansion has since then been continued unremittingly. The discount rate was raised time and again. Pressure on the reserves of commercial banks became more intense. As a result many people found it harder to obtain loans, and credit became more costly than it has been in a long generation. Nor were the restrictive measures taken by the government confined to monetary actions. In 1955 the stockpiling program was adjusted within the limits permitted by law and defense requirements, so as to relieve the shortages of vital materials felt by the civilian economy. Earlier plans to finance the new Interstate Highway Program by borrowing were abandoned in 1956, and additional taxes on gasoline and other automotive products were enacted to make this program self-financing. Proposals to cut tax rates continued to be resisted successfully. And the higher tax revenues, which the advance of prosperity kept generating, permitted a modest reduction of the federal debt in fiscal year 1956 and again in fiscal 1957, despite the recent increase of federal expenditures.

This is an impressive record. All the same, when governmental policies are viewed in their entirety, it is clear that the efforts to resist the inflationary pressures that developed after 1954 neither ranged as widely nor carried as much weight as the measures that had previously been adopted to resist recession. Nothing that was done to curb inflation matched the dramatic tax cuts of 1954 or the reduction in bank reserve requirements of both that year and the preceding year. No general increase in taxation was enacted by the Congress. No increase in reserve requirements was ever ordered by the Federal Reserve authorities. No issue of long-term bonds was put out by the Treasury between the summer of 1955 and the fall of 1957. The lifting of the discount rate was carried out in a series of small steps. The increase of minimum down payments in connection with federally underwritten mortgages came merely to 2 per cent of the purchase price. Even the security holdings of the Federal Reserve System had their ups as well as their downs, and they were practically as large at the end of 1956 as at the end of 1954.

Beyond this, the restrictive measures taken by the government were accompanied by other actions of an expansive character which culminated in 1956—a year during which wholesale prices rose sharply while consumer prices also resumed their advance. Increases in the pay of federal employees were enacted in 1955 and became effective in July of that year. An increase in the hourly minimum wage from 75 cents to a dollar became effective in March 1956, increasing directly the wages of two million workers in private industry. Price support levels for various agricultural crops were raised in 1956. Special export programs for agricultural products were pushed energetically. A new Soil Bank Program was enacted and government purchases for the school lunch and related programs were increased. Lending by the Small Business Administration was stepped up. Various of the special restrictions on housing credit that had been adopted during 1955 were either relaxed or dropped, and massive support of the mortgage market was extended by the Federal National Mortgage Association. The old-age insurance program was liberalized, with effects on the flow of incomes that were delayed, however, until 1957. Expenditures increased in connection with numerous other programs. Between July 1956 and July 1957, total federal expenditures on a cash basis rose 7.4 billion dollars over the preceding fiscal year, while cash receipts rose only 5.1 billion. In consequence, the cash surplus declined from 4.5 to 2.1 billion dollars.

Viewed individually, many—if not all—of the expansive actions taken by government during 1955 and 1956 were meritorious in high degree. They were inspired partly by considerations of the national defense, and partly by the concern with people's welfare which must go hand in hand with the encouragement of private enterprise in our times. With the nation's prosperity increasing, it seemed only natural to take some constructive steps in behalf of the sectors of our economy that had failed to participate in the nation's general progress or that felt the impact of credit restraints most severely. With wages rising rapidly in the private economy, it seemed only prudent to raise the pay of governmental employees. With tax revenues growing abundantly, it seemed only proper to use a portion of the increased wherewithal to reduce somewhat the outstanding public debt, and yet leave enough to increase defense outlays and expand other programs that seemed essential or socially desirable. All this was done. The increase in federal expenditures thus helped to swell the nation's aggregate monetary demand at a time when physical resources were already being strained by the rising demands of business firms, consumers, and state and local governments, many of whom also felt that their augmented spending was only natural, prudent, and proper. With the economic community at large, including the several levels of government, striving to add to consumption or to capital investment more quickly than the nation's workshops could add to production, some advance of both the wholesale and consumer price level became unavoidable.

It is true that federal spending increased much less rapidly than did the nation's total expenditure after 1954. It may justly be held, however, that there was a need for special restraint on the government's part at a time when the rest of the economy was displaying extreme exuberance. In the process of raising its expenditures and taking other expansive actions, particularly with regard to agriculture and wages, the policy of the federal government for containing inflation came to rest increasingly on the general credit restraints administered by the Federal Reserve System. This was a heavier burden than our monetary authorities could of themselves properly handle.

IV

The American people are nowadays broadly united on major goals of economic policy—a high and stable rate of employment in relation to the labor force, expanding production, improvement in living standards, and a reasonably stable consumer price level. The federal government has sought to promote these objectives. It has done this with increasing understanding that prosperity cannot be ordered or guaranteed by government officials.

A nation's prosperity rests fundamentally on the enterprise of individuals seeking to better themselves, their families, and their communities. It depends far more on what individuals do for themselves than on what the government does or can do for them. The government may, however, significantly influence the course of our economy by pursuing policies that stimulate private citizens to act in ways which will tend to sustain prosperity. Considerable success has attended governmental efforts in recent years to maintain an environment that favors higher production, expanding employment, and rising living standards. The purchasing power of the consumer's dollar has not, however, been maintained. It is true that the rise in the price level that has occurred since 1954 is moderate by historical standards. However, in view of the rigidity which of late has characterized the wage level and only to a lesser degree the price level during economic contractions, still greater moderation of price advances must be sought during economic expansions in order to prevent a creeping type of inflation in the future.

Although governmental resistance to inflation has significantly stiffened of late, it is difficult to avoid the conclusion that the government is not yet prepared to act as decisively to check inflation as it is to check recession. In the event of a recession, the general attitude of government is apt to be that everything which is at all reasonable must be done without much delay, and that if inflationary pressures develop later as a result of the stimulants that are applied, they will be dealt with in due course. On the other hand, once inflationary pressures emerge, the government is unlikely to proceed in the spirit that if a recession develops as a result of its restrictive measures, that difficulty in turn will be dealt with in good season. Rather, the attitude is apt to be that, while everything which is at all reasonable must be done to curb inflation, restrictive policies must not be applied on so vigorous a scale as to take any appreciable chance of bringing on or hastening a recession.

Such weighting of the scales of economic policy, however

slight, is probably unavoidable in the existing state of public opinion. While the government has the broad responsibility of leading the nation along sound economic channels, no Administration that is too far removed from the prevailing sentiments of the people can long continue to govern. When a threat of unemployment develops, a clamor for governmental intervention comes from all directions. On the other hand, when the price level begins rising, pressures for governmental action are less insistent. Not only that, but governmental steps to curb inflation are sure to be loudly resisted by many, while measures to curb unemployment are just as sure to be applauded in most quarters. There can be little doubt that although people generally and genuinely wish the consumer price level to remain reasonably stable, they also fear depression more than they fear inflation. The catastrophe of the 1930's is still fresh in our memories and the sort of inflation that we have had is rightly viewed as the lesser evil by comparison.

Our economic and political environment, however, has been radically transformed over the past quarter century. Serious depressions are no longer the threat they once were, while creeping inflation has become a chronic feature of recent history and a growing threat to the welfare of millions of people. Not only is a creeping inflation unnecessary to the continuance of prosperity, but it can in time become a grave obstacle to it —either because the inflation may get out of hand or because, if inflation should continue for many years its gradual inroads on the pocketbooks of people, their concern over inflation may mount to a point where they will be unwilling in the event of a recession to support any large governmental efforts to hasten recovery. These considerations are better understood today than they were only a few years ago. But they are not yet understood widely enough. Nor, speaking broadly, have people as yet developed the same sense of justice toward the sufferers from inflation that they have come to feel with regard to the sufferers from unemployment.

If we are to make better progress in dealing with inflation, the first requirement therefore is better and wider public understanding of the need for a solution. But we must also recognize the shortcomings of our recent public policies and try to improve upon them. However necessary and helpful a balanced budget and a restrictive monetary policy may be in the age-old struggle against inflation, it is doubtful whether they alone can cope with the threat of creeping inflation.

FIVE

The New Environment of Monetary Policy

I HAVE already attempted to demonstrate that the progress our nation has made in dealing with economic recessions has not yet been matched by similar progress in dealing with inflation. In grappling with the threat of depression, we have acted on a far larger scale than was ever contemplated during the 1920's. Not only do we command new tools for curbing recession, but we are willing to use them with promptness and vigor. More important still, our minds are prepared, should the need arise, for additions to the array of countercyclical weapons. In dealing with inflation, we have been less imaginative and less enterprising. It is true that the government is nowadays more concerned with the danger of inflation than it was in the immediate postwar period, and that foresight and courage have of late been mustered to check tendencies toward inflation as well as recession. Nevertheless, our intellectual, moral, and practical approach to the problem of inflation continues to suffer from earlier neglect. The heavy emphasis that the government has recently placed on a restrictive credit policy has served to bring us back to the best thought that ruled on the subject of inflation during the 1920's,

Millar Lecture at Fordham University, October 22, 1957. Reprinted, by permission of the publisher, from *Prosperity Without Inflation*, Fordham University Press, New York, 1957, pp. 43–65.

but it has done no more than that. In the meantime the economic world has changed profoundly.

I

The great expansion of governmental activities since the 1920's has reduced the economic area over which a restrictive credit policy can nowadays be effective. In 1929, federal expenditures on goods and services accounted for about 1¼ per cent of the dollar value of the nation's total output. Other forms of spending—interest payments, pensions, grants-in-aid to the states, and sundry subsidies—brought total federal expenditures to 2½ per cent of the nation's output. The outlays by state and local governments were a larger factor in the economy, but the combined expenditures of all our governmental units still accounted for less than 10 per cent of the nation's total output. Since then, governmental outlays have increased tremendously, in relation to the growth of the economy as well as in an absolute sense. During the past decade federal expenditures alone have ranged from 13.4 per cent of the dollar value of the nation's output in 1947 to 21.3 per cent in 1953 and 17.4 per cent in 1956. State and local outlays, which fell well behind federal expenditures during the 1940's, have also been catching up of late. The combined sum of federal, state, and local expenditures was over 104 billion dollars in 1956, or a little over 25 per cent of the nation's total output. In each of the four preceding years this percentage was still higher.

Federal expenditures are shaped by numerous and complex forces on the domestic and international fronts, but they are practically unaffected by the level of interest rates or the availability of credit. When federal revenues are high enough to finance larger outlays, as has been the case since fiscal year 1955, there is no need to resort to financial markets beyond meeting temporary cash needs and refinancing the debt that keeps falling due. On the other hand, when deficit finance is being practiced, the condition of the money market is not likely to count significantly among the factors that lead the government to enlarge the deficit or to reduce it. If the federal government should again find itself spending more than it raises in taxes, it will not be because money may be borrowed on easy terms. Nor would the government be inclined to reduce its spending merely because borrowing has become harder. In the last analysis, the federal government has considerable power to shape the markets for money and capital to suit its ends; and it may well choose to do that rather than permit high objectives of national policy to be thwarted by any tightness of credit.

State and local governments have no such financial independence. However, the rapid growth of population, a continuing trend toward suburban living, and the shortages that accumulated during the Great Depression and World War II have created in many communities a sense of urgency with regard to schools, parks, highways, water systems, and other public improvements. Some projects have of late been shelved here and there because of statutory ceilings on interest rates or because of the reluctance of local citizens to assume the burden of a rising interest rate. Also, offerings of revenue bonds and other issues of local authorities have in some instances been withdrawn or postponed because of the congested condition of the capital market. By and large, however, state and local governments have either enjoyed sufficient revenues to finance their desired scale of expenditure, or they have been willing to submit to higher interest rates. The benefits to be derived from most governmental projects cannot be calculated in dollars, and this of itself tends to blunt the influence of interest rates. At least during recent years, state and local expenditures have responded neither promptly nor on any large scale to general credit conditions.

But if government expenditures are largely sheltered from ordinary fluctuations in the credit market, so also are the operations of a part of the business world. Moreover, this part seems to have grown since the 1920's. Many business firms are able to finance their requirements—whether for new plant and equipment, or the accumulation of inventories, or the carrying of receivables—without any borrowing or without much borrowing. What these businesses do is to finance their requirements largely from internally generated funds—that is, undistributed profits, depreciation allowances, and related charges. From 1947 through 1956 corporations retained, on the average, 54 per cent of their profits. Between 1923 and 1929, on the other hand, retained corporate income averaged only 33 per cent. Depreciation funds and other allowances for capital consumption have likewise become of larger importance in corporate financing. In all, the internally generated funds of business corporations exceeded their externally raised funds—that is, new capital issues, bank loans, mortgages, trade debt, and other liabilities—by 42 per cent during the decade from 1947 through 1956. Between 1923 and 1929, on the other hand, corporate internal funds appear to have exceeded their external funds by about 10 or 20 per cent.

The requirements for external financing have, of course, increased greatly in an absolute sense. Not only that, but during the recent boom, corporations have found it necessary to turn increasingly to banks and the capital market to finance their vast expansion and improvement programs. Whereas internal funds exceeded external funds by 42 per cent over the full period from 1947 through 1956, this excess dropped to 26 per cent during the last two years of the period. Despite the recent revival of stock issues, borrowing has continued to be the preponderant source of external capital for corporations. However, in view of the steep rates of taxation that have ruled of late and in view of the rapidly growing use of amortizable loans, interest rates appear to have had less influence on corporate borrowing and investment than they had during the 1920's or earlier times of our history.

Interest charges are rarely a large element in business costs, and their practical importance has tended to become smaller as a result of high taxes. A rise in the rate of interest from 4 to 5 per cent will raise annual interest charges from $4,000 to $5,000 on a loan of $100,000. But with a basic federal tax rate of 52 per cent on corporate income, the net added cost to a sizable corporation that manages to stay in the black is $480, not $1,000. In fact, the net added cost is likely to be even smaller, since about two-thirds of the states nowadays levy a tax on corporate income which, while quite small relative to the federal tax, is not negligible either financially or psychologically. In the case of unincorporated businesses or households, the high rates of the personal income tax in the middle and upper income brackets likewise take some of the sting out of a rising interest rate. During the 1920's income taxes were, of course, much less formidable and therefore interfered less with the effects of interest rates. The federal tax rate on corporate incomes in those years was 13½ per cent at its highest, federal taxes on individual incomes were much lower than at present, and only a minority of states as yet imposed any income taxes. Hence, allowing for taxes, a rise of interest rates from, say, 4 to 5 per cent meant just about that during the 1920's, while nowadays it means roughly a rise of only half that size—that is, from 2 to 2½ per cent—for many borrowers, at least some of whom are sure to ignore so small an increase in cost.

Another factor that has served to blur the influence of a rising interest rate is the development and rapid growth during the past ten or twenty years of versatile instruments calling for systematic amortization of loans. Term loans to business running up to five or ten years were practically unknown during the 1920's. Nowadays, they are a significant item in the portfolios of many insurance companies as well as of commercial banks. The long-term fully amortizable mortgage was largely developed during the 1930's, in connection with governmental efforts to stimulate homebuilding activity. This type of loan, which was of interest mainly to savings and loan associations during the 1920's, now dominates the mortgage market. Consumer installment loans were already of some consequence during the 1920's, but they have grown immensely since then in relation both to consumer incomes and to retail trade. The essential feature of these newer loan instruments is that they can be tailored to the needs of the borrower. The interest rate remains, of course, one of the terms of the loan contract. However, since other terms can also be varied, the importance of the interest rate is often reduced or obscured.

A rise in the interest rate is never welcome news to a borrower. But a businessman is apt to be less troubled by a rise in the interest rate if other dimensions of the loan contract are adjusted to his liking; for example, by lengthening the term to maturity and arranging a convenient repayment schedule. Certainly, the size of the initial down payment and the amount of the monthly installment are more vital to the typical buyer of an automobile on credit than the precise level of the interest rate that must be paid on the loan. The same is true of the buyer of a television set, an air conditioning unit, or a new home. Indeed, the deterrent effect of higher prices, to say nothing of higher interest rates, can often be offset by lengthening the period over which the loan can be repaid or by reducing the required down payment on the purchase. Recent experience has demonstrated that such liberalization of the terms of loans can go on for a time on a very considerable scale in the face of a restrictive credit policy and rising market interest rates. During the greater part of 1955, credit terms were extensively liberalized on installment sales of automobiles and on veterans' mortgage loans. Although terms stiffened on mortgage loans in 1956, the average maturity of automobile loans continued to increase, particularly in the case of used cars. Even this year there has been little evidence of any significant tightening of terms.

Of course, direct rationing of available funds by lenders always goes hand in hand with the impersonal rationing through market interest rates. But if higher taxes and more flexible loan contracts have tended to reduce the restraining influence on the nation's business of a rising interest rate, other financial developments have served to lessen the control of the monetary authorities over the availability of loan capital.

The Federal Reserve System can exercise a decisive influence on the level of reserves and therefore on the total assets of its members, which are preponderantly commercial banks. The Federal Reserve System wields no authority, however, over other financial intermediaries such as life insurance companies, savings and loan associations, savings banks, investment companies, and pension funds. In the aggregate, institutions over which the Federal Reserve System has only an indirect and somewhat remote influence have been growing more rapidly than commercial banks. In 1955 the assets of commercial banks were about four and one-half times as large as in 1922. On the other hand, the combined assets of mutual savings banks, the postal savings system, credit unions, and savings and loan associations were about eight times as large. The combined assets of life insurance companies, other insurers, and private and public pension funds were sixteen times as large. The assets of government lending institutions and of investment

companies have increased still faster. As a result of these uneven trends, the assets of commercial banks, which at the end
of 1922 somewhat exceeded the combined assets of other
financial institutions exclusive of the Federal Reserve Banks,
amounted to only 52 per cent of the total assets of these other
financial institutions at the end of 1955.

The fortunes of commercial banks have not been subject to
any simple trend such as the statistics just cited may suggest.
The assets of commercial banks changed little in relation to the
assets of other financial institutions during the first two decades of the century. The relative position of commercial
banks then declined during the 1920's, but rose again between 1933 and 1945. It has declined sharply since then, and
now appears to be lower than at any time at least since 1900.
Although the assets of commercial banks increased 50 billion
dollars between the end of 1945 and the end of 1955, the assets
of other financial intermediaries, again excluding the Federal
Reserve Banks increased about 230 billion dollars. This dis-
parity of growth appears to be continuing. During 1956 the
assets of commercial banks increased 7 billion dollars, while
the assets of other financial intermediaries increased about 25
billion dollars.

Since the end of World War II the spectacular growth of the
assets of financial institutions other than commercial banks reflects only in small part the rise in stock prices. What it basically signifies is the efficiency of financial markets in assembling "idle" funds and putting them to work in commerce and
industry. This process not only can continue in the face of restrictions on the growth of commercial bank assets, but it is
even likely for a time to be accelerated by a restrictive credit
policy. A rise of interest rates increases the cost of holding demand deposits, on which commercial banks have been forbid-
den to pay interest since 1935. Hence, rising interest rates, es-

pecially if the movement is of considerable magnitude and duration, tend to stimulate both consumers and business firms to convert their cash balances into earning assets. This can often be done without any significant loss of liquidity. For example, when an individual draws on his checking account to buy a life insurance policy or to acquire savings and loan shares or to deposit funds in a mutual savings bank, he obtains against a financial institution a claim which can be readily converted into cash. The institution, in turn, having acquired ownership over a part of his demand deposit, now has additional money to lend to others who are likely to be active spenders. Much the same thing happens when a corporation buys the commercial paper issued by a sales finance company, especially when the transaction is handled through a repurchase agreement. In these and other ways the loans of financial intermediaries can for a time grow quite rapidly even when the reserves of commercial banks are severely restricted by Federal Reserve actions. This is precisely what has happened since 1954.

The rapid growth of financial institutions other than commercial banks is not, however, the only development of recent times that has tended to limit the control that the Federal Reserve System can exercise over credit expansion. The emergence of a large amount of federal government securities in the portfolios of commercial banks has had a similar influence. During the 1920's Treasury securities were a minor factor in the operations of commercial banks. For example, they accounted for 10 per cent of the assets of the member banks of the Federal Reserve System in mid-1922 and for only 8 per cent of their assets at the end of 1929. During the 1930's and during the war years, however, a large part of the rapidly growing federal debt found a home in commercial banks. At the beginning of 1946 the member banks held 57 per cent of their assets of over 138 billion dollars in the form of Treasury securities. Bank holdings of government debt have considerably diminished since then, both in amount and in relation to their total assets. Nevertheless, Treasury securities still amounted to 58 billion dollars, or about a third of the total assets of the member banks, at the end of 1954 when the recent boom was getting actively under way.

These large holdings of government securities add immeasurably to the flexibility of bank management. In particular, they enable commercial banks to replenish their supply of loan funds, if they so wish, and thereby to circumvent for a time the restrictions that the Federal Reserve authorities may impose on their reserves. A bank does not like to disappoint any of its regular customers. Nor, for that matter, does it care to turn down a new applicant of substance and reputation. After all, if his needs are met in whole or in part, he may well bring his future business to the bank which was willing to go to some trouble at a time of credit stringency to accommodate him. To the extent that a bank holds short-term Treasury securities, it can acquire funds for loan expansion without sustaining an appreciable capital loss. The disposal of long-dated securities is a more costly method of raising loan funds at a time of rising interest rates. However, a higher interest rate on a new loan will often compensate a bank for the loss it sustains by selling bonds. Even when that does not happen, the need to look after a customer may of itself induce a bank to reduce its holdings of long-term Treasury issues.

In fact, commercial banks have responded to the surging demand for credit in the recent expansion by disposing of both short-term and long-term securities on a very considerable scale. The loans and investments of all commercial banks increased only 9.2 billion dollars between the end of 1954 and the end of 1956, or by 6 per cent over the two-year period.

Their outstanding loans, however, increased by 19.7 billion dollars or 28 per cent. This huge expansion of loans by commercial banks was accompanied and made possible in large part by a reduction of 10.4 billion dollars in their holdings of federal obligations.

The great volume of outstanding federal securities has increased the financial maneuverability of all types of financial institutions, not only of commercial banks. Thus, the assets of mutual savings banks and insurance companies increased very substantially during 1955 and 1956. The inflows of cash on account of new savings and debt repayment were not sufficient, however, to enable the managers of these institutions to make all the loans or acquire all the private or state and local securities that they deemed advantageous. Hence they disposed, in the aggregate, of 3 billion dollars of their holdings of federal obligations. The Treasury securities sold by them and by commercial banks were largely bought, on balance, by individuals, by the federal trust funds, and by various state and local investment accounts. In 1955, when the recent spurt in plant and equipment expenditures was still in its early stages, business corporations added a little over 4 billion dollars of Treasury securities to their holdings. In the following year, when outlays on investment were much larger and the stringency of the money and capital markets was greater, they disposed of almost 5 billion dollars of their securities. Thus, the huge sales of government securities by financial institutions during 1955, and both by them and business corporations during 1956, served— along with other devices to which I have alluded—to mobilize the nation's cash and put it to work in the nation's markets. This process went on in spite of and partly in response to the efforts of the Federal Reserve System to restrain the expansion of credit and, through that, the expansion of spending across the nation.

II

I have suggested that various financial developments—the growth of government expenditures, our steep tax rates, the lesser dependence of corporations on external financing, the greater flexibility of loan instruments, the relative decline of commercial banks among financial intermediaries, and the large holdings of Treasury securities by financial institutions—have all tended to reduce the effectiveness of traditional monetary restraints. Of course, these are not the only financial developments of recent times that bear on monetary policy. Nor have all the changes in our financial environment worked in the same direction. Surely, the breakdown of the international gold standard has made it possible to base our monetary policies to a greater extent on domestic considerations than was feasible during the 1920's. Other recent developments, such as the emergence of a large volume of real estate mortgages underwritten by the government, have made it easier to shift funds from one part of the country to another or from one financial institution to another. The large holdings of government securities by financial institutions, business corporations, and the general public have had a similar effect. But if these factors have facilitated the transmission of Federal Reserve pressures on commercial banks to other parts of the economic community, they have also facilitated ways of escape, at least temporarily, from these pressures. On balance, there appears to be little doubt that the net effect of the vast changes that have occurred in recent times in the realm of finance has been to blunt to some degree the effectiveness of Federal Reserve policies aiming at the restraint of the nation's spending.

This does not mean that the Federal Reserve authorities have inherently less power than they had during the 1920's. In a theoretical sense their power to restrain expansion is fully as large or even larger. For not only are they able to exert pressure on commercial banks by selling government securities, of which they hold a great abundance, but they can raise the reserve requirements of the member banks—a power they did not have in the 1920's. Viewed in the abstract, there is almost no limit to what the Federal Reserve System can accomplish, despite the narrowing of the base to which its policies apply. Just as the Federal Reserve System is capable of offsetting a shift from demand deposits to time deposits in commercial banks, so it could offset a shift of demand deposits from individuals to financial institutions. If the Federal Reserve authorities sought to prevent the assets of all financial institutions, taken in the aggregate, from increasing, they could in principle force a sufficient reduction of commercial bank assets to compensate for the growth in the assets of other financial institutions. All this, and indeed much more, may be said of the powers of the Federal Reserve System. The essential point of the preceding analysis, however, is that in order to achieve a particular effect on the nation's total expenditure in today's environment, the degree of credit restriction which needs to be taken is likely to be appreciably greater than was the case a generation ago. But if our economic and financial environment has changed, the political environment has changed still more and the changes have not been of a kind that favor highly restrictive credit policies.

The Employment Act of 1946 pledges the federal government to "utilize all its plans, functions, and resources" to foster economic expansion and to help prevent depressions. The Federal Reserve authorities, being members of the government, are bound by this statutory declaration of policy. In principle, a restrictive credit policy at a time of surging demand is entirely in harmony with the objectives of the Employment Act. Although not all depressions spring from excessive exuberance during periods of prosperity, that has been the course of events in the past altogether too often. Once extensive speculation gets under way—whether in commodities or securities or real estate—the foundations on which the nation's prosperity rests become insecure. So it is also when the quality of newly extended credit seriously deteriorates, or when a competitive rush develops to construct physical facilities that, in the aggregate, are well beyond current requirements. Of late, these teachings of experience have counted heavily in the economic thinking of government officials outside as well as within the Federal Reserve System. But if concern over the continuance of prosperity has at times led to credit restrictions, it has also led to a gradual application of these restrictions. Now that our government is committed to doing what it can to promote maximum production and employment, the Federal Reserve authorities are fairly bound to pursue a policy of credit restraint with considerable caution, lest the application of restraints bring on the very decline of aggregate economic activity which it is the responsibility of government to try to prevent.

The virtual avoidance of general credit restraints over the long stretch from 1933 to 1951 has also left its mark on current thought and practice. The earlier policy was based on the belief, which came to be held rather widely in professional and political circles, that on the one hand, general credit controls could check a boom with dangerous ease and, on the other hand, that they could do little to speed recovery once a depression developed. This exaggeration of the restrictive power of credit controls was, on a superficial view, strikingly confirmed by the course of events in early 1953. The pressure on bank reserves then exercised by the Federal Reserve authorities, together with a substantial issue of 3¼ per cent bonds by the Treasury, was interpreted by many in the financial community as a signal that interest rates would soon rise further and that it would become more difficult to obtain credit. Something of a scramble for money developed, interest rates rose briskly for a few weeks, and some dealers were undoubtedly embarrassed. These happenings in financial markets were not, however, a typical response to a moderate degree of credit tightening. More than anything else, they reflected the bewilderment of a financial community that had become accustomed to stable interest rates and had forgotten how a restrictive credit policy works. Government officials could overlook the criticism that "tight money" brought on the industrial recession which became visible around mid-1953. They knew better, as did many others. However, they could not escape the fact that they had misjudged the psychology of financial markets. The memory of this minor embarrassment understandably made them more cautious in the next encounter with economic excesses.

Moreover, government officials—the Federal Reserve authorities among them—must reckon with the opposition that restrictive credit measures often arouse in business, labor, and political circles. The influence of Federal Reserve actions on the wage policies of trade unions and the pricing policies of business firms is, at most, indirect. Surely, as we have recently seen, a new round of wage and price increases can occur in the face of a restrictive credit policy. But once a higher consumer price level has been established, it becomes unrealistic to look to the Federal Reserve System for a restoration of the former price level. All that may reasonably be expected of the Federal Reserve System is that it will do everything it can, within its limited powers, to keep the price level from rising further. A credit policy that is sufficiently restrictive to bring down the price level is, to be sure, always possible. But a policy which did that would in all likelihood bring down also the volume of employment. Federal Reserve officials are likely to shrink from such a course, not only because of their responsibility under the Employment Act, but also because they are apt to feel, whether consciously or not, a wholesome concern over the political uproar that would follow.

Another practical factor that has tended to limit the application of credit restraints is the recurring need of the Treasury to borrow money. Of late, this has usually involved the refunding of outstanding debt rather than the issue of new debt. But in view of their magnitude and frequency, the refinancing operations of the Treasury are still a very formidable obstacle to the consistent pursuit of a restrictive credit policy. For example, apart from the weekly rollover of bills and three special issues of bills, the Treasury entered the money and capital markets four times in 1956: in March to refinance 9.5 billion dollars of its securities, in July to refinance 12.9 billion, in August with a new issue of 3.2 billion, and in December with a refinancing of 9.1 billion. In 1955 the Treasury made even more trips to the financial markets and raised still larger sums, and so it has also been this year. Treasury debt operations, of course, are not a new thing for the Federal Reserve System. During the 1920's, however, the federal debt was a smaller factor in financial markets. Not only that, but the debt was then being reduced steadily and a smaller proportion of the outstanding debt was of a short-term character.

The current financing problems of the Treasury stem largely from the short maturities of a great part of the outstanding public debt. This creates not only administrative difficulties for the Federal Reserve System; it also tends, however subtly, to impart a bias to monetary policy. During a time of economic boom, a Secretary of the Treasury may well feel that, unless credit expansion is restricted, commodity prices are likely to rise swiftly, upset his budgetary calculations, and eventually cause economic trouble all around. He may therefore favor a restrictive policy and even assume a certain leadership in its behalf. At the same time he cannot entirely overlook the fact that when a forthcoming Treasury issue carries a higher interest rate than the one falling due, it must raise at once, however modestly, the government's expenditures. Nor can he ignore the possibility that, in the absence of support by the Federal Reserve System, a newly projected Treasury issue may, besides being poorly received in financial markets, seriously upset the prices and yields of outstanding securities, both public and private. If he communicates such thoughts to the Chairman of the Federal Reserve Board, he is merely acting in the line of duty. And in fact, all this is so clearly understood and recognized that the Federal Reserve authorities can be counted on to take the Treasury's needs into account without being prodded. The practical result is that restrictive credit actions, which are otherwise deemed desirable, are not infrequently postponed or that easing actions, which are otherwise deemed undesirable, are temporarily undertaken. Once the Treasury issue is out of the way and more or less absorbed, the Federal Reserve authorities are again free to act. But neither the economy nor human sentiment ever stands perfectly still. Once a restrictive action has been delayed, some subtle change in the one or the other may cause further delays. In the end, not only is the timing of Federal Reserve actions apt to be somewhat distorted from the viewpoint of the interests of the general economy, but the entire range of actions taken in the course of a boom is likely to be somewhat less restrictive than it would have been if the Treasury's trips to the financial markets for substantial sums had come less frequently.

III

I have already commented on one of the two major risks that unavoidably accompany a policy of general credit restraint— namely, that if the policy is pushed too far, it may hasten or bring on a business recession. The second risk is that if such a policy is continued over a considerable period, it may have undesirable side effects on the character or structure of the nation's economic activity. With increasing frequency, the charge has of late been made that a restrictive credit policy has uneven effects on the economy, that general credit restraints are selective in their practical effects, and that small businesses, homebuilders, prospective homebuyers, and local governments, especially school districts, bear the main brunt of general credit controls. The intensity with which these criticisms have been urged is of itself a fact with which government officials, including the Federal Reserve authorities, have had to reckon. Beyond that, and in the degree to which the criticisms are valid, they raise the question whether the side effects of general credit restraints may not offset some of the economic benefits that could be gained by their more vigorous application at a time of economic exuberance.

The financing difficulties of state and local governments appear to have been exaggerated in recent discussions. It is true that some municipal issues ran into trouble as early as 1955, while postponements of corporate issues did not come into public view until 1956. But there is little evidence that school bonds have suffered to any great extent in recent markets. In the nine critical months from July 1956 to March 1957 school bond issues were marketed at the highest rate yet recorded. Unsold bonds were only 3 per cent of the dollar amount of school bond offerings during this period. Taken in the aggregate, the capital issues of state and local governments, just as the capital issues of business corporations, have been exceptionally heavy this year.

The experience of small businesses during the recent period of general credit restraint appears to be a more serious matter. It is necessary to distinguish, of course, between the financing difficulties of small businesses that are of a chronic nature and those that are peculiar to a time of credit stringency. The ability of a small enterprise to expand is undoubtedly affected by our high tax rates, which severely limit the profits that can be ploughed back into business. Also, a small firm typically has little or no access to the public markets for capital. All this applies to times when credit conditions are easy just as it applies to a time of credit stringency. It is claimed, however, that when the reserves of commercial banks are under pressure, the financing problems of small firms are apt to become aggravated. Most banks, to be sure, will do everything they can to look after the needs of their regular customers, small or large. But if it is hard to turn down or to meet only in part a request for a loan by any sound business firm, it may be especially hard when the firm is large and powerful. In any event, a large firm of good reputation which cannot obtain credit from one bank can ordinarily shop around and eventually obtain a loan from another institution or, perhaps, float a public issue. Opportunities of this type are far more limited for the typical small business.

These judgments are based on general impressions. Facts on this important subject are unavailable on a precise and comprehensive basis. There are, however, various scattered pieces of evidence. First of all, we have the experience of the Small Business Administration, which received almost twice as many applications for loans in 1956 as in 1955. Not only that, but the percentage of approved applications rose from 38 in 1955 to 49 in 1956 without, apparently, any change in credit standards. Second, there is a special study by the American Bankers Association, based on a sample of large banks, which shows that the dollar amount of outstanding loans of under $50,000 increased a little over 14 per cent between the end of August 1955 and a year later. This is a considerable increase. Yet the commercial, industrial, and agricultural loans of weekly reporting member banks, which cover a larger sample of the big banks, show an increase of 21 per cent. Taking the two sets of figures together, it would appear, therefore, that the dollar amount of business loans in excess of $50,000 increased by something more than 21 per cent. Third, we have the quarterly compilations of new short-term loans, classified by size of loan, and covering a sample of large banks in nineteen cities which report to the Federal Reserve Board. According to this sample, the dollar amount of new loans ranging from $1,000 to $10,000 declined 4 per cent between 1955 and 1956, while there was an increase of 3 per cent in the loans from $10,000 to $100,000, of 9 per cent in loans from $100,000 to $200,000, and of 42 per cent in loans of still larger size. Fourth, we have the quarterly financial statements for manufacturing corporations compiled by the Federal Trade Commission and the Securities and Exchange Commission. From these figures it appears that the largest corporations, those with assets of over 100 million dollars, increased their indebtedness to banks by a substantially larger percentage between 1955 and 1957 than did small- or medium-sized corporations. The evidence is less clear, however, when long-term debt, beyond that already included in bank loans, is also considered.

These statistics leave much to be desired. The first piece of evidence, drawn from the experience of the Small Business Administration, tells nothing of the difficulties that some large firms experienced in obtaining credit. The second piece of evidence, which relates to the change in the total of outstanding bank loans of under and over $50,000, rests on different samples. The third piece of evidence, which refers to new bank loans of varying size, is restricted to a sample of large banks and therefore is apt to understate the over-all increase of small loans relative to large loans. A similar bias is likely to flow, at a time of generally rapid loan expansion, from fixed-size classes for loans. The fourth piece of evidence, which refers to outstanding bank loans of manufacturing corporations of differing size, is subject to uncertain defects of coverage. Furthermore, it makes no allowance for the changing composition of industry which is always an important feature of a cyclical expansion in business. A similar limitation attaches also to the second and third pieces of evidence. There are still other difficulties that attach to the statistics cited. Nevertheless, it is difficult to escape the broad but definite impression that, although the financing problems of small business have been greatly exaggerated and although interest rate differentials have in fact moved in favor of smaller businesses, the recent credit restraints have had a greater impact on the availability of credit to small businesses than they have had on the large firms.

It also seems clear that credit restraints have had a part in the recent decline of the homebuilding industry. In December 1954, housing starts, taken on a seasonally adjusted basis, reached a level exceeding 1.4 million units. They have declined since then to a level of about 1 million. Overbuilding in some localities, higher construction and land costs nearly everywhere, and a more selective, if not also a lessened, demand have contributed to the decline, but credit conditions appear to have been the most important single factor. Interest rates are a fairly large element in the cost of home ownership, particularly for families in low income brackets. To some degree, therefore, rising interest rates would of themselves tend to restrict the volume of homebuilding. Legal impediments to the free movement of interest rates on federally underwritten mortgages, however, have made matters much worse.

With the rise of interest rates during the recent boom, the maximum interest rates fixed by law or regulation for federally underwritten mortgages soon became unrealistic and these mortgages could ordinarily be placed or sold only at a discount. The practice of discounting, however, is poorly understood and sometimes arouses intemperate criticism. To avoid possible embarrassment on this account, some financial institutions concentrated increasingly on conventional mortgages. The supply of money for underwritten mortgages, on which the homebuilding industry has come to depend very heavily, was therefore reduced. At the same time, as a result of the provision of law which practically requires the builder to absorb any discount on mortgages guaranteed by the Veterans Administration, the builder's profit tended to dwindle as the discounts became larger. Hence the inducement to build was diminished. In short, in view of our housing legislation with its special regulation of interest rates and discounts, the recent policy of general credit restraint acted as a selective credit control on homebuilding. It would, of course, be equally correct to say that, in view of the recent policy of general credit restraint, our housing legislation acted as a selective credit control. Changes in the law governing discounts which were passed by the Congress this year have accentuated this difficulty, and they are likely to do so again under conditions of tight credit.

IV

I am led by this lengthy discussion of financial trends to three broad conclusions. First, since various economic and political developments of recent times appear to have reduced the effectiveness of Federal Reserve restraints on over-all credit expansion, we must discipline our expectations of what can be accomplished through general credit controls. There is little doubt that, given enough time, the Federal Reserve System is still capable of checking any large-scale expansion of aggregate demand. The process of economizing on cash cannot be stretched indefinitely by households or by the business community. As the holdings of Treasury securities by financial institutions are reduced and as the cash balances of individuals and corporations become smaller in relation to their transactions and contingent needs, the avenues of escape from the pressure applied by the Federal Reserve authorities on the reserves of commercial banks are bound to become fewer and narrower. This process, however, takes considerable time. Since 1954, we have experienced a credit shortage in the sense that interest rates have risen sharply and also in the sense that many have borrowed less than they would have liked or wanted to borrow. We certainly have not had a credit shortage in the sense that the amount of credit expansion has been small. In the meantime, as everyone knows, the price level has risen disconcertingly.

Second, although the side effects of a restrictive credit policy are of little consequence if the policy is applied over a few months, they cannot be safely ignored if the policy is extended over years. The traditional assumption that general credit controls exercise something like a uniform impact on different sectors of the economy appears to be invalid. When the government embarks on a restrictive credit policy, it does this with a view to restraining the growth of total expenditure, not to benefit one type of activity or to injure another. In practice, however, some branches of activity, such as those in which the federal government itself is engaged, are untouched by general credit restrictions. In other activities, such as consumer install-ment buying, the effects are seriously felt only after a very sub-stantial lag. On the other hand, small businesses and the home-building industry are apt to feel the impact of general credit restraints fairly promptly and more keenly. But not only do general credit restrictions have selective effects, it also appears that these effects may interfere with some key objectives of na-tional economic policy—such as the extension of home owner-ship, the promotion of sound neighborhoods, and the mainte-nance of an environment in which small and new businesses, which are a vital source of innovation in our economy, have a reasonable opportunity to survive, prosper, and grow. The government has therefore recently sought to reduce the un-even impact of credit restrictions by enlarging the loan funds available to the Small Business Administration, and by adopt-ing a variety of measures in behalf of housing.

Third, in view of the limitations that attach to restrictive Federal Reserve policies, it would be unwise to depend on the Federal Reserve System as our sole or principal guardian of the stability of the dollar. If the struggle against creeping infla-tion is to be successful, we must proceed simultaneously on numerous fronts. General credit controls have an important place in any responsible program for protecting the stability of the dollar. However, they need to be accompanied by other measures of policy that, in the first place, will reduce the burden that needs to be carried by our monetary authorities and, in the second place, improve the chances of success in their special sphere of activity.

SIX

Economics and Our Public Policy of Full Employment

DURING the nineteenth century, full employment was just a dream of a small band of reformers. Today it is a firmly established objective of public policy through the greater part of the world, including our own country. The Employment Act, which was passed by the Congress in 1946, states plainly that it is the continuing responsibility of the federal government to create and maintain "conditions under which there will be afforded useful employment opportunities, including self-employment, for those able, willing, and seeking to work." [1] This moral commitment to full employment has been reaffirmed time and again by successive Presidents and successive Congresses. There can be no doubt that it expresses faithfully the prevailing sentiment of the American people. What we debate nowadays is the scale, the timing, and the precise character of employment policies, not the need to strive

Lecture at Rice University, April 18, 1963, originally published in *The Nation's Economic Objectives,* E. O. Edwards (ed.), University of Chicago Press, 1964. Reprinted by permission of Rice University and the publisher.

[1] This Act, except for recent minor amendments, is conveniently reproduced in *Economic Report of the President,* January 1954, Appendix B.

for full employment or to use the powers of government to move the nation towards this goal.

The pursuit of full employment has naturally served to enhance the role of economists in the formation of public policy.[2] Government officials charged with the responsibility of administering the Employment Act need to know how economic trends have been developing. They need to form judgments about the demand for labor and its supply in the months or years ahead. They need to shape or readjust policies to relieve existing unemployment. They need to devise ways of minimizing unemployment in the future. In view of the frailty of much of economic knowledge, the economist cannot often speak with the impersonal authority of science on these vital matters. His power to predict the future is as yet very limited. As is true of other men, his economic judgments are influenced by ethical intuitions and philosophical attitudes. These limitations of economics and of economists must be understood. It is well, however, not to underestimate the power of economics to define and disentangle the issues with which policymakers are concerned. If economists cannot be implicitly trusted to lead the nation to the goal of full employment, they can at least clarify the nature of the goal and the obstacles that may be encountered by taking this or that route to it.

I intend to take advantage of the quiet setting of Rice University by discussing some issues surrounding the goal of full employment. I do so in the belief that a clearer notion of what full employment means may help our nation to deal with its unemployment—a problem which President Kennedy has recently characterized as "our number one economic problem." [3]

[2] See "An Economist in Government" by the present writer, *Columbia University Forum*, winter 1957.

[3] *Manpower Report of the President*, March 1963, p. xi.

I. CAUSES OF UNEMPLOYMENT

The causes of unemployment are complex and many. We usually associate it with business recessions or a lagging rate of economic growth, and we are apt nowadays to attribute both the one and the other to a deficiency of aggregate demand. However, even if the business cycle vanished, a troublesome volume of unemployment would remain.

In the first place, seasonal variations of economic activity will continue. At certain seasons of the year, a considerable number of workers will still be laid off or lose their jobs in the construction industry, in the garment trades, in the automobile industry, in vacation resorts, and in many other places and activities.[4]

In the second place, the fortunes of individual firms, industries, and communities will still vary enormously. The economic impact on working people will therefore be uneven. Here and there, men and women will become unemployed as new technology renders their skills obsolete, or as factories move to new locations, as old mines become exhausted, as construction projects reach completion, or as both old and new businesses shut down or reduce their operations because they are unable to compete successfully against their rivals. Inevitably, some interval often elapses before those who have lost jobs can find employment once again.

In the third place, the disappearance of the business cycle will not of itself eradicate certain differences among people that count in our labor markets. In all probability, the rate of

[4] It is perhaps worth noting that the seasonal corrections of monthly figures of unemployment, as practiced by statisticians, merely redistribute the unemployment that occurs within a year. They do not serve to reduce the annual level of the figures. Nor should they do so; this function belongs to economic policy, not to statistical contrivance.

unemployment will therefore remain higher for young persons than for the labor force at large, for Negroes than for native whites, for women than for men, for older workers than for those in the prime of life, for those with little schooling than for educated persons, for the physically handicapped than for those free from disability, and for lethargic people than for those who proceed with energy and initiative. Needless to add, the rate of unemployment will also be higher for men and women who harbor somewhat romantic notions about their worth than for those who adjust readily to market conditions.

The significance of these familiar observations should be clear. What they mean is that a risk of unemployment is present for the individual even in times of prosperity, that whether times are good or bad the risk is uneven for different parts of the working population, that this risk increases materially during business recessions, and that it may remain uncomfortably large when economic recovery proceeds slowly. These are reasons enough for public policy to concern itself with unemployment. But if the goal of full employment is to be of constructive aid in diminishing unemployment, it must be framed with an eye to actual characteristics of people and the conditions under which they live and work.

II. FULL EMPLOYMENT AND OTHER VALUES

In popular discussions, the goal of full employment is sometimes described in phrases that are so sweeping as to suggest that it would be well if every man, woman, and child worked twenty-four hours every day. Of course, no one wants or means that. Everyone recognizes the infirmities of childhood and old age, that human endurance has its limits, that much of leisure is sanctioned by custom or religion, and that a free society leaves it up to an individual to decide whether to work or not. When we speak precisely, we do not therefore identify the unemployed with the jobless. Instead, we consider as unemployed only those among the jobless who are able, willing, and seeking to work. If all persons of this category actually succeeded in finding jobs, employment would surely be at a maximum while unemployment would disappear.

This seems to be the objective of public leaders when they assert, as men often do in a mood of exuberance, that the elimination of unemployment is a basic goal of our society. For example, the Council of Economic Advisers recently declared that "ideally, all persons able, willing, and seeking to work should be continuously employed." [5] Statements such as this convey a noble sentiment, but they can hardly be taken literally. I doubt if anyone who has seriously thought about the matter really believes that the complete elimination of unemployment would be ideal or even good for our type of society, in contrast to one that is rigidly governed by custom or authority.

We can put what I say to a test by a little reflection. Let us provisionally agree that full employment means a condition of zero unemployment. This, let us say, is the goal towards which public policy should be directed. Let us suppose, next, that the rate of governmental spending is sharply increased in the interest of stimulating the economy and that a large and well-sustained upsurge of private spending follows. Employment in most lines of activity will therefore rise progressively, unemployment will diminish, and the economy will move towards the established goal. As the process of expansion gathers momentum, young men and women embarking on their careers will find it easier to obtain suitable work; members of minority groups and many of the physically handicapped will

[5] *Economic Report of the President,* January 1962, p. 44.

discover that they and their services are wanted; and not a few women who took jobs because their husbands were temporarily out of work will resume their normal family responsibilities. Hence, there will be ample cause for satisfaction in the improved performance of our economy.

Prosperity, however, has a habit of creating problems of its own. When the demand for all sorts of commodities and services steadily increases and unemployment decreases, costs of production and prices do not stand still. In the early stages of expansion, increases of output can commonly be achieved without significant addition to overhead costs. As output keeps growing, this source of economy diminishes and eventually vanishes. Technological and managerial advances continue, of course, to be made at a thousand points. Their favorable influence on costs is offset, however, as older equipment is again put to use, as the quality of newly hired labor declines, as hours of work lengthen and overtime rates are paid, as fatigue grips both managers and their employees, as workers become more restless and independent, and as deliveries of needed materials or equipment become less dependable.

These developments would in time raise costs of production even if wage rates remained constant. That, however, will not happen. With aggregate demand continuing to expand, labor shortages will appear first in this trade or community, then in another, and so keep multiplying. Wages will therefore rise on a wide front, and they would do so even if trade unions were few and weak. Prices will likewise rise under the pressure of expanding demand, sometimes advancing before, and sometimes after, wages have risen.

Not all of us, of course, will be troubled by the higher prices that now have to be paid for consumer goods. Indeed, most of us may point with pride to the power of our economic system to provide employment for more and more people who are less fortunate than we, but who also want to live decently, raise families, and give their children a good start in life. Many of us will have a more personal cause for rejoicing—either because our incomes have risen faster than the cost of living or because the market value of our holdings of common stocks or real estate has soared. There will be some among us, however, whose savings have been accumulated chiefly in the form of bank deposits, savings bonds, or life insurance. There will be others, too, whose salaries or wages have failed to keep in step with the rise in the cost of living. There will be still others whose livelihood depends on a pension, annuity, or some other type of fixed income. These groups will not be indifferent to the rise of prices. Nor will economists, public officials, and others who ponder the future as they watch speculation spreading, economic injustices multiplying, the balance of payments deteriorating, and—perhaps also—the world's confidence in the dollar declining.

The advance of costs and prices will therefore arouse some skepticism about the ideal of full employment that we postulated. Symptoms of shortage, besides that of soaring prices, will add their mite to this changing mood.[6] In view of the scarcity of labor, more and more of us will find that we must deal with a salesgirl whose understanding is faulty, or that we must get along with a janitor who seems never to be around, or that we must defer to the plumber who arrives a week after we had discovered a leaky pipe, or that we must learn to wait patiently for the new sofa that was promised for the wedding anniversary we celebrated three months earlier. So great is the variety of human nature and of personal circumstance that, notwithstanding the persisting advance of prices and the mounting of personal inconvenience, there will still be some

[6] Cf. Bertil Ohlin, *The Problem of Employment Stabilization*, New York, 1949, chap. 1.

among us who continue to espouse with fervor the goal of zero unemployment. But there will now be others, and their number is likely to swell as the expansion of aggregate demand becomes more intense, who will not only question the practical wisdom of their earlier ideal but will actually complain that the economy is suffering from overfull employment.

Once this stage has been reached, the simple concept of full employment with which we started will have lost its usefulness for public policy. True, all or most of us may still believe sincerely in full employment, but this will now mean different things to us, reflecting our individual values, attitudes, and circumstances. Compassion for the unemployed will weigh heavily in the scales, but other values will also count—among them a concern about the cost of living, industrial efficiency, the rate of economic growth, the scope of governmental authority, the level of taxes, the balance of payments, the prestige of our country abroad, to say nothing of such earthly matters as personal convenience in riding trains or shopping. This diversity of values is, of course, the condition in which we find ourselves in actual life, and it is one reason why economists, among others, differ in the advice they give to lawmakers.

III. FUNCTIONS OF SOME UNEMPLOYMENT

If my analysis has run close to the track of human sentiment, it follows that zero unemployment, apart from being unattainable,[7] would not really be a desirable condition for our society.

[7] Popular impressions to the contrary, some unemployment has persisted even in the U.S.S.R. See Warren W. Eason, "Labor Force Materials for the Study of Unemployment in the Soviet Union," and the discussion of this in *The Measurement and Behavior of Unemployment,* Special Conference 8, Universities-National Bureau Committee for Economic Research, Princeton University Press for National Bureau of Economic Research, 1957; also, I. Kaplan, "A Questionnaire Study of the Causes of

But if that much is true, we should recognize that not all unemployment is evil, and that some unemployment actually serves a useful function from the viewpoint of the individual or that of society. Although this proposition may appear strange to some of you, let us consider the case for it.

To begin with, some of the unemployment experienced by young men and women when they look for their first regular job is linked to our national tradition of freedom. Having a job is obviously important to them, and there are times when any job is better than none. Ordinarily, however, some picking and choosing helps young people to decide what they would like to do and how they can make the most of their capabilities. This, of course, results in a certain amount of unemployment. The only conceivable way of avoiding it would be to have young people take the very first job that came along. Such a rule of conduct would hardly recommend itself to them or, for that matter, to older men and women when they decide to reenter the labor force.

Unemployment arises voluntarily also among those who already have jobs. Independent businessmen sometimes discontinue one business before they establish another. Employees frequently leave their jobs before they have found new work. Some workers quit because they become dissatisfied with the rate of pay; or because they see no opportunity or insufficient opportunity for advancement; or because they do not like their work, or their working conditions, or the neighborhood where they live. Others leave because they think that their talents can be put to better use elsewhere; or because they wish to try out different jobs, or live in different places before settling down; or because they are moved to sudden anger by a foreman's or

Labor Turnover in the Industry of the Economic Councils," *Problems of Economics* (IASP Translations from Original Soviet Sources), December 1961, pp. 42–47.

colleague's injury to their feelings; or because they decide to seek or to follow husbands, wives, or sweethearts. Migration from job to job occurs at all stages of life, but it is especially common among young folk, who have both more opportunity and better reason for experimenting. To the extent that unemployment arises from the striving of men and women to escape the limitations of one environment and to seek out the opportunities of another, we may justly regard it as useful both to the individual and to society.

But if the exercise of freedom by new job seekers or by established employees creates some unemployment, so also does the exercise of freedom by employers. Individual employees are undoubtedly injured in the process. This fact warrants steady search for constructive ways of easing personal adjustments, but it should not blind us to the advantages that accrue to society from the exercise of freedom. In every group enterprise—whether it be a business firm, a government bureau, or a university—a certain degree of discipline is essential if the efforts of the group are to prosper. Individuals who are incompetent, undependable, or dishonest must be subject to the risk of dismissal, or else order and efficiency will suffer. Moreover, we could not have an efficient economy if employers who closed down their shops were required to support in idleness the men who previously worked for them, or if those who remained in business but needed fewer workers—whether because of dwindling markets or of technological changes—still had to retain their earlier work force on the payroll.

Industrial efficiency depends not only on the maintenance of certain standards of job performance and on the ability of every enterprise to dispense with labor that is no longer needed. Industrial efficiency depends also on the ability of an enterprise to maintain smooth operations and to meet unforeseen contingencies. We have already seen how the normal activities of consumption are impeded when unemployment tends to vanish. But if inability to locate a plumber, or a laborer, or a spare part may cause trouble or inconvenience to households, it will also impede the efficiency of business firms. Just as stocks of raw materials help to insure the continuity of production, so does the existence of a certain number of people seeking work help to insure the continuity and efficiency of production and thereby also contributes to the stability of total employment itself.[8]

The upshot of these remarks is simply that some unemployment is necessary or desirable from the viewpoint of a society that values freedom, equity, and efficiency. More specifically, we must have some unemployment if new entrants into the labor force are to be free to choose among jobs, if employed individuals are to be free to change jobs, if employers are to be free to replace unsatisfactory workers or to dispense with those whose services they no longer require, if business firms are to be able to carry on their productive operations with reasonable continuity and efficiency, and if the purchasing power of the dollar is to maintain some semblance of stability.

IV. MINIMUM RATE OF UNEMPLOYMENT

These broad but basic considerations may be stressed differently by individual economists. All economists recognize, however, that if the concept of full employment is to serve public policy constructively, it must at least allow for seasonal variations in economic activity and for the familiar frictions of the labor market. Since the adoption of the Employment Act, economists have also been under pressure to add precision to

[8] The need of continuity could, of course, be met in part by hoarding labor, but only at the cost of efficiency and the fluidity required for growth. See also pp. 189–190 in this connection.

the concept of full employment. This has proved to be a difficult and sometimes a very disconcerting task.[9]

An obvious starting point of the quest for precision is the Act's specification of the goal of "maximum employment." Some students have reasoned that since the Act takes maximum employment as the objective of public policy, it is desirable—even if not strictly necessary—to express this magnitude numerically. Others have gone further and argued that unless the objective of full employment is expressed by a definite number, policymakers will not know the magnitude of the gap in activity that needs to be filled and therefore will be unable to devise satisfactory public policies. In line with this thinking, the Council of Economic Advisers declared in its Report of March, 1961, that an unemployment rate of 4 per cent is a reasonable target for full utilization of resources.[10] In this pronouncement the Council merely used a figure which had gradually become something of a convention in economic circles during the postwar period. The Council, however, took the novel step of making this figure official.

The use of a 4 per cent unemployment rate as a criterion of full employment in our country can be rationalized in different ways. One possible justification is that when unemployment has been at that level or lower, it does not appear to have been much of a political problem. This argument will hardly satisfy those who believe that the American people need to apply a more exacting standard to the performance of their economy. Another possible justification is that the average unemployment rate during peak years of the business cycle works out for

[9] See E. G. Nourse, "Defining our Employment Goal under the 1946 Act," *Review of Economics and Statistics*, XXXVIII, May 1956.

[10] *Hearings on January 1961 Economic Report of the President, Joint Economic Committee*, 87th Cong., 1st sess., p. 326.

the period since 1900 to a figure that is close to 4 per cent.[11] This historical generalization is surely not irrelevant to a practical judgment concerning full employment, but it too will not satisfy those whose hearts are set on a different numerical goal. After all, there is nothing sacred about an average, especially when it varies with the precise period covered and with the treatment accorded to extreme cases, such as the war peak in 1918 or the depressed peak in 1937. Those who deem a 4 per cent unemployment rate too high can always point to historical instances when the rate was lower, while those who deem 4 per cent too low can point to inflationary conditions in years when the rate was at that level or even higher.

Of course, criticism of the 4 per cent figure along these lines is not directed against the desirability of numerical targets as such. But if what I said previously about the subtle role of human attitudes and values is valid, any unemployment rate that identifies full employment in the minds of people at one time may fail to do so at another time, for example, if prices begin rising swiftly. On this view, the presence or absence of full employment must be judged with reference to the entire complex of conditions that bear on a nation's economic health.

Still another criticism is that it really makes little difference whether the unemployment target is, say, 3 or 5 per cent. The point here is that the two figures are very close, that they imply an employment target of either 97 or 95 per cent, and that the economy will be doing about as well at one level of activity as at the other. This way of thinking must appear strange, if not irresponsible, to those who see and judge the economic world in terms of its unemployment. To them it

[11] Based on official data and Stanley Lebergott, "Annual Estimates of Unemployment in the United States, 1900–1950," in *The Measurement and Behavior of Unemployment* (cited in n. 7), pp. 215–16.

makes a great deal of difference where the unemployment target is set. According to their lights, if unemployment happens to be 5 per cent, then the distance from full employment will be twice as large with a target of 3 per cent as with one of 4 per cent. One who believes that compelling human or economic factors favor 3 per cent can therefore urge with a show of plausibility that whatever increase of governmental spending is being proposed to move the economy to the 4 per cent goal is merely half of what is required.

In view of the rich diversity of such judgments, it is not surprising that a storm of criticism from both the left and the right followed the Council's announcement that a 4 per cent rate of unemployment is a reasonable goal for full utilization of the nation's resources. The Council responded by explaining that the figure is simply "an interim goal, a way-station." [12] Needless to say, this modification will also not satisfy everyone, although the nebulous part of the new official goal is perhaps its strongest feature. The crucial weakness of the Council's 4 per cent figure is not that it is arbitrary. On the contrary, this figure is sufficiently grounded in experience to be useful on many occasions. The difficulty is rather that any numerical goal of full employment, once it has been made official, can be easily misinterpreted and become an obstacle to rational economic policy in a changing world.[13] For instance, if several hundred thousand teenagers or women suddenly entered the labor force and sought temporary, part-time jobs, unemployment could jump from 4 to 5 per cent but that would have little economic significance and require no change in public policy. On the other hand, even an unemployment rate of 3

[12] See *Economic Report of the President,* January 1963, p. 42; also *ibid.,* January 1962, pp. 44–48.

[13] Cf. my comments in *Hearings on January 1955 Economic Report of the President, Joint Committee on the Economic Report,* 84th Cong., 1st sess., pp. 43–45.

per cent could be dangerous to a nation if it rose to that level in the course of a new recession. The threat at such a time would not be the unemployment that exists, but rather the cumulating force of recession that could in time carry unemployment to 6 or 8 per cent or even higher.

V. CRITERIA OF FULL EMPLOYMENT

There is no need to dwell further on the point that full employment cannot be wisely identified with a fixed numerical target. This conclusion, however, will not make life easier for the makers of federal economic policy. True, it may help them avoid some costly mistakes, but they also need positive assistance in interpreting their duties under the Employment Act.

As far as I know, there are only two passages in the Act that give any promise of eventually bringing some precision to its employment objective. One is the specification of the goal of "maximum employment" which, as we have just seen, easily leads to unhappy arithmetical debates. But the Act also specifies, as I noted at the beginning of this lecture, that the federal government has the responsibility of promoting conditions that will afford "useful employment opportunities . . . for those able, willing, and seeking to work." [14] This passage does not invite absolute numerical targets of employment or of the unemployment rate. It will not suit those who seek the illusory comfort of precise targets. It nevertheless provides, in my judgment, a more useful handle for a public policy of full employment.

The central thought of this passage of the Employment Act is simply that ample employment opportunities are of great social or public importance. Let us now pursue this thought in the light of our earlier conclusion that some unemployment is

[14] See n. 1.

socially desirable. That conclusion rested on a tacit assumption which very much needs to be made explicit, namely, that unfilled jobs exist. Clearly, new entrants into the labor force will be unable to exercise their freedom to choose among jobs if there are no jobs to be filled. Nor will those at work be able to exercise their freedom to change jobs if there are no vacancies. Nor, speaking more generally, will those who are seeking jobs, whatever the cause of their searching, be able to get work unless jobs are being created or vacated. It follows that job opportunities—or, more narrowly, vacant jobs—are absolutely vital. It further follows that if the number of job vacancies equaled the number unemployed, there would then be sufficient employment opportunities to permit, in principle, a job for all who are able, willing, and seeking to work.

This line of reasoning leads at once to a basic criterion of full employment, namely, equality between the number of jobs seeking men and the number of men seeking jobs. Of course, these quantities need to be considered in terms of the market place. If the prevailing wage in a given trade happened to be approximately twenty dollars a day, it would make little sense to treat a man who holds out for thirty dollars as being unemployed. It would likewise be pointless to treat an employer who is willing to pay only ten dollars as having a real vacancy. In other words, we need to think of the relation between unemployment and job vacancies in terms of actual market conditions. Furthermore, we need to recognize that it makes a good deal of difference to the general welfare, and therefore also to public policy, whether equality between the number of unemployed and the number of job vacancies comes to rest at a figure of three million or thirteen million. Taking all these considerations together, full employment may be said to mean that the number of vacant jobs at prevailing wages is as large as the number unemployed and that the labor market is so organized that everyone who is able, willing, and seeking to work already has a job or can obtain one after a brief search or after undergoing some training.[15]

Let us now see how helpful this interpretation of full employment can be in formulating public policy. First of all, the criterion of equality between the number of unemployed and the number of vacant jobs poses squarely what in the economic sphere is perhaps the major policy problem of our generation, namely, whether aggregate demand at a particular time is deficient and, if so, what action the government can wisely take. Many of us have become accustomed to attribute every drop in general economic activity—more recently also every sign of sluggishness in the rate of economic growth—to a

[15] Stated more formally, equality between the number of vacant jobs and the number unemployed is a necessary but not a sufficient condition of full employment. The two other conditions are, first, that the equality holds at prevailing wages, second, that the labor market is so organized that practically all of the unemployed could obtain a job after a brief search or after obtaining some special training. Cf. W. H. Beveridge, *Full Employment in a Free Society*, New York, 1945, pp. 18–20, 124–31.

Equality of job openings and job seekers, at prevailing wages, could emerge at a high level of unemployment. In that event, the obstacle to full employment would not be the level of aggregate demand, but rather that the unemployed lack the highly intricate skills that are wanted, or that they choose not to practice them, or that they are located in the wrong places, or that they lack information about available jobs, or that legal wage minima are out of line with conditions in some markets. Even this statement is incomplete, for it assumes that adjustments must be on the side of supply, whereas some could in fact be made by those demanding specific types of labor.

The present concept of the goal of full employment would require for its full implementation detailed statistics on the structure (occupational, geographic, sex, age, etc.) as well as on the over-all level of both job vacancies and unemployment. However, even if we had nothing more than national totals, we would still be able to judge whether or not existing unemployment was due to a deficiency of aggregate demand. In deciding this issue, both job vacancies and unemployment would need to be expressed in seasonally adjusted form.

deficiency of aggregate demand, and we are therefore apt to urge the government to compensate for any deficiency that we believe exists. This way of thinking is often sound, practically useful, and socially beneficial. It rests, however, on an excessively simple view of the economic process. There can surely be difficulties on the supply side as well as on the demand side; for example, when a protracted strike in a major industry or a concentration of geographical shifts of businesses brings economic trouble, including unemployment. In diagnosing the state of the economy, it is critically important therefore to check the number unemployed against the number of job vacancies before concluding that aggregate demand has become deficient or to what degree this has happened.

Let me be more specific. I think that informed citizens will generally agree that our economy has suffered in recent years from excessive unemployment. There is less agreement, however, about the causes of the unemployment or the proper remedy for it. According to one school of thought—I shall call it the expansionist school—the principal cause is a more or less chronic shortage of aggregate demand. According to another school of thought—to which I shall refer as the structural school—the principal cause is found in the rapid piling up of economic changes, which have been creating more jobs than can be filled in some occupations and communities while substantial unemployment is being created in others.

Each school has presented impressive evidence to support its position, but neither the one nor the other has been able to demonstrate conclusively that its diagnosis is the right one. Thus the expansionist school stresses the recent failure of business investment in fixed capital to match earlier economic performance, the reduced rate of growth of total production since 1957, and the higher rate of unemployment since then. These facts may be granted; but they still leave open the vital question whether the number unemployed has been larger or smaller than the job vacancies. Unless this question is resolved, there is bound to be at least some lingering doubt about the characteristic remedy of the expansionist school—namely, easy credit, larger federal expenditures, lower tax rates, or some combination of these policies for increasing aggregate demand.

The structural school, in its turn, stresses the existence of extensive shortages of scientists, teachers, engineers, doctors, nurses, typists, stenographers, automobile and TV mechanics, tailors, domestic servants, and some other types of labor. In view of these shortages, it denounces the fiscal remedies proposed by the expansionists as being circuitous and needlessly costly. A far more effective way of dealing with unemployment, according to the structuralists, is to focus policy on better organization of the labor market—for example, by disseminating fuller and more timely reports on occupational trends, by bringing together pertinent data on every unemployed individual and every vacant job in a pool of information coordinated by employment exchanges,[16] by improving the existing system of vocational training and guidance, and by extending as soon as experience justifies it the retraining programs that have been established under recent legislation. All this and even more may be granted by the expansionists without budging from their position. They can properly insist that the mere existence of shortages in various occupations or communities

[16] Electronic computers open up exciting possibilities for the future. With their aid, an unemployed worker expressing his need or preference to an officer of an employment exchange might be referred in a matter of hours, if not minutes, to a list of potential employers (outside his community if there are none in his own) who need that type of employee. Employers could be served in a similar way. If all this seems remote, the main reason is that our Federal-State Employment Service has failed to flourish.

by no means discredits their thesis that, taking the nation as a whole, unemployment substantially exceeds the unfilled jobs.[17]

These recent discussions have served to illustrate once again that inadequate knowledge of the causes of economic difficulty is by no means a bar to strong opinions on the part of economists or of others. This is unavoidable when a problem like unemployment, about which men feel deeply, becomes a subject of public concern. It is not so much the exaggeration by this or that school that I find deplorable, as the complete absence of national statistics on job vacancies. The Employment Act has now been on the statute books nearly twenty years. It has come to serve as a sort of "constitution" for economic policy-making.[18] Its authority is constantly invoked by both public officials and private citizens. Its emphasis on ample employment opportunities is widely applauded. In its name all sorts of governmental programs are debated or undertaken to expand aggregate demand. Yet our nation has thus far failed to take the trouble to equip itself with the facts needed to determine whether, when, or to what degree, aggregate demand is deficient. If over-all national statistics on job vacancies existed, and if they were supported by data on job openings and unemployment in individual occupations and communities, much of the debate between the expansionists and the structuralists could be resolved on a factual basis.[19] Controversy

[17] My own speculations on this issue, if of any interest in this connection, are expressed, among other places, in the Preface to Thomas B. Curtis, *87 Million Jobs*, New York, 1962, and in a statement at *Hearings on January 1963 Economic Report of the President, Joint Economic Committee*, 88th Cong., 1st sess.

[18] See A. F. Burns, "Some Reflections on the Employment Act," *Political Science Quarterly*, LXXVII, December 1962.

[19] There is some reason to hope that the report of the Gordon Committee will be more successful than an earlier effort by the Council of Economic Advisers in getting a national system of job vacancy statistics or-

about public policy would doubtless continue for reasons to which I have already alluded, but it would proceed along more constructive channels, concentrating on future prospects and needs of the economy—a subject on which men are bound to hold different opinions.

VI. EFFECTIVENESS OF LABOR MARKETS

The concept of full employment that I have sketched may be helpful to policymakers also in other ways. By focusing on job opportunities as well as on job shortages, on employment as well as on unemployment, this concept should help to keep the healthy and the pathological aspects of economic life in perspective. Moreover, it should help to make students of public policy more alert to structural problems of our economy. As I have already noted, even if the business cycle vanished, unemployment would remain troublesome. Even if there were never any shortage of aggregate demand, the mutual adjustments of supply and demand for labor would often proceed slowly. Hence, whatever one may think of the merits of the controversy between the structuralists and the expansionists, there can be no doubt that unemployment would be very substantially reduced through better organization and functioning of the labor market.

This aspect of the unemployment problem has not received the attention it deserves on the part of economists. For example, economists frequently urge extension of the coverage of unemployment insurance and liberalization of benefits on the ground that such reforms would make the unemployment-insurance system a more powerful stabilizer of personal in-

---

ganized. See President's Committee To Appraise Employment and Unemployment Statistics, *Measuring Employment and Unemployment,* September 1962, pp. 25, 199–202, and Appendix B.

comes and of consumer buying. This argument, which I think is valid, does not justify the tendency to neglect the supply side or the interaction of supply and demand. There is a serious need to study how the structure of the unemployment-insurance system may need to be modified to promote better adjustment of the supply of labor to the prevailing demand. Indeed, it is doubtful if the advantages sought from extended or liberalized insurance benefits will be realized unless they are accompanied by extensive structural reforms.[20]

Another problem that deserves the attention of economists is that while many workers have recently been unemployed or have had to be content with part-time jobs, many others have been working overtime or holding down extra jobs. For manufacturing, accurate data exist on overtime and they disclose a disturbing development. In 1956, a year of booming business, overtime accounted for three hours of the average workweek. In 1962, when business activity was sluggish, overtime was equally abundant, although the number of manufacturing workers had in the meantime fallen by 8 per cent. One possible explanation of this increasing tendency to keep people on overtime is the steady growth of fringe benefits, the cost of which to a business firm tends to vary with the number of men employed rather than with the number of man-hours worked. Another possibility is that employers are gradually learning that disputes about work rules are fewer when they resort to overtime than when they add to their work force and therefore need to rearrange some of the jobs. These and other hypotheses require the most careful study by economists. For if it is really true that collective bargaining and some of our social legislation are tending to complicate the unemployment prob-

[20] Cf. the writer's comments in the *Proceedings of the Fourteenth Annual Meeting of the Industrial Relations Research Association*, December 1961, pp. 198–200.

lem, it would be well to turn at once to exploring ways of reducing the dangerous side effects.

The very high unemployment rate among young people in recent years is still another problem that cannot be understood in its entirety in terms of the theory of deficient aggregate demand. More recognition needs to be given to what the increasing emphasis of our society on academic training and college education is doing to the minds of young people. The dignity of honest labor, whether skilled or unskilled, is no longer stressed by parents or teachers as it once was. Not all youngsters, however, are capable of climbing high on the competitive educational ladder. Some lack the interest, or the intelligence, or the emotional stability to do so. When they are told on all sides that life holds out little for a person who lacks a good education, it is not surprising that many young men and women, who could have become good workers at some trade, drop out of school and join the ranks of casual labor. Whatever the answer to this distressing problem may be, we can be quite sure that the mere expansion of aggregate demand will not solve it.

The main reason more attention has not been devoted to this and other peculiarities of labor markets is the preoccupation of economists with the problem of demand. The belief has developed and is now widely held that, whatever the cause or causes of unemployment may be, a sufficient increase of aggregate demand will in time work an effective cure. On an abstract plane this theory seems quite valid, as I in fact have shown by analyzing what would happen for a time if the government constantly kept injecting new money into the income stream. But I also concluded that demonstration by stressing the revulsion of feeling that would eventually be stirred by any such experiment.[21] There are limits to the amount of inflation,

[21] See pp. 179–182 of this paper.

and the inefficiency and inconvenience associated with it, that our country will tolerate. Indeed, these limits are more severe in actual life than in my illustration. The practical significance of this is that the discontent aroused by a large inflationary experiment would be likely to lead to its discontinuance before enough of a dent had been made in structural unemployment.[22] Not only that, but massive political resistance could develop to any early repetition of the experiment even on the modest scale that might be needed to deal with that part of unemployment which, in the event of a recession, is really due to an insufficiency of aggregate demand.

I am well aware of the need for further research on the problem of business cycles and on the more general problem of maintaining aggregate demand at satisfactory levels. I surely hope that such research will go forward at Rice University and elsewhere. I particularly hope that economists will seek better understanding of the subtle forces that shape the confidence that businessmen, investors, and consumers have in their own and the nation's future. But I also feel that far more of the best thought of economists needs to be devoted to the several structural aspects of unemployment that I singled out for attention, as well as to related problems such as the influence of the minimum wage and current ways of administering welfare programs on the supply of labor, the influence of prejudice on the job opportunities of older men and minority groups, the effectiveness of both old and new training and retraining programs, the feasibility of reducing seasonal fluctuations in employment, and so on. If I am also right in thinking that comprehensive statistics on job vacancies are a vital miss-

[22] Given the number of vacant jobs and the number of unemployed for the entire nation, the smaller of the two figures (or either one if they are equal) may be taken as a rough indication of the size of the structural problem.

ing link in our entire system of economic intelligence, there is plenty of useful work ahead for economists.[23]

It is by patient extension of the still small area of knowledge and understanding that economics has made its principal contribution to public policy in the past. That is also the way in which new usefulness to our public policy of full employment will be found in the future.

[23] The new annual report on manpower (see n. 3) should foster a more balanced approach to the problem of unemployment. This report is required by the Manpower Development and Training Act of 1962.

SEVEN

The Problem of Unemployment

SINCE EARLY 1961 our nation has experienced increasing abundance and prosperity. Production, both in the aggregate and on a per capita basis, has risen substantially and with little interruption. The like has been true of employment, the flow of incomes, consumer buying, and corporate profits. Our growing prosperity, moreover, has been shared widely by the nation's families, communities, and businesses. And yet, the good times of recent years have been clouded by unemployment.

Although the rate of unemployment has gradually diminished, it has consistently remained above 4 per cent—that is, above the "interim target" which the managers of our national prosperity have set for implementing a full employment policy. To find an unemployment rate as low as 2 or 3 per cent, it is necessary to go back to the decade preceding the recession of 1953–54. To find an unemployment rate as low as 4 per cent, it is necessary to go back to the boom of 1956 and early 1957. In 1964, our best year since then, unemployment averaged 5.2 per cent. And although the unemployment rate has moved

Fairless Lecture at Carnegie Institute of Technology, November 2, 1965. Reprinted, by permission of the publisher, from *The Management of Prosperity*, Carnegie Institute of Technology, New York, 1966, pp. 33–50.

below 5 per cent this year, it was still nearly 4.5 per cent at the time of the most recent survey.

The persistence of sizable unemployment in the midst of increasing prosperity has been a disquieting experience to thoughtful Americans. An unemployment rate of 4.5 or 5 per cent is high for any country, and it is uncomfortably high for a nation that aspires to greatness. For that very reason, it is important to approach our unemployment problem searchingly and yet guard against exaggeration.

An unemployment rate of, let us say, 5 per cent does not mean, as social critics sometimes suggest, that one out of twenty breadwinners is anxiously pacing the streets in search of any sort of job to enable him to feed his family. Taken as a whole, unemployed workers in our country are neither a static nor an impoverished group. Normally, a high proportion of those who are unemployed in a particular month are either working again or are out of the labor force the following month. Most unemployed men with family responsibilities manage to find jobs within a few weeks. Moreover, they usually can draw unemployment insurance or dip into their savings while looking for work. A large fraction of the unemployed consists of married women, teenagers, or pensioners, who often wish only part-time or intermittent work. Not a few of the unemployed have given up their jobs to search for better opportunities or a different style of living. Some of the unemployed actually have a job but have not as yet reported for work or are absent from their present job while looking for another, or are waiting to be recalled when the temporary shutdown at the plant where they work, lasting perhaps two or three weeks, has ended. On the other hand, some of those counted as employed are doing temporary or part-time work when they would much prefer to have regular full-time jobs.

We may draw at once two inferences from these facts. First,

minor and not unreasonable adaptations of unemployment figures may change their look. For example, if all those having a job were omitted from the unemployment count, and if the unemployment figure itself were expressed as a percentage of the total labor force including the armed forces, instead of the civilian labor force alone as is customary, the unemployment rate would be lowered by about 0.5 per cent; that is, an unemployment rate of 5 per cent would usually become 4.4 or 4.5 per cent. Second, the reported unemployment for any month or year does not tell us nearly enough either about the waste of resources or about the human cost that is connected with unemployment. To deal with the unemployment problem intelligently, it is necessary to know what types of people are unemployed and how strenuously they may be looking for jobs.

We are on safer ground in making relative comparisons of unemployment over time, but even here we must be cautious. Although our statistics of unemployment have been compiled on a virtually uniform basis during the postwar years, they are insensitive to gradual changes in the character of unemployment. One of the telling advantages that wealth brings to an individual or to a family is a widening of choice. Clearly, a relatively poor man is under greater pressure to take a job than a man of substantial means. The former may need to settle on a job promptly, while the latter can bide his time and explore opportunities more thoroughly. And what is true of men is even more true of their wives and children. Unless supplementary income is needed to provide the necessities of life, the main breadwinner is likely to encourage his wife to hold out for a job that is reasonably attractive, and he is especially likely to urge his son to look for a post that has something of a future. But if the growth of individual and family incomes has tended to make people more selective about jobs, it has for that very reason tended to lengthen the usual interval of unemployment. The spread of unemployment insurance, and more liberal welfare programs generally, have also worked in that direction. The great merit of these social measures is that they maintain the flow of income on a modest scale even during periods of unemployment, so that even poor men may practice some of the discrimination in job choosing that comes as a matter of course to the well-to-do. Our statistical measures, however, do not recognize this voluntary aspect of unemployment, nor the fact that our growing prosperity and social legislation are tending to increase it.

Another factor that needs to be considered is the changing structure of the labor force. Although men are still the nation's primary workers, accounting even now for about two-thirds of the labor force, both the interest of women in gainful work and their opportunities have been growing rapidly. Women accounted for 56 per cent of the growth in the adult labor force during the eight years from 1948 to 1956, and they accounted for a still larger fraction—65 per cent—of the growth during the next eight years. Also, as the war babies have been coming of age, young workers have become a larger factor in the labor market. The number of teenagers in the labor force was practically the same in 1956 as in 1948; but they have become much more numerous since then. The increasing role of married women and young people in industry must be kept in mind in interpreting statistics of employment or unemployment. Since women commonly have responsibilities as wives, mothers, or housekeepers, they tend, on the average, to work fewer hours and less regularly than men. For example, about 48 per cent of the women who worked in 1963 were part-time or intermittent workers, while only 21 per cent of the men can be so classified. And just as family duties make women prone to part-time and intermittent work, so attendance at school has similar consequences for many youngsters. That this factor is of some consequence is evident from the fact that in recent years a little over half of the teenage labor force has consisted of students.

The emergence of a large part-time and intermittent work force is one of the neglected aspects of the changing structure of the American economy. The growth of this part of the labor force has been substantial. Not only are women an increasing part of the nation's work force; it also appears that the proportion among them who seek part-time or intermittent work is tending to become larger. And although the great majority of men continue to be regular full-time workers, the proportion who work part-time or intermittently is also rising—indeed, it is rising faster than among women. Taking the entire working force together, we find that the part-timers and the intermittently employed accounted for 27 per cent of the population with work experience during 1950, for 29 per cent in 1957, and for 31 per cent in 1963. This upward drift reflects, on the side of demand, the rapid growth of trade, clerical tasks, and service occupations. On the supply side, it reflects the spread of public and private pensions, as well as the growing participation of married women and students in gainful employment. Elderly men on a pension can often get along without steady full-time jobs, and not a few of them are driven to part-time or intermittent work by the penalty imposed by our social security system on those whose income exceeds the low statutory maximum.

The changing structure of the labor force has left its mark on both the character and the magnitude of the unemployment problem. Whether unemployment is viewed from the side of efficiency or that of welfare, the unemployment of a student seeking a summer job or the unemployment of a housewife

seeking part-time work cannot be readily equated with the unemployment of the family breadwinner who needs a regular
full-time job. Furthermore, the increasing participation in the
labor force of women, youngsters, students, part-timers, and
intermittent workers—these, of course, are overlapping groups
—is exerting upward pressure on the unemployment rate.

A new entrant into the labor force rarely finds or takes a job
immediately; in other words, he is unemployed for a time.
These unavoidable intervals of unemployment tend to be repeated for intermittent workers, among whom part-timers are
a large and increasing group. Women, whose role in the economy is growing, are typically less inclined or less able than
men to end their unemployment by taking a job in another
city. Indeed, they are even less prone to move to another
occupation or to another firm within the city of their residence.
That, of course, is one reason why the unemployment rate is
characteristically higher for women than for men. Also, the
unemployment rate for young men and women is consistently
much higher in our country than for adults. There are many
reasons for this—among them, the limited or utter lack of experience of young people, their low seniority status, and their
healthy propensity to test their aptitudes and opportunities by
experimenting with different jobs. My point at the moment is
merely that youngsters are an increasing part of the nation's
total labor force, and that students—who often seek part-time
or intermittent work and whose mobility is necessarily very
limited—are a large and growing part of the youthful labor
force. Although it is difficult to determine the degree to which
the various and complex changes in the character of the labor
force are tending to influence the unemployment rate, I do not
think there can be much doubt that the general effect is upward. One thing we know definitely—persons seeking part-

time jobs are an increasing part of unemployment. In 1964 one out of every six unemployed workers was looking for a part-time job, in contrast to one of thirteen a decade earlier.

Facts such as these deserve more recognition than they usually receive. Certainly, an unemployment rate of 4 per cent, or for that matter any other fixed figure, is an excessively crude guide to economic policy. It would be an error of judgment, however, to leap to the conclusion that unemployment of the magnitude experienced by our nation since 1957 is not a serious matter. Much of our unemployment has been concentrated—and still is—among low income groups, particularly Negroes, whose political voice is now becoming stronger. Unemployment contributes to crime and social tensions, and in recent years it has contributed also to racial strife. Moreover, unemployment tends to be a disrupting influence on people in every station of life, particularly in a society—such as ours—which is accustomed to identifying work with virtue. The fact that growing affluence has made people more selective about jobs, or that some individuals could give up gainful employment without inviting economic hardship, or that many individuals now prefer part-time work, does not mean that jobs have become less vital to personal happiness or individual fulfillment than they were a generation ago. Abundance as well as equality of opportunity is still the great American dream. No matter how we qualify the interpretation of unemployment figures, they do tell us that in recent years our nation has not succeeded as well as it did during the early fifties, or during other periods of prosperity, in enabling men and women— whether young or old, married or single, rich or poor—to fulfill the normal desire of having a job and thus finding usefulness.

The uneven impact of unemployment on people is perhaps its harshest feature. Factory workers and office workes may share the same roof, but the risk of becoming unemployed is much larger for the former than the latter. When a slump in sales or some technological improvement leads a business firm to cut back its work force, the brunt of the adjustment is usually borne by ordinary production hands, especially those with low seniority status, while the supervisory and clerical employees are affected little, if at all. Again, seasonal factors are of little importance in some industries, but a major disturbance in others. Certainly, civil servants or even workers in the steel and automobile industries do not experience protracted periods of seasonal slack such as are common in the construction industry or in food canning or in the garment trades. The business cycle also impinges very unevenly on the lives of working people. When a recession develops and employment declines, the rate of decline is typically much larger for wage-earners than for the self-employed, for blue-collar workers than for white-collar workers, for manufacturing or mining employees than for those engaged in the service trades, and for workers in the durable goods branch of manufacturing than for those in the nondurable branch. These disparities of risk are at the very heart of the unemployment problem. Indeed, if all workers were subject to the same unemployment hazard, in the sense that the unemployment experienced during any year was shared evenly, a 5 per cent unemployment rate would mean at worst an unpaid—and perhaps unplanned—vacation of about two and a half weeks for everyone. Production would still suffer, but not necessarily the morale or the welfare of people.

The fact that the risk of unemployment has lately become disproportionately high for some major segments of our working population is therefore a troublesome development. Last year the unemployment rate for adult females was a third higher than for adult males. This is the largest such discrepancy in a dozen years. In 1963 the unemployment rate for teenagers was three and a half times that of adult males, and in 1964 this ratio became still larger. There is no precedent for such extreme differentials, at least in the postwar period. The differential between whites and nonwhites has also widened ominously. Since 1955 the unemployment rate for all nonwhites has been rather consistently more than twice that of white workers. In the forties and early fifties, the difference between the two groups was much smaller. In the case of male teenagers, the average ratio of the nonwhite unemployment rate to that for whites was 1.1 for the years between 1950 and 1954, then rose to 1.6 during 1955–59, and reached 1.7 during 1960–64. In the case of female teenagers, the corresponding ratios were 1.5, 2.2, and again 2.2. I do not think that these wider differentials can be explained simply by the persistence of a relatively high rate of unemployment. I find, for example, that the comprehensive unemployment rate was the same in 1950 as in 1964, and yet all these differentials were then appreciably smaller.

The heavy impact of recent unemployment on teenagers, women, and Negroes means, of course, that unemployment has lately become increasingly concentrated among relatively inexperienced and unskilled workers. Available statistics do not enable us to differentiate very precisely between the skilled working population and the unskilled group. However, since experienced and more skilled workers predominate among married men, the unemployment rate for this group gives a clue to what has been happening in the market for skilled labor. So too, although more crudely, does the unemployment rate for adult males or the unemployment rate for insured workers. If we go back to the eighteen-month stretch from January 1956 to June 1957, when the economy was booming and jobs were plentiful nearly everywhere, we find that the unemployment rate averaged 2.4 per cent for married males,

3.4 per cent for adult males, and 3.4 per cent again for insured workers. In the years that followed, the unemployment of these groups became much higher; but by 1964 they began to approximate the 1956–57 boom level, and by the second quarter of this year they were fully back to that level. Meanwhile, the unemployment rate of teenagers, nonwhites, and women has persistently remained above the 1956–57 rates. This year, the gap has narrowed sharply for women, but not for nonwhites or teenagers.

These divergent trends suggest a sort of dual economy, with persistent shortages of skilled labor existing side by side with surpluses of relatively unskilled or inexperienced labor. The first Manpower Report of the President, issued in March 1963, strongly emphasized the prevalence of unemployment, and yet noted a shortage of scientists, teachers, engineers, doctors, nurses, typists, stenographers, automobile and TV mechanics, tailors, and some other types of labor. Since then, the increase of help-wanted advertising indicates that recruitment efforts by employers seeking skilled labor have mounted. And there are also other indications of increased inequality in the distribution of work among our people. During the boom of 1956–57, one out of every eighteen or nineteen workers engaged in moonlighting, and so it was still in 1963 and in 1964—although the rate of unemployment had become much higher. Meanwhile, overtime work at premium rates, which averaged 2.6 hours per worker in manufacturing during the boom of 1956–57, rose to 2.8 hours in 1963, 3.1 hours in 1964, and 3.4 hours in the first half of this year. In view of the extensiveness of overtime, it need surprise no one that part-time idleness—that is, the extent to which individuals seeking full-time work find themselves on part-time schedules—has been running lower this year and last than it did during the boom of 1956–57. Clearly, serious shortages in some major sectors of the labor market have been existing side by side with high unemployment, much of it of a long-term character, in other sectors.

In our dynamic economy, shortages in some parts of the labor market frequently accompany surpluses elsewhere without becoming a matter of national concern. They are apt to become that, however, when the correction of the disequilibrium proceeds slowly; that is, when geographic pockets of chronic depression emerge or when persistently high unemployment develops in some major industries or occupations or other social groups. Two schools of thought on the unemployment problem have made their voice heard in recent years. According to the expansionists, whose views have dominated public policy in recent years, the fundamental cause of our relatively high rate of unemployment is a deficiency of aggregate demand. The structuralist school, on the other hand, claims that the fundamental cause is the intensified tempo of economic change, which has created more jobs than can be filled in some occupations and communities while substantial unemployment exists or is being created in others. In principle, these differences of diagnosis could be settled by comparing the size and composition of unemployment with the number and composition of vacant jobs. Unhappily, despite the general excellence of our statistical system, even rough statistics of job vacancies are unavailable on a nation-wide basis. The protagonists of the two schools have therefore had to rely on indirect and circumstantial evidence.

In the early stages of the debate, the expansionists tended to minimize the importance of structural changes. They took their stand on the theoretical ground that once aggregate demand increased sufficiently, the groups that have been suffering from abnormally high rates of unemployment would find their position dramatically improved. By and large, the structuralists conceded the theory. They insisted, however, that the improvement would come much too slowly, that it would involve the nation in inflation, and that the problem of unemployment could be solved without this heavy cost by concentrating on policies for better matching of jobs and workers. As the discussion proceeded, the gap between the two schools narrowed. The evidence amassed by the structuralists gradually led the expansionists to give greater weight to geographic, occupational, industrial, and other imbalances in the labor market. Also, since the new labor market policies proposed by the structuralists often required additions to governmental expenditure, they were to that extent welcomed by the expansionists. The expansionist school has persisted, however, in denying that structural factors are a greater cause of the unemployment of the past few years than they were in earlier times.

As far as I can judge, the expansionist theory is sounder in what it claims than in what it denies. In view of the fact that our nation experienced a recession in 1957–58, that the recovery which followed was incomplete, that another recession occurred in 1960–61, and that a good part of 1962 was marked by sluggishness, there can be little doubt that a deficiency of aggregate demand was a major cause of unemployment during much of the period since 1957. However, there are cogent grounds for believing that if the pressure of aggregate demand had remained at the boom level of 1956–57, the unemployment rate would still have been higher in recent years than it was then. In addition to the factors I have already noted, statistics on productivity suggest that the displacement of labor through technological and other improvements in industry has proceeded somewhat faster during the past few years than it did during the late fifties. To the extent that this has occurred, it has complicated the adjustment of the supply of labor to the changing requirements of employers. At any rate, with a part-time and intermittent work force growing, with a tendency toward voluntary unemployment increasing, with the employment opportunities of the unskilled declining, and with inequality in the distribution of work increasing, it appears that our economy has been changing in ways that make it harder to achieve full employment merely by stimulating aggregate demand. If this generalization is valid, as I am increasingly inclined to believe, it would be wise to devote much more attention than we are giving to policies for facilitating the mutual adjustment of supply and demand in the labor market.

Fortunately, recognition of this need is increasing. While the dominant emphasis of economic policy in the past few years has been on the expansion of aggregate demand, numerous programs have also been initiated to improve the functioning of the labor market. These programs run the gamut from training people for available jobs to helping workers relocate where the jobs are or bringing new jobs to depressed areas. I cannot stop to examine or evaluate these programs. Surely, some suffer from being spread too thinly, and others are handicapped by overlapping authority or conflicting provisions. But what is chiefly important, the new activities being directed to the training or retraining of unemployed or poorly adjusted workers seem to be very promising. At first, these activities were focused exclusively on vocational skills. They are now being broadened to include also instruction in the rudiments of language, arithmetic, and personal conduct. Although these new educational efforts are still being conducted on a small scale, they are likely to expand as experience is gained and as the needed teaching and counseling staffs become available. We must not overlook, however, the lesson to be drawn from earlier experience with vocational education, namely, that constant vigilance is needed to assure that the teaching and counseling are realistically geared to the changing job requirements of employers. In 1918, when federal concern with vocational education started, less than 30 per cent of those enrolled in federally aided vocational classes received instruction in home economics or agriculture. Incredible though it may seem, this proportion had grown by 1963 to over 60 per cent, while technical education languished.

Our governmental authorities recognize that the success of the new training programs will depend heavily on the effectiveness of the federal-state employment service. Modern high-speed electronic computers and telecommunication have opened up exciting opportunities. With their aid, it should be possible for an unemployed person to walk into a local employment office, express his need or preference for work, and be referred in a matter of hours, if not minutes, to a list of plausible jobs in his own community, or—if none are available there—to jobs in more distant places. Employers seeking to fill vacancies could be similarly served. If the employment service took full advantage of modern technology and began to function in this manner, our labor market—or rather that part of it being served by the public employment system—would become so organized that supply and demand could, in principle, be matched almost instantly. Some reduction of the level of unemployment, perhaps a very substantial reduction, is virtually bound to be achieved through such a reform. The results, of course, would be all the better if some practical way could be devised of coordinating the activities of public and private employment offices.

The effectiveness of the new training programs in reducing unemployment will depend also on how speedily and how accurately the authorities can detect shifts in occupational and industrial trends. Although good statistics are not enough to make good forecasts, they are an indispensable tool to the analyst and forecaster. Statistics on unemployment have already proved very helpful in the analysis of labor market trends, but there is as much need for statistics on job vacancies as for statistics on unemployment. Recent research and experiments have demonstrated that useful statistics on job vacancies can be collected on a current basis, and the Department of Labor has therefore sought an appropriation for this purpose. In view of the need for job vacancy statistics on the part of administrators of the new training programs as well as local school authorities, vocational counselors, personnel officers, and practical economists concerned with labor market problems, I have no doubt that the Congress will in time provide the necessary funds; but it would be wise to take early steps to supply this vital missing link in our system of economic intelligence.

Besides devoting energy to new labor market programs, it is desirable to reappraise older governmental programs that influence the efficiency of the labor market. One of these is the social security system which has strengthened our economy and brought blessings to many millions, but which has also had some unhappy side effects. Whatever may be said of present eligibility requirements for unemployment insurance, they have not been adjusted sufficiently to cope with the increasing trend toward part-time and intermittent work. Too many individuals are tempted to work for a short time, then leave and draw unemployment insurance. Also, too many employers manage to attach workers to their establishments by a combination of subnormal wages and the assurance of unemployment benefits during protracted periods of seasonal slack. Of course, the employees of such subsidized firms often become unemployed only in a technical sense. The same is true of workers who have just retired on a pension and yet draw unemployment insurance. To the extent that these conditions prevail, they cry out for remedy. If such abuses were stopped or substantially reduced, our actual as well as statistical unemployment would be somewhat lower, and there would be the added advantage that public policy could then look more favorably on the liberalization of benefits for the great mass of the unemployed who are truly willing and seeking to work.

More important still, there is a need to improve our understanding of the effects of minimum wage laws on the workings of the labor market. I have already noted the great influx of women and teenagers into the labor force in recent years. This major development in the market for relatively unskilled labor has been reinforced, on the supply side, by migration of both whites and Negroes from farms to the cities. Meanwhile, many employers have been finding ways of economizing on costs by substituting machinery or other automatic devices for unskilled or semiskilled labor. In these circumstances, in order to perform the function of bringing the demand for labor and its supply into mutual adjustment, the price of unskilled labor should have declined in recent years relative to the price of skilled labor.

As far as I have been able to learn from the meager accessible data, this did not happen. For example, records for the construction industry show an increase in average hourly wages of 40 per cent between 1956 and 1964 for skilled labor and 50 per cent for common labor. During the same period, the average hourly wage rose 36 per cent for skilled maintenance workers in manufacturing plants, and the increase was the same for unskilled workers. Again during this period, the minimum union wage rose 41 per cent for drivers engaged in local trucking and 43 per cent for their helpers. Systematic date for office employees go back only to 1958. Here we find that the average wage of office boys has risen more since 1958 than that of accounting clerks, and that the average wage of file clerks has risen more than that of any other group of female office workers. These comparisons, it should be noted, are useful only in judging the skilled-unskilled differential of a particular industry or group. They cannot be used to compare industries, since the samples differ and so too does the treatment of fringe benefits.

If the wage trends that I have cited are at all representative, it appears that the skilled-unskilled wage differential has lately been out of equilibrium; in other words, unskilled labor has been relatively overpriced. One reason for this development is the tendency of trade unions to press for uniform or even narrower wage differentials between skilled and unskilled work. Another and more powerful reason is the minimum wage legislation of our federal government. During the postwar period, the minimum wage per hour has been raised four times, first in January 1950 when it went up from forty to seventy-five cents, next in March 1956 when it rose to a dollar, then in September 1961 to a dollar and fifteen cents, and in September 1963 to a dollar and a quarter. Each time the minimum was raised, it was set at approximately half of the average manufacturing wage. However, the statutory minimum was only 29 per cent of average hourly earnings in manufacturing just before the increase of 1950, while the corresponding figure reached 40 per cent just before the increase of the minimum in 1956, 43 per cent before the increase in 1961, and 47 per cent before the increase in 1963. There has thus been a strong upward drift across the years in the actual ratio of the minimum wage to the average wage. This drift is most simply indicated by the fact that the minimum wage rose 67 per cent between early 1956 and 1964, while average hourly earnings in manufacturing rose 34 per cent. Meanwhile, the federal minimum has become effective over a greater range of industry, and many states have likewise raised or expanded the coverage of their minimum wages.

When the statutory minimum wage rises, the effects spread

out. In the first place, forces are set in motion to restore previous differentials, so that there is a tendency for the entire lower end of the wage structure to be lifted. Secondly, the higher minimum has an influence on prevailing attitudes and opinion. Not a few uncovered workers are apt to feel that they too are entitled to a higher minimum and that nothing else would be just. This sentiment is often shared by others, including businessmen in the community, so that even some reluctant employers give way. However, the mere raising of the statutory minimum does nothing of itself to improve the productivity of workers, and it therefore also does nothing to enhance their worth to employers. In a large and complex economy such as ours, there is always some range of substitution, depending on relative costs, between skilled and unskilled workers or between labor and machinery of this or that degree of automaticity. The broad result of the substantial increase of the minimum wage in recent years has therefore been a curtailment of job opportunities for the less skilled workers. With unskilled labor being overpriced, employers have been using relatively more capital or skilled labor and relatively less unskilled labor. Large firms have frequently made this adjustment in the course of expanding their operations, while many small businesses that previously managed with a helper or two have learned to get along with just one or without any.

These broad observations are borne out by statistical evidence. During the postwar period, the ratio of the unemployment rate of teenagers to that of male adults was invariably higher during the six months following an increase of the minimum wage than it was in the preceding half year. The ratio of the unemployment rate of female adults to that of male adults has behaved similarly. Of course, the unemployment of teenagers and women depends on a variety of factors—certainly on business conditions as well as on the minimum wage. I have tried to allow for this in a more refined analysis. It appears, whether we consider the unemployment rate of teenagers or that of women, that its primary determinants are, first, the general state of the economy as indicated by the unemployment rate of adult males, second, the ratio of the minimum wage to the average wage in manufacturing. The influence of the wage ratio turns out to be particularly strong in the case of nonwhite teenagers. According to my equation, it appears that in the absence of any change in the general state of the economy, another increase of twenty-five cents in the minimum wage would be likely to raise the unemployment rate of nonwhite teenagers by as much as eight percentage points. This, I need hardly say, is a very disturbing estimate. However, the same equation also indicates that a reduction of the ratio of the minimum wage to the average wage tends to lower the unemployment rate. In other words, the slow reduction of this ratio since 1963, when the minimum wage was last set, has contributed somewhat to the improvement that has recently taken place in the teenage unemployment rate. Of course, the effort made during the past few months to enroll teenagers in various training programs has also contributed modestly to this result.

The subject of minimum wages is surrounded by human emotion and political commitment. Compassionate concern for the poor does credit to our age, and yet the programs to which it gives rise can be effective only to the degree that they meet the test of economic soundness. The surest way to improve the income of poor people is to help them become more productive. However, some unfortunate people are so handicapped that they cannot become more productive. Hence, there is also something to be said for a society that would assure a minimum income for every family. Legislation of a minimum hourly wage does no such thing. It helps some of the poor and harms others—often those who need help most. In view of our nation's newly aroused interest in the problem of poverty, economists can no longer ignore, as they virtually have, the minimum wage.

Beyond the questions that I have discussed, there is a great need for more vigorous research on labor market problems. The rate of unemployment today is appreciably lower than it was a year or two ago, and it may before long reach 4 per cent—a level that economists often associate with "full employment." That condition, however, would still mean extensive unemployment for some significant parts of the working population. Partly for this reason, and partly also because the labor force will probably rise more rapidly in the years ahead, we should prepare for the future by improving our basic knowledge. According to a study by the Bureau of Labor Statistics, seasonal variations in industry and trade account for at least 20 per cent of total unemployment in a good business year. This major source of unemployment is not receiving the attention it deserves. The growth of overtime is another subject that calls for research. While scarcity of skilled labor may well be the principal cause of this development, other causes have been suggested. One is the steady expansion of fringe benefits, the cost of which to a business firm tends to vary with the number of men employed rather than with the number of man-hours worked. Another is that employers are finding that disputes about work rules are fewer when they resort to overtime than when they rearrange jobs in the process of adding to their work force. Still another factor is that some large employers seek to regularize the number of jobs in order to maintain good community relations, and this necessarily means more overtime when sales are brisk. These and other suggested causes of the growth of overtime need to be thoroughly investigated. Still another highly important subject for research revolves around the need for business planning of technological improvements or of shifts in plant location so as to ease the problem of adjustment for the employees.

Let me say, finally, that in this discussion I have assumed that the managers of national prosperity will seek to maintain aggregate demand at a high level. I have not stressed this need, because at present there is little danger that the state of demand will suffer from neglect. The danger is rather that philosophical commitment to the theory of deficiency in aggregate demand has now become so strong that it will lead us to seek solutions without attending sufficiently to the structural causes of unemployment.

EIGHT

Aggregate or Structural Approaches to Full Employment

THE EMPLOYMENT ACT which we celebrate today has had its share of the vicissitudes of fortune that go with life. The bill originally proposed by Senator Murray ran into massive opposition in the House, and many anxious months elapsed before the Congress hammered out an acceptable compromise. The machinery established by the Act has not always functioned smoothly or as its designers may have hoped. At times, the findings by the Council of Economic Advisers have lacked the detachment or the lustre of science. At times, the pronouncements of the Joint Economic Committee have suggested excessive partisanship or haste. In one year the Congress refused to vote a full year's appropriation for the Council's activities, and its ability to survive became doubtful. Despite such occasional setbacks, the moral authority of the Employment Act has grown with the passage of time. Indeed, in the span of a mere twenty years, the Act has acquired the force of an economic constitution. The President, his Council of Economic Advisers, the Congress, in some degree the entire

Address on twentieth anniversary of Employment Act, Washington, D.C. Reprinted from *Twentieth Anniversary of the Employment Act of 1946: An Economic Symposium*, Joint Economic Committee, Eighty-Ninth Congress, Second Session, February 23, 1966, pp. 27–33.

executive and administrative establishment, including the Federal Reserve Board, now function under this "constitution" when major economic policies are developed.

As befits a constitution, the Employment Act lays down general principles and procedures, but gives little guidance on how the Federal government is to discharge its new responsibility of promoting "maximum employment, production, and purchasing power." To be sure, the Act stresses the importance of proceeding "in a manner calculated to foster . . . free competitive enterprise." This constraint reaffirms our nation's commitment to the principle of freedom, but it does no more than that. The Act also specifies that the means employed in furthering its objectives must be consistent with the "needs and obligations" of the Federal government, with "other essential considerations of national policy," and with "the general welfare." In view of this broad language, our successive presidents have been able to deal under the umbrella of the Employment Act with such objectives of policy as stability of the general price level, faster improvement of productivity, equality of opportunity, and equilibrium in the balance of payments. However, the Act itself is entirely reticent on these matters, and therefore gives no clue to the way in which any of these objectives is to be sought, or how the pursuit of one or another of them may aid or limit the achievement of "maximum employment, production, and purchasing power." In short, the Act practically leaves the means for dealing with recession, unemployment, or inflation to judgment concerning the individual case.

The flexibility inherent in the Employment Act has proved very helpful to government officials charged with its administration. Indeed, economic life is so full of surprises that it is doubtful if the Act could have survived if the Congress had prescribed some formula, whether the one suggested by the

Murray bill or any other, for achieving maximum employment —to say nothing of maximum production or purchasing power. At the same time, the sweeping but imprecise mandate of the Act has imposed an extremely difficult task on the Council of Economic Advisers and the Joint Economic Committee, and beyond them on professional economists as a class.

Taking the past twenty years as a whole, the administrators of the Employment Act have concentrated on the maximization of employment, but they have not neglected other major objectives of national policy. By and large, our economy has performed well during this period. We have preserved the essentials of freedom in a revolutionary age, when many other nations have lost or destroyed their freedom. Our economy has continued to grow in size and efficiency. We have made great strides in moderating the business cycle, and the fruits of industry have been widely distributed among our people. The Employment Act has contributed to these achievements by introducing elements of order into economic policymaking and by providing assurance to both businessmen and consumers that economic storms would not be left to themselves. We must not, however, gloss over the lapses from full employment during the postwar period, or the series of recessions, the deterioration in the value of the dollar, the chronic deficit in the balance of payments, and the persistence of pockets of poverty in our land of plenty. If the efforts of the administrators of the Employment Act have not always been successful, the reason in large part is that they have worked with tools that are much too crude.

We need, in particular, better ways of determining whether, when, or to what degree unemployment can best be attacked by over-all monetary and fiscal policies. Our nation has relied preponderantly on such policies during the past few years on the ground that aggregate demand was deficient. This approach has certainly not been wanting in plausibility. In view of the fact that we experienced a recession in 1957–58, that the recovery which followed was incomplete, that another recession occurred in 1960–61, and that a good part of 1962 was marked by sluggishness, there can be little doubt that a deficiency of demand was a major cause of unemployment during much of the period since 1957. However, the Council's calculations of the gap between actual and potential output, quite apart from being fragile, cannot be treated as measures of demand shortage. If aggregate output falls short of its potential, the gap may have nothing to do with any weakness of demand. It may instead reflect obstacles on the side of supply or a failure of the constituent parts of demand and supply to adjust sufficiently to one another. Since the structure of our economy keeps changing, these changes as well as difficulties on the demand side must be reckoned with in a scientific diagnosis.

Let me note briefly a few of the structural factors. First, welfare programs have grown very rapidly in recent years. A great merit of these social measures is that they maintain a flow of income during periods of unemployment, so that even poor men may practice some of the discrimination in job choosing that comes as a matter of course to the well-to-do. Our statistical measures, however, do not recognize this voluntary aspect of unemployment, nor the fact that our social legislation together with increasing prosperity have been tending to increase it. Second, women and teenagers have become a much larger factor in the labor force since the late fifties. But women are less inclined or less able than men to end their unemployment by taking a job in another city. Indeed, they are less prone than men to move to another occupation or another firm within the city of their residence. Moreover, married women commonly seek only part-time or intermittent work. And since a large proportion of the teenagers in the labor force are students, they also frequently seek part-time or intermittent work. But a new entrant into the labor force rarely finds or takes a job immediately; in other words, he is unemployed for a time. Since these unavoidable intervals of unemployment are repeated for intermittent workers, the volume of unemployment has tended to rise as the intermittent work force has grown. Third, the obstacles to rapid adjustment in the labor market have lately become larger. The pace of technological change has quickened. The supply of part-time workers has increased with sudden rapidity, while the evolution of demand has been gradual. Also, the legally prescribed minimum wage has risen much faster than the average wage at the very time when the ranks of unskilled and inexperienced workers were swelling. Hence, shortages of some types of labor and in some communities have coexisted with surpluses in others to a larger extent than before.

It is developments such as these that the structuralist school has emphasized rather than any deficiency of aggregate demand. And just as the expansionist school has sought to fortify its claims by an impressive array of evidence, stressing in particular the depressed state of business investment in fixed capital between 1957 and 1963, so the structuralist school has marshalled considerable evidence on the high and rising level of overtime work, on the concentration of unemployment among less educated workers, on the jump in the ratio of the unemployment rate of Negroes to that of whites since the mid-fifties, on the exceptionally high ratio of the unemployment rate of teenagers to that of adult males during the past three years, and so on. Most structuralists have been entirely ready to grant that easy money, lower tax rates, and larger Federal expenditures—that is, the remedies favored by the expansionists—would reduce unemployment. They have insisted, however, that more lasting effects would be achieved by attending to the structural causes of unemployment, and that the risk of inflation would also be reduced in the process. Although their views were heeded to some degree, as the Manpower Development and Training Act of 1962 and related legislation testify, the expansionist theory proved more congenial to the mood of our times. Had it done so to a lesser degree, I believe that unemployment would now be no higher while the danger of inflation would be smaller than it has become.

My purpose on this occasion, however, is not to press the relative merits of this or that school of economic thought. My basic point is rather that existing information has prevented economic investigators from reaching the precise diagnosis of the unemployment problem that the Employment Act so plainly requires. The Act declares that the Federal government has the responsibility of promoting "conditions under which there will be afforded useful employment opportunities . . . for those able, willing, and seeking to work." To discharge this responsibility, statistics are needed to determine to what degree, if any, the aggregate demand for labor falls short of the number of "those able, willing, and seeking to work"—that is, of the supply of labor. But the aggregate demand for labor includes the unfilled jobs as well as those that are being manned, just as the aggregate supply of labor includes the unemployed workers as well as those who have jobs. Hence, to determine the relation between aggregate demand and supply, information is needed on three magnitudes—employment, unemployment, and job vacancies. Unhappily, while we have comprehensive statistics on the first and the second, the data on job vacancies are fragmentary, and it has therefore been impossible to bring either the expansionist or the structuralist theory to a decisive test.

If I read the Employment Act correctly, its implementation

requires continuous, carefully compiled, and comprehensive statistics on job vacancies. It may be interesting to know whether the existing unemployment rate is above or below 4 per cent, but neither this conventional figure nor any other can be relied upon to identify maximum employment—or its equivalent in common usage, full employment. What really matters for the purposes of the Employment Act is not what figure on unemployment appears to correspond best to the concept of full employment, but how the amount of unemployment that actually exists compares with the number of job openings. When unemployment exceeds job vacancies at prevailing wages, the demand for labor is clearly insufficient to provide employment for everyone who is able, willing, and seeking to work. At such a time, a deficiency of aggregate demand exists, and a governmental policy that relies on monetary, fiscal, or other devices to expand demand is, in principle, suited to the nation's needs. On the other hand, when the number of vacant jobs is equal to or larger than the number of the unemployed, there is no deficiency of demand. A government that is seriously concerned about inflation will not seek to expand demand at such a time, but will instead concentrate its efforts on securing better matching of the men and women who seek work with the jobs that need to be filled. By equipping ourselves in the future with more of the information needed to determine the true state of demand, we should be able to pursue the objective of full employment with less danger of causing serious inflation.

This objective will be promoted by other improvements in economic information. Our statistical system is the best in the world, but it is not keeping pace with the needs of our times. We learn, for example, that unemployment amounted to 3.3 million this January. What precisely does this figure tell us? A short answer is that it reports the number of jobless persons who are able, willing, and seeking to work. This answer, however, is incomplete and in some respects misleading. In the first place, the figure includes an unknown number of individuals who, while they are willing to work and are seeking work, are so handicapped physically or psychologically that they would be unable to hold down a job even in a very tight labor market. Second, the unemployment figure includes several hundred thousand persons who actually have jobs; specifically, those who are waiting—whether of their own choice or the employer's—to start work within thirty days, those who are searching for a new job while they are absent from work, and those who have been temporarily laid off but have definite instructions to return within thirty days. Third, the unemployment figure includes an undetermined number who are not looking for work diligently. A man who applied for a job as much as sixty days ago, but made no other effort to find a job while waiting for a reply to his application, may still be counted as unemployed. Fourth, the unemployment figure includes a certain number of persons, again of unknown magnitude, who are not looking for work in any sense, either because they are temporarily ill, or because they are waiting to be recalled from an indefinite layoff, or because they believe that no work is available in their community or trade. On the other hand, the unemployment figure omits some, perhaps many, persons who have stopped looking for work because they have established that acceptable jobs are unavailable within their geographic reach. Clearly, the unemployment figures which serve as a basis for much of our policy-making are highly technical and somewhat dubious aggregates. Not only is it desirable to refine the concept of unemployment; we also need to learn how to assemble and use statistics of unemployment so that the parts which cannot be readily influenced by broad fiscal or monetary policies may be approached by more direct measures.

Other branches of our statistical system also show signs of age and need to be revitalized—notably, the records of prices and wages. The quotations that enter into price indexes of industrial commodities at wholesale are largely based on list prices rather than actual market transactions. But in the course of an economic upsurge, such as we have been experiencing, discounts tend to become smaller, concessions fewer, and premiums more frequent or larger. By neglecting these changes, our price indexes have understated the advance of the wholesale price level since mid-1964. If more accurate price indexes had been available, we might have realized sooner that the remarkable period of general price stability which began in the late fifties had come to an end, at least temporarily.

Despite their element of bias, the wholesale price indexes have the merit of comprehensiveness—an advantage that our measures of wage changes lack. The fullest set of figures published by the Bureau of Labor Statistics pertains to hourly earnings of production workers in manufacturing. These figures represent hours paid for, not hours worked, and hence do not allow for the increasing number of hours paid for but not worked. They do not include fringe benefits—a factor that has become of major importance to employers and employees alike. A sizable and increasing fraction of employees are classified as "nonproduction" workers, and they are not covered at all in the wage statistics. Finally, it is well to note that employees in the goods producing industries are now outnumbered by those in the service industries, and that the statistical coverage of wage rates and earnings in the service industries is meager.

But the records that are used most widely and on which businessmen as well as government officials have come to rely most heavily are the estimates of gross national product—that is, the nation's total output of goods and services. These figures not only inform us on past and current economic conditions, but also serve as a basis for much of the forecasting in which economists and others necessarily engage. As is true of so many parts of our statistical system, the gross national product estimates are more dependable than comparable data for most other nations. They are not, however, as good as they should be. The July 1965 issue of *Economic Indicators,* for example, reported that the gross national product in 1964 was 623 billion dollars. The next month's issue reported the appreciably higher figure of 629 billion for the same year. In fact, had it not been for certain changes of definition that accompanied the statistical revisions, the latter figure would have been 640 billion. Or to cite a more nearly current example, the increase between the first and second quarters of 1965 was reported in successive issues of *Economic Indicators* as 9.2, 9.5, and 11.2 billion dollars, while the increase between the second and third quarters was reported as 11.0, 11.6, and 12.7 billion. While I admire the constant striving of statisticians for promptness, precision, and conceptual relevance, I also suspect that the initial underestimates of the growth in our nation's output last year may have contributed to the somewhat tardy realization by policy makers that slack in the economy was vanishing. I have wondered over the years, and still do, how much might have to be added to the cost of gathering our statistics so as to reduce, if not eliminate, the need for sizable revisions in the future, and whether the resulting benefits would not greatly outweigh the cost. I hope that the Joint Economic Committee, which has often taken the initiative to improve our statistical system, will seek answers to these questions.

Let me say, finally, that the implementation of the Employment Act requires, besides better information, more realistic models of the workings of our economy than are now current. Contrary to widespread notions, neither the labor force nor the output per man-hour grows steadily and smoothly, year after year. Nor is the gap between actual and potential output like a bathtub that merely needs turning on of the fiscal faucet to be filled. Experience teaches that productivity increments tend to decline as full employment is approached. If this tendency is overlooked by the makers of policy, the bathtub may overflow. Experience also teaches that confidence is a basic factor in economic life, and that it therefore makes a difference, even if we cannot express it in a mathematical equation, how we seek to fill gaps. Arithmetically, one dollar in the Federal budget is like any other, but from an economic viewpoint the individual dollars differ. The great success that attended the recent reduction of income tax rates cannot be attributed solely to the arithmetical magnitude of the fiscal stimulus. It was also due to the fact that the government took numerous steps to improve confidence after the unhappy steel price episode of April 1962, that the fiscal stimulus adopted in early 1964 took the form of a tax reduction instead of an increase in expenditures, and that the tax reduction became effective over the entire range of personal and corporate incomes instead of being limited, as some well-meaning citizens had urged, to individuals at the lower end of the income scale. But just as confidence may be strengthened by creating a better environment for enterprise and investment, so also can it be damaged by imprudent management of governmental finances or by arbitrary interference with the workings of labor and commodity markets.

I wish to congratulate the present Council of Economic Advisers and the Joint Economic Committee on their efforts to bring our evolving economic knowledge to bear on the nation's economic condition. They need not be reminded of William James' pragmatic maxim that "we have to live today by what truth we can get today, and be ready tomorrow to call it falsehood."

NINE

Wages and Prices by Formula

IN RECENT years our nation's economic policy has been focused largely on the problem of unemployment. The reasons for this concern are plain. The recovery from the recession of 1957–1958 failed to develop momentum and came to a halt in the spring of 1960 when the unemployment rate was still above 5 per cent. The new recession that followed proved to be mild and brief. But when the labor force is growing and becoming more productive, even a minor recession of business activity can have serious repercussions. In the early months of 1961 unemployment reached 7 per cent, and the new Administration, as was generally expected, embarked promptly on an expansive economic policy.

At first the Administration placed its emphasis on increasing federal expenditures and on creating as much monetary ease as the state of our balance of payments might allow. Later, with unemployment still hovering around 6 per cent, the need for a more effective policy became clearer. Official interest gradually shifted from raising federal expenditures to carrying out a sweeping reduction of income tax rates, which still bore the stamp of the Great Depression and World War II. After a pro-

Murray Lecture at State University of Iowa, November 10, 1964. Reprinted, by permission, from *Harvard Business Review*, March–April 1965.

tracted debate, Congress recognized the importance of revising the tax system, and lower tax rates for individuals and corporations became law. Meanwhile, the Administration promulgated more liberal rules for figuring depreciation on tax returns, took some steps to improve the matching of jobs and skills in labor markets, and pressed for an extension of monetary ease.

By and large, the economy has responded well to the new direction of economic policy. Of late, production and employment have increased materially, and the unemployment rate has been moving gradually downward.

I. PROGRESS WITHOUT INFLATION

In pursuing its expansive economic policy, the Administration has been aware of the risk that unbalanced budgets and rapid additions to the money supply may set off a new wave of inflation. That can hardly be a pleasant prospect for any government under modern conditions. The impact of inflation on the purchasing power of families living on pensions or other types of fixed income is severe. Also, inflation commonly bears harder on those who work for a salary than on wage earners, and it deals harshly with anyone whose plans for the future depend on savings accumulated in the form of bank deposits, shares of savings and loan associations, government savings bonds, and the like. These injustices of inflation tend to breed political discontent, and so, too, does the widespread awareness that inflation is often the precursor of recessions. When costs and prices begin advancing rapidly, experience has shown that speculation in inventories and overbuilding tend to develop, that the strength of economic expansion tends to be undermined in the process, and that prosperity is then liable to give way to recession.

Moreover, the precarious condition of the balance of payments has lately added a dimension of risk to inflation that we, unlike an earlier generation of Americans, cannot ignore. Since 1958 our country has experienced a massive outflow of gold and a still larger increase in its short-term liabilities to foreigners. The United States has continued to serve as banker of the world; but any banker whose reserves dwindle while his demand liabilities keep mounting will inevitably invite caution on the part of those who deal with him.

Fortunately, our wholesale price level has recently remained stable while much of the rest of the world has suffered inflation. This development has served to keep down the deficit in our balance of payments, but it has not sufficed to eliminate it. Therefore, if our price level should rise in relation to that of competing nations, our exports would tend to diminish relative to imports. Unless major steps were taken to counteract such a development, the deficit in our international accounts would become larger, and this could lead to a run on the dollar and its ultimate devaluation. The attending financial crisis would unsettle commercial and industrial markets throughout the world. It would leave a legacy of fear that could result in a lasting constriction of international trade and investment. Worse still, it might injure fatally our country's foreign prestige and, therefore, its capacity for political leadership of the Free World.

Clearly, the risks of inflation are formidable, and they are recognized as such in informed circles both within and outside government. Thus, in formulating the nation's economic goals, the President's Economic Report of 1962 emphasized "the achievement of full employment and sustained prosperity," and urged such an achievement "without inflation."

But how can inflation be avoided? Government authorities have approached this question pragmatically since 1960, just as they did during the 1950's and in earlier times. They have, however, made it plain that they would be disinclined, as long as the economy is still operating short of full employment, to seek general price stability by imposing monetary or fiscal restraints. And the one need that they have stressed above all others is that wages and prices be set in "responsible" fashion by private parties—in other words, that trade union leaders and business managers need to moderate their economic power in ways which will take account of the national interest in preventing inflation.

II. ADVENT OF GUIDEPOSTS

Exhortation with regard to prices or wages is by no means a novel practice of government. In its days of secular authority, the Church spoke firmly on the need for just pricing. In later times governments often blamed profiteers for increases in food prices. In the postwar period it has become customary for governments to stress the importance of stability in the *general level* of prices rather than the rectitude of individual prices. As of old, however, the authorities seek to limit private power in the marketplace by moral suasion. In today's world, as everyone knows, some trade unions can raise wages beyond the level that would prevail in a competitive labor market, just as some corporations have the power to push prices above competitive levels.

It is understandable enough, therefore, why our successive presidents in the postwar period have seen fit to lecture the private community on the need for noninflationary conduct. General Eisenhower, for example, warned during his presidency that "businesses must recognize the broad public interest in the prices set on their products and services" and that "greater stability of the general level of prices" is unlikely unless the national average of increases in wage and salary rates and related labor benefits remains within the limits of national productivity gains."

In the last few years governmental pronouncements of this sort have become more frequent and louder. In fact, the urging of moderation on private parties has reached a scale that marks something of a break from the earlier policy of dealing with inflation. On the one hand, the classical weapons of monetary and fiscal restraint, which in the past were relied on as the main defense against inflation, are now frowned on. On the other hand, general appeals to public responsibility are being implemented by wage and price guideposts. Trade unions and business firms, in other words, are no longer merely asked or admonished to moderate their private power in the public interest; they are advised with a show of specificity how this can best be done.

Once exhortation has been fortified by formula, it can no longer be dismissed as sheer rhetoric. It then takes on new authority over the minds of men, and its capacity for good or ill becomes much greater.

The guideposts have been a major part of the Administration's economic policy since early 1962, when they were first set forth by the Council of Economic Advisers. What are these guideposts or guidelines?

1. *Wages*—This guideline specifies that the annual rate of increase in wage rates, including fringe benefits, should be equal in a particular firm or industry to the annual trend increase in national productivity, that is, to the average annual percentage rate of growth over a term of years in the output per man-hour of the economy at large.

2. *Prices*—This guideline specifies that when the trend of an industry's productivity rises less than the national trend of productivity, its prices "can appropriately rise enough" to accom-

modate the rise in labor costs per unit of output that conforms to the wage guideline; and that when an industry's productivity rises more rapidly than the national average, its prices "should be lowered" in keeping with the decline in unit labor costs.

The Council originally characterized its pronouncement on the guidelines as a contribution to public discussion of how the national interest may be judged in the case of private wage and price decisions. The guidelines were certainly not intended to be interpreted as directives to industry or labor. In fact, they were described by the Council as "general guideposts" which still had to be reconciled in individual situations with "objectives of equity and efficiency." In other words, "specific modifications" were required to adapt the guidelines "to the circumstances of particular industries."

The more important types of modification that would be likely to arise in practice were actually listed by the Council. For example, the suggestion was advanced that wage increases should exceed the "general guide rate" if the bargaining position of workers in a particular industry or locality had previously been weak or if an industry was unable to attract sufficient labor.

As was bound to happen, however, it was the crisp formula of the "general guideposts," not the qualifications or disclaimers, that mainly caught the public eye. And, with the passage of time, the Administration has itself become bolder. The January 1964 Report of the Council no longer speaks of the guidelines as a contribution to public discussion of how the national interest may be judged; instead, it describes them as a "standard" for private wage and price decisions. The Report of 1962 had avoided specifying the annual trend increase of national productivity on the ground that this was "a large and complex subject and there is much still to be learned." The Report of 1964, on the other hand, is free from all methodological doubts and presents without qualification a figure of 3.2 per cent as the annual trend increase of productivity in the private economy that is currently applicable. The Report of 1962 had indicated that the "general guideposts" were "only first approximations" that would need to be adapted extensively "to the circumstances of particular industries." The Report of 1964, on the other hand, states flatly that the guideposts "can cover the vast majority of wage and price decisions" and, while the modifications that had been suggested earlier "still apply, . . . it must be emphasized that they are intended to apply to only a relatively few cases."

Thus, the official position, as now developed or clarified, is that the national interest can be best served by setting wages and prices in accordance with the formula of the general guidelines—not, to be sure, in every instance, but almost that.

III. GUIDEPOSTS VS. COMPETITIVE MARKETS

As every economist knows, there are only two ways of raising the real earnings of labor. They can be raised by (1) increasing output per man-hour of work or (2) enlarging the share of total income that accrues to wage and salary workers.

Of these two sources, the first is basic, and it has always been vastly more important in our country than the second. The guidelines have the great merit of calling attention to this fact. Taking the economy as a whole, it is the cost of labor that dominates production costs. If the cost of labor per unit of output rises, business firms will ordinarily seek to protect their profit margins by raising prices. But a rise in wage rates, using this term broadly so as to include fringe benefits, need not involve a rise in production costs. It will do that only if the rise in the hourly wage rate is proportionately greater than the increase in output per man-hour. Therefore, if the average percentage increase in wage rates across the nation merely equals the average percentage increase in output per man-hour, the general level of prices could remain stable without reducing the fraction of the nation's output accruing to stockholders and other income claimants.

By expressing this basic truth, the guideposts have helped to direct the attention of thoughtful citizens to ways of raising output per man-hour—ways such as investing in more and better tools of production, improving the education and skills of workers, improving the quality of management, and eliminating featherbedding and restrictive trading practices.

Public enlightenment, however, has been an incidental aspect of the guideposts. Being a tool of policy, they point to a course of action. Their essential purpose is to curb inflation—or, more precisely, to permit monetary and fiscal policies to stimulate production and employment without stirring up inflationary pressures from trade unions or corporations. And if the guidelines for prices and wages were generally observed, it is indeed true that the existing links between the flow of money to markets, on the one hand, and the flow of goods and services to purchasers, on the other, would be broken. In such a world the levels of wages and prices would be governed by formula, and they would no longer reflect the changing forces of market demand and market supply—as they now do.

If the policy of the guideposts became fully effective, it would therefore change drastically the workings of our commodity and labor markets, and thereby modify—for better or worse—the character of our economic system. Let us try to visualize a little more definitely how the guideposts, if they were generally and fully respected, would work out in practice.

Statistical records stretching back into the nineteenth century demonstrate that, although the over-all productivity of our economy occasionally declines, its trend has been steadily upward. If this continues to be true, as we may reasonably suppose, general observance of the guidelines will result in higher wages every year, regardless of the stage of the business cycle or the level of unemployment or the state of the balance of payments. The rise of wages will be the same, on the average, in years of recession as in years of prosperity; but in any given recession the rise of wages could easily be larger than in the preceding years of prosperity. Furthermore, the average wage will tend to rise in any given year by the same percentage in every firm, regardless of its profitability or the state of the market for different kinds of labor.

However, general observance of the guidepost for prices will not freeze individual prices or the relations among them. What it would tend to freeze is (1) the general level of prices and (2) the ratio of individual prices to unit labor costs of production. The tendency of the price-cost ratio to remain constant will be stronger in some industries than in others. Strictly speaking, the guidepost for prices specifies merely that the ratio of price to unit labor cost of production should not rise; it does not argue against a decline of the price-cost ratio. Hence, firms or industries experiencing a weak demand for their products or keen foreign competition may need to be content with prices that decline relative to their unit labor costs. On the other hand, firms or industries that are favored in the marketplace would be unable to raise prices relative to their unit labor costs even if their incoming orders were many times as large as their production. Nor would they be able to raise prices to compensate for increases in costs of production other than those of labor.

The broad effect of these tendencies would be to keep more

or less constant the percentage share of the national income—
or of national output—going to labor. Changes in the use of
capital relative to the use of labor, whether upward or downward, could still have a large influence on the size of the national income but not on the proportion of income accruing to
labor. Unless major shifts occurred in the occupational or
industrial distribution of employment, any fluctuation in labor's percentage share of the national income would be due
primarily to the discrepancy between the movement of over-all
productivity in a particular year and the corresponding trend
increase. Nonlabor income, in the aggregate, would also tend
to be a constant percentage of the national income.

It is well to bear in mind, however, that since profits are
only a fraction of nonlabor income, the share of profits in the
total national income could either rise or decline. In the postwar period, the amount paid by corporations on account of excises, customs duties, property taxes, licensing fees, and other
indirect taxes has risen more rapidly than their net output. If
this trend continues, the income share of investors in the corporate sector will tend to undergo a persistent decline, while
that of labor will tend to remain constant.

In the hypothetical economy that I have sketched,
monopolies—whether of business or labor—would no longer
have the power to push up the price level. Put more precisely,
if trade unions and business firms complied voluntarily with
the guidelines, they would relinquish any market power that
they have not yet used or that they might gain in the future.
This is worth noting, but it is not the main point.

The fundamental point of the preceding analysis is that general observance of the guideposts would throttle the forces of
competition no less effectively than those of monopoly. The
point is important because, unlike much of the rest of the
world, the rivalry among U.S. business firms is very keen. Even

in industries where a few corporations dominate the market—as in the case of automobiles, steel, and aluminum—each corporation competes actively against the others in its industry, against rival products of other industries, and against foreign suppliers. Competition in labor markets is also stronger than casual references to labor monopoly may suggest. After all, only a little over a fourth of the population working for wages or salaries is unionized, and many of the trade unions are weak. By and large, it is competition—not monopoly—that has vast sweep and power in our everyday life. Since free competitive markets would virtually cease to exist in an economy that observed the guidelines, this transformation of the economy merits serious reflection.

To be sure, compliance with the guidelines would be voluntary in the economy we are considering. That, however, may not mean much. For when economic freedom is not exercised, it is no longer a part of life. As far as I can see, an economy in which wages and prices are set voluntarily according to a formula suggested by the government would be almost indistinguishable from an economy in which wages and prices are directly fixed by governmental authorities. In either case, the movement of resources toward uses that are favored by the buying public would be impeded. In either case, the tendency to economize on the use of what happens to be especially scarce, whether it be materials or labor or equipment, would be weakened. In either case, since prices will no longer tend to equate demand and supply in individual markets, some form of rationing would need to be practiced.

In all likelihood, therefore, a shift from our present market economy to one of voluntary compliance with the guidelines would adversely affect efficiency. It would also adversely affect the rate of economic growth and the rate of improvement of the general standard of living.

It is true, of course, that controlled economies can and do escape complete rigidity. The exigencies of life do not permit their authorities to be blind to considerations of efficiency or social harmony, so that price and wage edicts have to be modified here and there. Black markets tend to develop, and—despite their unsavory character—they often perform a useful function in facilitating production. Moreover, managers gradually become skillful in "gray practices," such as reclassifying labor in order to escape the wage restraints or modifying products in order to escape the price restraints. Our hypothetical economy of voluntary compliance would also have its safety valve; that is to say, the guidelines would be modified in "a relatively few cases" in the interest of equity or efficiency. However, gray or black markets, which impart some fluidity and resilience to authoritarian economies, could not exist in the economy of voluntary compliance that we have been considering here.

IV. ARE THE GUIDES WORKABLE?

This theoretical sketch of how our economy would work if the guidelines were generally and fully observed has blinked institutional factors—such as the adjustments caused by the disappearance of auction markets, the new role of trade unions, and so on. Moreover, our theoretical sketch has tacitly assumed that voluntary compliance with the guidelines is merely a matter of will. Life is not that simple. Even if everyone responded to the government's plea for "cooperation" and sought faithfully to act in accordance with the guidelines, it would frequently be difficult or actually impossible to do so.

There is, first of all, a vast gap in our statistical arsenal. To comply with the guideline for wages, businessmen would need to know the trend increase of the over-all output of the nation per man-hour. Once this highly complex magnitude had been estimated by the government, it would presumably be subjected to outside review, revised if need be, and accompanied by a specification of the boundaries of the year (if a year be the interval) to which it would apply. All firms dealing with labor, except those newly established, would then know what wage adjustment was expected of them.

Compliance with the price guideline would be infinitely harder. For this purpose, every company would need to know the trend increase in the productivity of its own industry and how this increase compares with the trend increase of over-all productivity of the economy. Such information is not generally available, nor is it readily usable.

The productivity indexes now being published, besides being often out of date, lump together a great variety of products. In time, more detailed and more current indexes of productivity will doubtless be constructed, but there are limits to what is statistically feasible. Even if measures of this type become available for each of a thousand or ten thousand industries, much confusion or perplexity will still remain. Should a manufacturer of bricks, for example, be guided in his pricing by an index of productivity for the stone, clay, and glass group or by an index confined to brick manufacture? If the latter, is the pertinent index a nationwide measure, one confined to his region, or perhaps to his locality or plant? How should a manufacturing firm proceed when its output is not standardized or when it makes a hundred different items, instead of just one product? If the appropriate index is not available, as may long remain the case for many firms, especially in the service trades, what is the best "proxy" for it? Will the judgment of a company's management on such issues, even if made entirely in good faith, be acceptable to others—such as its trade union, the Council of Economic Advisers, or the general public—who also seek only what is right? Better statistics on productivity will reduce these difficulties; however, they cannot possibly remove them.

Another puzzling problem would be posed by changes in the composition of labor that is used in industry. Consider, for example, the case of a company that has recently decided to employ more skilled workers of different sorts and less unskilled labor. Since skilled labor is compensated at a higher rate, the average wage per hour that is paid by the company to its workers will go up, quite apart from any wage increase that may be needed for the individual grades of labor. Let us now suppose that the wage guidepost calls for an increase of, say, 3 per cent. Then the company's employees will naturally expect an increase of this size in their individual rates of pay. But may not the company's personnel executive, who has become steeped in the mathematics of the guidelines, properly insist that the average wage has already gone up this much or more on account of the more intensive use of skilled labor and that no increase of wage rates is therefore warranted by the government's guideline? Will the trade union's representative grasp this statistical subtlety? Will he not argue that the guideline requires an increase of 3 per cent, that other organizations are putting through such increases, and that simple justice requires that the same be done by this company? Suppose that the personnel executive perseveres and finally convinces the union's representative. Will the latter, in turn, be able to persuade the company's employees? Can we even be sure that the company's board of directors will be convinced by the argument of its personnel officer? In view of modern trends that emphasize the use of higher skills, this sort of difficulty would be bound to occur frequently in an economy of voluntary compliance.

A related puzzle with which businesmen would need to

grapple arises from changes in the composition of output. Suppose that a firm has two plants, that each of them makes a unique product, that the output per man-hour is constant in each plant, but that the two plants differ in efficiency. If the wage guidepost calls for a 3 per cent increase in wages, it might appear, since no improvement of productivity has occurred in either plant, that a corresponding increase in the price of each of the two products is justified by the guideline for prices. But are price advances really proper if the firm has shifted some workers from the less efficient to the more efficient of its two plants and thereby raised the output per man-hour of the entire firm as much as or more than the trend increase of national productivity? In that event, does the guidepost for prices require that the productivity of each plant be taken separately or that the two be taken in combination?

Another problem that businessmen and trade-union leaders would need to face is whether the modifications of the guideposts that the Council of Economic Advisers has officially sanctioned apply in a particular case. In assuming, as I have, a general willingness to comply with the guidelines, I have not meant to abstract from human nature entirely. Since the modifications suggested by the Council are phrased in very general terms, men acting in good faith may feel that their situation is precisely the kind of rare case that permits some departure from the guidelines. But will business managers and labor leaders always or even frequently agree in their interpretation of what modifications are permissible? In any event, is it not likely that the modifications will turn out to be numerous, rather than, as now intended by the Administration, relatively few?

In view of these and many other problems that are bound to arise in practice, the guidelines would prove unworkable over a very large segment of industry, even if everyone sought conscientiously to observe them. To deal with this critical difficulty, a new governmental apparatus might need to be established; its function would be to spell out detailed rules and to interpret them in individual cases. Although there is no way of telling just how such an agency would work, it seems reasonable to expect that not a few of its clarifying rules and interpretations would be arbitrary, that its advisory rulings would at times involve considerable delay and thereby cause some economic trouble, and that the rulings themselves would have at least some inflationary bias. These factors inevitably cast a cloud over the preceding analysis of how an economy of voluntary compliance would function, but they hardly make the prospect more inviting.

V. SPECTER OF CONTROLS

I have as yet said nothing about the aspect of guidepost policy that has aroused the most skepticism—namely, the likelihood of general observance on a voluntary basis. In recent years unemployment has been fairly large, and many industries have had sufficient capacity to increase output readily. Under such conditions, upward pressure on prices cannot be great. Even so, the guidelines have been sharply criticized or defied by powerful segments of the business and labor community. The critical test of the inhibiting power of the guidelines will come, of course, when both labor and commodity markets become appreciably tighter—and this test may come soon. If the recent wage settlement in the automobile industry is at all indicative, expectations of a high degree of compliance with the guidelines are hardly warranted. Similar experiments in other countries also suggest that general price stability will not long be maintained through voluntary restraint.

But once the government in power has committed itself to a policy, it may become difficult to move off in a new direction. A strong commitment to the policy of the guidelines inevitably means that any extensive private defiance would, besides frustrating the government's anti-inflation policy, injure its prestige. There is always a possibility, therefore, that failure to comply voluntarily with the guidelines will be followed by some coercive measure. This might initially take the form, as has frequently been proposed, of a review by a governmental board of the facts surrounding the price or wage changes that are being contemplated. The thought behind proposals of this nature is that once the facts are clearly developed, the force of public opinion will ordinarily suffice to ensure "responsible" actions by corporations and trade unions.

No one can be sure whether this expectation will be fulfilled. But if it is, the governmental review board will have virtually become an agency for fixing prices and wages. If, on the other hand, the board's reports were flouted with any frequency, the next step might well be outright price and wage fixing by the government. It would seem, therefore, that from whatever angle we examine the guidelines, direct controls pop up dangerously around the corner.

This danger must not be dismissed as an illusion. Although the guidelines are still in their infancy, they have already hardened, as I previously indicated. Nor has the evolution of the Administration's thinking concerning the guidelines been confined to a literary plane. In April 1962, only three months after the announcement of the guidelines, the Administration moved sternly to force the leading steel companies to cancel the price increases that they had just posted. This interference with the workings of a private market had no clear sanction in law, and it caused consternation in business circles. Fortunately, a crisis was avoided by a prompt and concerted effort of the Administration, in which President Kennedy himself took the leading part, to restore business confidence.

Since then, the government has been more cautious. But it has continued to espouse the need for moderation in the matter of wages and prices, and now and then has even gently rattled its sword. Early in 1964 President Johnson requested the Council to reaffirm the guideposts. He emphasized his commitment to this policy by adding that he would "keep a close watch on price and wage developments, with the aid of an early warning system which is being set up." Last summer, when intimations of a rise in the price of steel appeared in the press, the President lost no time in declaring that such action would "strongly conflict with our national interest in price stability."

VI. TOWARD SOUNDER POLICIES

As this account of recent history suggests, the guidepost policy may, under the pressure of events, move our nation's economy in an authoritarian direction. The danger may not yet be large, in view of prevailing political attitudes, but it could become serious in a time of trouble or emergency. And this is not the only risk, as I shall presently note. However, the fact that many citizens both within and outside government favor the guidelines must also be considered, for it means that they see smaller risks or larger advantages in this policy than I do.

It may readily be granted that the guidepost policy has the meritorious objective of blunting the power of monopolists to push up the price level. This is the feature of the policy that its proponents often stress. Indeed, they are apt to argue that it matters little in practice whether or not the bulk of the economic community pays any attention to the guidelines—as long as the major corporations and trade unions do so.

But if the guidelines are circumscribed in this fashion, they are still subject to the criticism of interfering with the competitive forces of the markets in which many major corporations actually operate. Moreover, the absence of a precise indication of what firms, industries, or trade unions are covered by the guidelines can create a mood of uncertainty that will militate against compliance. Not least important, the effectiveness of the guidelines in curbing inflation becomes doubtful when their application is restricted. For the very limitation on wage and price increases in the guideline sector of the economy would facilitate increases in the uncovered sector whenever an expansive economic policy generated a monetary demand that grew faster than the supply of goods and services.

Another argument frequently advanced in favor of the guideposts is that if they were in fact respected on a sufficient scale, then profit margins would tend to be maintained and the chances of prolonging the current business expansion would therefore be improved. This consideration is bound to count in men's thinking at a time when our nation is striving to reduce unemployment and to spread prosperity. We must not, however, become so absorbed in today's problems that we overlook those that will haunt us in a later day. If the guidelines may stretch out the expansion now by helping to maintain the relatively high profit margins of prosperity, may they not at some later time stretch out contraction by serving to maintain the low profit margins of recession?

Let me add, also, that I recognize that the guideline policy was adopted by the Administration only after it had given serious consideration to alternatives. The thought of its economists apparently is that, in general, monetary and fiscal tools must be used to promote expansion as long as the economy is not operating at full employment; that other devices must therefore be employed (in the absence of full employment) to prevent inflation; that policies aiming to increase competition or to improve productivity cannot accomplish much in the short run or cannot be pushed hard for political reasons; that direct controls of wages and prices cannot and should not be seriously considered under peacetime conditions; that consequently, there is only one major way left for curbing immediate inflation—namely, through devices of exhortation; and that the guidelines for wages and prices are merely a promising specific application of the technique of exhortation.

Space will not permit me to unravel this complicated argument, but I at least want to suggest why I think it may be faulty. Once the government looks to trade unions and business firms to stave off inflation, there is a danger that it will not discharge adequately its own traditional responsibility of controlling the money supply and of maintaining an environment of competition. In the past our own and other governments have often found it convenient to blame profiteers, corporations, or trade unions for a rising price level. Only rarely have they pointed the finger of blame at their own policies—such as flooding the economy with newly created currency or bank deposits.

To the extent that the government relies on private compliance with its guidelines for prices and wages, it may more easily be tempted to push an expansive monetary and fiscal policy beyond prudent limits. Besides, it may fail to resist strongly enough the political pressure for higher minimum wages, larger trade union immunities, higher farm price supports, higher import duties, more import quotas, larger stockpiling programs, and other protective measures that serve either to raise prices or to prevent them from falling.

One of the major needs of our times is to give less heed to special interest groups and to reassert the paramount interest of consumers in vigorous competition. The political obstacles to reducing artificial props for prices are undoubtedly formidable. However, reforms of this type—supplemented by more stringent antitrust laws, effective enforcement of these laws, and reasonable steps to curb featherbedding—are likely to contribute more to the maintenance of reasonable stability in the general price level than will the guidelines for wages and prices on which we have recently come to rely.

Another major need of our times is for better guidelines to aid the government itself in formulating and carrying out its economic policies. The widespread tendency of attributing most existing unemployment to a deficiency of aggregate demand is an oversimplification. When the amount of unemployment is larger than the number of job vacancies at existing wages, the aggregate demand for labor is clearly insufficient to provide employment for everyone who is able, willing, and seeking to work. At such a time, a deficiency of aggregate demand exists, and a governmental policy that relies on monetary and fiscal devices to expand demand is, in principle, well suited to the nation's needs. On the other hand, when the number of vacant jobs is equal to or larger than the number of the unemployed, there is no deficiency of aggregate demand. A government that is seriously concerned about inflation will not pursue an expansive monetary and fiscal policy at such a time, and—instead of lecturing the private community on the need for moderation—will itself lead the nation in a policy of restraint. This does not mean its concern about unemployment will cease but, rather, that it will direct its policy measures toward better matching of the men and women who seek work with the jobs that need to be filled.

A sensible guideline for monetary and fiscal policy is, therefore, not the volume or rate of unemployment as such, but the relation between the number of the unemployed and the number of job vacancies. As yet, such a guideline is merely a theorist's dream because statistics on job vacancies hardly exist in our country. There are grounds for hoping, however, that this condition will be corrected in another few years, so that we will become better equipped for promoting our national goals.

The problem of achieving and maintaining prosperity without inflation in a free society is a very diffcult one. We must be willing as a people to seek out and to explore new ways of meeting this critical challenge of our times. But we also must remain mindful of the lessons of past experience—particularly, the need for prudent control of the money supply and the need for maintaining and enhancing the forces of competition. The progress that we make will depend heavily on the economic understanding of citizens and the intensity of their interest in public policies.

TEN

The Quest for Full Employment and Economic Stability: 1960-1966

SINCE THE END of World War II, full employment, rising productivity, and a stable price level have been major objectives of economic policy in the United States, as they have in every other industrial country. All segments of our society—businessmen and labor leaders, farmers and urban workers, educators and legislators—now accept and endorse these objectives, particularly the need for full employment. Each year the President's Economic Report reaffirms allegiance to the principles of the Employment Act of 1946. Each year the Joint Economic Committee appraises the President's program for promoting "maximum employment, production, and purchasing power," and prods both the Congress and the executive to pursue whatever measures seem needed to achieve or maintain full employment and economic stability. Each year scores of governmental, business, labor, and civic groups, besides many hundreds of individual economists and other intellectuals, join in the continuing debate on the most appropriate means of achieving the broad economic objectives

Lecture at American Enterprise Institute, April 11, 1967. Reprinted, by permission of the publisher, from Arthur F. Burns and Paul A. Samuelson, *Full Employment, Guideposts and Economic Stability*, American Enterprise Institute for Public Policy Research, Washington, D.C., 1967, pp. 1–39.

on which Americans are so generally agreed. The present meeting is one of many such efforts to seek better ways of moving toward our national objectives.

I

The constant attention that we give to public economic policies is proof enough, if any were needed, that the economy rarely performs as well as we think it should. True, we have made considerable progress toward full employment and economic stability in our generation, and we have accomplished this while preserving the essentials of political and economic freedom. Financial crises, which frequently disrupted economic life in earlier times, no longer exacerbate our troubles. Expansions of aggregate economic activity have tended to become longer. Contractions have become both shorter and milder, and the business cycle has lost much of the terror that it held for our fathers. Not only that, but the trend of output per man-hour, which is the most vital source of improvement in the general welfare, has moved upward faster than in earlier decades of this century. These gains are impressive when viewed against the background of past experience. However, the yardsticks that we apply to the performance of the economy have also tended to become more exacting, and in any event we have not escaped our share of disappointments. While the level of both employment and production has been generally high and rising during the past twenty years, we have experienced some troublesome recessions. Even in years of extremely brisk activity, such as 1956 and 1966, large groups of people—notably Negroes and teenagers—have continued to be subject to a higher risk of unemployment than the working population at large. And even those workers who have had the good fortune to hold down steady jobs at rising wages have found that their improved money earnings, and also their accumulated savings, are partly illusory on account of the upward tendency of prices.

Economic instability has not yet vanished in our country, any more than it has vanished in any other country that values freedom sufficiently to practice free enterprise on a major scale. Nor, for that matter, has it vanished in the Socialist world where economic life is largely organized on the basis of state edicts. For example, Czechoslovakia experienced a recession in 1963, Communist China suffered a great depression after 1959, Yugoslavia has found it prudent to encourage many of her workers to look for jobs in Western Europe, the Soviet Union has suffered substantial unemployment of the seasonal and frictional type, and Poland has struggled for years with the burden of inefficiency resulting from the practice of requiring its industrial enterprises to absorb more workers than they need. And just as it is impossible to find, whether we look West or East, any final solution to the problem of unemployment, so also it is difficult to find substantial stability of the price level anywhere. Indeed, the advance of the price level of our total output, although it has reduced the purchasing power of the dollar by about 40 per cent during the past twenty years, still ranks as one of the better records of the postwar period.

These imperfections of economic achievement, both in our own past and in other parts of the world, need to be recalled at a time when the course of our economy has again become sluggish. Only two years ago we boasted that the economic expansion which started early in 1961 had already proved more durable than any of its predecessors under peacetime conditions. Now, despite a tremendous upsurge of federal expenditure, which is bound to continue for some time on account of the war in Vietnam, many economists are concerned that our nation may once again be on the brink of recession. Only a short time ago the view was spreading in business and governmental circles that monetary and fiscal policies would henceforth adjust the aggregate demand for goods and services so closely to what the economy can produce at full employment that the danger of recession need no longer be taken seriously. Now, many economists are questioning the skill of governmental policymakers and some are even suggesting that governmental policies have a chronic tendency to destabilize the economy. Any such sweeping generalization can hardly be justified. Nevertheless, in view of recent shifts of fortune and opinion, it may be useful to stop and consider some of the difficulties in the management of prosperity; in particular, how public policy drove the economy forward after 1960, why rapid expansion has temporarily given way to sluggishness, and what guidance can be derived from these experiences for the future. That is my purpose in this evening's lecture.

II

The main source of our national prosperity has always been the hopefulness, initiative, skill, and energy of the American people. By and large, we have also been blessed with good government and with public policies that have left large scope for the expression of these qualities. The increasing attention of government to the problem of full employment and economic stability has led in our generation to ever-changing permutations of policy and they too have left their mark on the character and rate of economic progress. This has been singularly true of the years since 1960 which have been characterized by much boldness and innovation of governmental policy in the economic sphere. History, however, does not divide itself neatly into stages or periods. What happened after 1960 was conditioned by developments in the immediately preceding years.

Taken as a whole, the decade of the 1950's experienced substantial advances in production, employment, and living standards. The later years of the decade, however, brought difficulties in quick succession. The recession following the Korean War came to an early end under the impetus of stimulative governmental policies. But as so often happens in a modern economy, the confidence of the business community soon spilled over into excessive exuberance. During 1956, business construction and the machinery and equipment industries forged ahead at an extremely rapid rate, while the output of the consumer goods trades became sluggish and homebuilding actually slumped. The average level of prices advanced swiftly in wholesale markets, but costs of production rose faster still and profit margins shrank. These and other imbalances gradually undermined the process of expansion. In July 1957, a recession got under way; and although it proved to be brief, it was the sharpest decline of aggregate activity in the period since World War II. The recovery that followed was strong at the outset, but it soon faltered and it did not return the nation to full prosperity. In the spring of 1960, when the unemployment rate was still 5 per cent, the economy again lapsed into recession. During this decline of activity, total output held up exceptionally well. But when the labor force and productivity keep increasing, the mere cessation of growth in physical output suffices to create trouble. Unemployment mounted during 1960 and reached 7 per cent in the spring of 1961.

The unsatisfactory performance of the economy in the late 1950's can be blamed in part on governmental timidity or excessive concern over inflation. There were, however, good reasons for concern and caution. The inflation of 1956–57 was fresh in people's memories. President Eisenhower and other high officials realized that the advance of prices would have been smaller if they had moved as promptly and as energetically to curb the excesses of the boom as they had previously moved to check the post-Korean recession. It was only natural that men in authority were resolved not to repeat the mistake. But once the recession started in 1957, the government could not very well remain aloof. Some prominent officials and many private citizens urged a prompt reduction of personal and corporate income tax rates. They pointed out that the nation was still functioning with a tax system that had developed under wartime conditions, and they argued that a lightening of the tax burden would strengthen incentives, enlarge economic horizons, and thereby release fresh and enduring forces of expansion. This compelling plea went unheeded because of fear of budgetary consequences. Instead, credit conditions were eased and federal spending was allowed to expand. The decisions to increase spending did not come at once; they came in a long series, sometimes grudgingly, and thus spread out over months. But when the successive small accretions were finally added up in late 1958, it was discovered that they came to a much larger total than our fiscal authorities had either planned or advocated—indeed, that they made a larger dent in the budget than, say, the $5 billion tax cut that was then being urged would have entailed.

The main impact of the new federal spending programs came after the economy began recovering. A cash deficit of $13 billion, which still stands as the largest annual deficit since 1946, piled up in the fiscal year ending in June 1959—a year of continuous business expansion. This emergence of a huge deficit at a time of rather rapid economic advance was merely the most dramatic of a series of developments that cast doubt on the financial policy of the government. Over a long stretch of history, it had been characteristic of the level of wholesale prices to fall during contractions of aggregate activity, thereby erasing all or part of the advance that had occurred during the expansion phase. In the recession of 1957–58 wholesale prices departed from rule, actually rose, and thus gave fresh support to the widely held theory that we are living in an age of inflation. This sombre view about the future was reinforced by the deterioration in the balance of payments. During 1958, imports rose sharply, exports fell, and our stocks of gold were cut by two billion dollars. More ominous still, foreign financiers, who hitherto appeared to have unbounded faith in American finances, began to whisper serious doubts whether the integrity of the dollar could be counted on in the future.

Financial developments during 1958 and the fears which they engendered thus strengthened the determination of governmental authorities to try to prevent, now that the economy was again advancing, the sort of excesses that had led to an inflationary boom during 1956–57. Both our international political position and the interests of the domestic economy clearly required better management of prosperity. Having moved too slowly to restrain the preceding expansion, they were ready to move with all necessary speed this time. Still embarrassed by the increase of the discount rate in August 1957, which came when the boom was already turning into recession, the monetary authorities now took steps to restrain the expansion of credit almost as soon as the first blush of economic recovery was recognized. Before 1958 ended, free reserves of the commercial banks were already wiped out. Pressure on reserves was sharply intensified during 1959. In consequence, the money supply began to decline and interest rates moved up with extraordinary speed. Meanwhile, the budgetary authorities brought the expansion of federal spending to an abrupt halt. Since tax revenues continued to pile up as economic activity grew, the budget moved from an enormous deficit in early 1959 to a sizable surplus twelve months later. Taken together, these fiscal and monetary measures accomplished one of the most violent shifts on record from a policy of stimulation to a policy of restraint.

The abrupt shift of policy proved more restrictive than government officials planned or expected. Largely as a result of their actions, the economic expansion that started in April 1958, came to a premature end and unemployment rose at a time when it was already excessive. These unhappy consequences, however, had their redeeming side. The very abruptness and magnitude of the policy shift routed an inflationary psychology, demonstrated that ours need not be an age of inflation, forced businessmen to reduce waste and improve efficiency, created sufficient slack in the labor market to impede substantial wage increases, and thus reestablished stability in costs and prices. That these conditions were produced without causing a collapse in the state of confidence was an accomplishment of no small significance. The aggregate demand of final buyers, both domestic and foreign, kept growing throughout the recession of 1960–61. Fortunately, the monetary authorities reduced the discount rate one month after the recession started in 1960, instead of raising it one month later as in 1957. The easing of credit helped to maintain aggregate demand and thereby hastened the end of the inventory adjustment. Fiscal policy, in the meantime, remained stubbornly quiescent. Governmental authorities were in no mood to tolerate larger expenditures, nor would they countenance a tax cut which was again being urged by capable and disinterested citizens. In February 1961, economic expansion resumed and the administration's expectation of an early upturn was vindicated; but before this happened, the nation's electorate decided in a close presidential election to entrust power to the Democratic party.

III

In the course of the campaign of 1960, John F. Kennedy promised that if he were elected president, America would get moving again. He lost no time in giving a new and bolder twist to economic policy. Although his administration can hardly be credited with initiating economic recovery in 1961, it did assume at once a very active role in nursing the recovery and in turning what might have been an ordinary expansion into a remarkable upsurge of the economy. Both political and economic circumstances favored an expansionist policy. On the one hand, the danger of inflation seemed quite remote after three years of stability in average wholesale prices and in unit costs of production in manufacturing. On the other hand, the persistence of slack in industrial capacity and in the labor market created a sense of impatience with conservative financial policies. Something new was expected of the new administration. The merits of an expansionist fiscal policy—particularly the advantages of a reduction of income taxes over an increase of governmental expenditures—had been extensively debated since 1957, and the nation was in a mood to try some fiscal experiments.

In the first year of his administration, President Kennedy chose to move cautiously. By and large, he left it to his advisers to popularize the teachings of the "new economics," to give a scholarly dress to the theory of using fiscal devices to close the gap between actual and potential output, to create a vision of an economy that might soon be recession-proof, to demonstrate that the full-employment surplus (or deficit) is a better index of the degree of fiscal stimulation than the actual deficit, to show that the quest for actual budgetary balance could be self-defeating, and to quiet any lurking fears of inflation by suggesting guidelines for the proper behavior of prices and wages. The President himself was more concerned with advancing specific policies for which the public was prepared —such as speeding of procurement and construction in the interests of recovery, raising agricultural price supports, liberalizing social security, lifting the minimum wage, extending governmental programs for education and introducing health insurance for the aged. To be sure, the President did recommend an investment tax credit, but he coupled it with tax increases that would prevent any loss of revenue to the Treasury. He also suggested legislation for stand-by authority under which the President could temporarily reduce individual income tax rates and accelerate spending on public works; but he was much too wise about political matters to expect these measures to win congressional approval in any near future. President Kennedy's caution was plainly reflected in his Budget Message of January 1962, which called for a small surplus in the next fiscal year.

Even at the outset, however, the budgetary practice of the new administration was less orthodox than the President's rhetoric. Plans for federal spending were repeatedly revised upward during 1961, and actual expenditures followed suit. A surplus in the cash budget of $3.6 billion in 1960 was followed by a deficit of $6.8 billion in 1961—the first of an unbroken series of deficits that is still continuing. Monetary policy also eased and gave strong support to the liberal expenditure policy. As expected, consumer spending responded to these stimuli and so too did investment in inventories. Business investment in plant and equipment failed, however, to develop the vigor that is characteristic of the recovery stage of the business cycle. By the first quarter of 1962, new orders and contracts for plant and equipment were merely 13 per cent higher than a year earlier, in contrast to increases of 86 per cent, 43 per cent, and 31 per cent during the corresponding stage of the three preceding expansions. Unemployment diminished, but its rate of decline was abnormally slow. Evidently, the recovery was not proceeding as well as had been hoped, despite the large fiscal and monetary stimuli.

The weak link in the chain of economic recovery was business investment in fixed capital. In popular discussions, this was generally attributed to the existence of excess industrial capacity. However, a good deal of idle capacity always develops in the course of a business slump, and yet this condition has never been a bar to brisk expansion of investment once confidence recovers. New firms are then established in larger numbers; existing firms in turn speed investments associated with innovation; firms that have done well despite the slump enlarge their capacity in anticipation of stronger markets; while many of the firms that have fallen behind in the competitive race finally embark on substantial programs of modernization. If these responses were not strongly felt in 1961, the reason was a want of sufficient confidence. Overinvestment in 1956–57, the steadily rising trend of wages, the tendency of profit margins to shrink during the past dozen years, the sharply reduced rate of economic growth during the past three or four years—all these factors contributed to business caution, and so too did the coming of a new administration whose economic policies could not as yet be fairly assessed. Many businessmen were concerned that trade unions, which had contributed to the victory of the Democratic party at the polls, would soon become bolder in their demands for higher wages and larger fringe benefits. Some feared that larger governmental spending, however favorable to markets in the short run, would in due course be followed by higher taxes. Others feared that direct controls of prices might eventually be undertaken by the government in order to check the inflationary pressures that would result from its fiscal and monetary policies, and still others were concerned on all these grounds.

The uneasiness of the business community reached a climax in April 1962, when President Kennedy moved sternly to force the steel companies to rescind the price increase that they had just posted. This action by the President had no clear sanction in law and it caused consternation in business circles. Men reasoned that if the government could coerce or punish the steel industry today, it might move next against the automobile industry or the aluminum industry or any other. Since the beginning of 1962 economic recovery had shown some signs of hesitation. Now, with confidence shaken and a large inventory adjustment in the steel industry unavoidable, the continuance of business expansion became more doubtful. The stock market reflected the mood of the time by experiencing its sharpest break of the entire postwar period. Orders for machinery and equipment were cut back here and there. Private borrowing stopped rising, raw materials prices softened, profit margins narrowed, and unemployment stopped declining. The curve of industrial production, which had risen smartly until April 1962, flattened out for the rest of the year.

Fortunately, an imminent recession was forestalled. Recognizing that the government's handling of the steel price problem had disturbed the business community, President Kennedy turned at once to the difficult task of rebuilding confidence. In one address after another, he and his lieutenants now stressed the dependence of our national prosperity on free markets, higher profits, and larger investment in fixed capital. These reassurances were soon followed by measures to reduce the tax burden borne by the business community. In July 1962, the Treasury announced that business firms could henceforth reckon their income taxes on the basis of shorter and more realistic estimates of the life of depreciable facilities. This basic tax reform was long overdue and it was welcomed by businessmen. With the President's prodding, the Congress enacted later in the year an investment tax credit which had already been proposed in 1961, but which was now substantially modified to make it more acceptable to the business community.

In the late summer of 1962 the President made his boldest move. His studies of the tax policies of other countries had convinced him that our tax system was a heavy drag on enterprise and investment. In view of the slowdown of the economy, a "quick" temporary tax cut had its appeal, but the Ways and Means Committee of the House of Representatives was more interested in permanent reform and legislation of this character could not be adopted quickly. In the circumstances, the President concluded that the time was right to announce his intention to request the Congress at the beginning of the next session to adopt a sweeping reform of the income tax, the main thrust of which would be a massive reduction of tax rates for corporations and for individuals in every income bracket. This tax proposal marked a radical departure in economic policymaking. In 1958 and again in 1960, when the country was experiencing recession, a tax cut had been repeatedly urged as a recovery measure that promised prompt results. Now, the purpose was to remove the fiscal drag on an expansion which was still under way, to extend thereby the advance of prosperity, and to risk fiscal deficits for an indefinite period to realize this objective.

The new tax policies and the new tone of governmental pronouncements had the desired effect on business and investor sentiment. Fears of hostile governmental intervention in the day-by-day activities of business firms subsided. Although many businessmen did not like the budgetary implications of a massive tax cut at a time when a deficit was already in the making, they also were quick to see that stimulation of the economy through tax reduction would serve to strengthen the private sector of the economy. In any event, the policy of favoring investment was a significant departure from the traditional policy of the Democratic party, and this fact was not lost on the business community. With optimism reviving and the state of inventories in better shape, economic conditions in late 1962 were ripe for a new wave of expansion. By the end of the year, business commitments for investment in fixed capital began rising again, and fears of an early recession soon vanished.

In all, about a year and a half elapsed between President Kennedy's announcement of his plan for tax reduction and its actual enactment. There were two major reasons for the long delay. First, the President's fiscal program, as presented to the Congress early in 1963, called for numerous revisions in the tax laws as well as a general tax reduction; and while the latter was welcomed widely, the former evoked powerful opposition. Second, the President projected an increase of budget expenditures of $4.5 billion for the next fiscal year besides a net tax reduction of over $10 billion. Many influential citizens who supported a reduction of taxes were sharply opposed to a simultaneous increase of expenditure on the ground that such a fiscal policy would entail a protracted series of deficits. The fate of the President's program therefore seemed very uncertain for a time. But as the issues surrounding the program were debated within and outside the halls of Congress, it became increasingly apparent that the President's main objective was the tax reduction, and that he would yield ground to his opponents on other parts of the fiscal package. More and more citizens therefore came to feel that they would not need to wait much longer for a reduction in taxes. Finally, in March 1964, when Lyndon Johnson was already carrying the burdens of the presidency, the tax cut became law. But months before that, the growing expectation of its adoption stimulated individuals and business firms to plan and spend more daringly. The expansion of economic activity, which was gradually cumulating of its own momentum, thus moved ahead on a wave of increasing confidence. The gross national product, expressed in real terms, rose 4 per cent between 1962 and 1963 and well over 5 per cent between 1963 and 1964.

IV

By early 1964, the expansion of economic activity had already lasted longer than the average duration of a business-cycle expansion. Nevertheless, the economy gave every indication that the advance would continue. Throughout 1964, as production and employment continued to rise, the structure of economic activity remained well balanced. A much faster pace in the output of business capital goods than in the output of consumer goods was only beginning. The ratio of inventories to sales in major branches of production and trade remained low or moved still lower. The wholesale price level was substantially steady. Although consumer prices kept rising, the advance was gentle. Although wages kept increasing, they advanced at nearly the same rate as the over-all improvement in productivity, so that unit costs of production remained quite stable. Profits grew with the volume of business, besides benefiting from revisions in the tax laws—among them, a reduction of income tax rates which became effective during the year. Stock prices moved up, but no faster than corporate earnings. With prices in our wholesale markets steady, while much of the rest of the world practiced inflation, exports rose sharply and a larger surplus on merchandise trade piled up than in any year since 1947. Meanwhile, interest rates remained fairly steady. In view of the still precarious state of the balance of payments, the monetary authorities sanctioned a moderate rise of short-term market rates of interest; but the interest rates of largest significance to businessmen—customer rates on bank loans, bond yields, and mortgage yields—remained at or below the level reached at the bottom of the recession in 1961.

Moreover, while federal revenues in 1964 continued to fall short of expenditures, the deficit now reflected lower tax rates rather than any further increase of spending. In the debates that preceded the Revenue Act of 1964, some citizens had urged larger federal spending as the best way to stimulate the economy, others argued for tax reduction, and still others felt that it would be well to travel both roads at the same time. President Kennedy was favorably inclined to the mixed approach, but he put much the heavier emphasis on tax reduction. Even so, the Congress balked. The preamble to the House bill explicitly assigned top fiscal priority to tax reduction, with debt reduction next. This meant, as Congressman Wilbur Mills explained to the House, that the nation was choosing tax reduction, and rejecting larger spending, as its "road to a bigger, more progressive economy." In order to assure adoption of the tax cut, President Kennedy assented to the preamble and President Johnson did likewise a little later. Indeed, in his first Budget Message, presented in January 1964, President Johnson called for smaller expenditures under the administrative budget in fiscal 1965 than in fiscal 1964. With this much assured, the Senate promptly passed the House bill with only minor revisions. And in line with the new fiscal policy, federal spending actually stopped rising for a time. From the third quarter of 1963 to the first quarter of 1965, cash expenditures remained virtually constant. Thus, private enterprise and private demand once again became the great energizing force of the economy.

At the end of 1964, economic activity had already been advancing for almost four years. The expansion was proving remarkably durable, but it was not yet exceptionally rapid or intense. This very fact, no less than the deliberate economic planning of the time, contributed to the prolongation of the advance. If the investment in plant and equipment was sluggish at the start, this facilitated more vigorous activity later. If the investment in fixed capital and in inventories was checked in 1962, that too contributed to greater activity later. If the shift toward public policies that were more mindful of business interests took place gradually, that in its turn helped to keep business optimism within moderate bounds. The expansion was thus the product of many causes, and not the least among them was the inheritance of price and cost stability. As late as 1964 there was still a fair amount of slack in the economy, and this condition continued to exercise a restraining influence on the market behavior of both businessmen and labor leaders. The fact, moreover, that productivity improved somewhat faster after 1960 than in the preceding quinquennium made it easier for business firms to pay higher wages without incurring higher costs per unit of output. In the environment of rough stability of costs and prices that ruled until 1964, there was little reason to accumulate inventories as a hedge against inflation. Nor was there any need to rush investments in fixed capital on the ground that costs were likely to be appreciably higher next year than now.

Thus, our economy in 1964 had the qualities of order and balance, besides considerable momentum from within the private sector. To be sure, signs were not lacking that the vigor of expansion was rapidly reducing the slack in productive capacity. Prices of sensitive raw materials had begun rising in spirited fashion as early as the fall of 1963. By the late summer of 1964 a significant increase had already occurred in the number of business firms reporting slower deliveries of merchandise. In the closing months of 1964, price increases in wholesale markets—while usually quite small—had become rather widespread. Toward the end of 1964 the unemployment rate for married men—who constitute, of course, the more skilled and experienced part of the labor force—had dropped to the level that ruled during the boom of 1956–57. By the end of the year, the length of the average workweek in manufacturing was already at the level reached during the Korean War. However, in the exhilarating economic and political atmosphere that ruled in the closing months of 1964, it was easy to overlook these and other indications of increasing pressure on the nation's available resources.

V

Clearly, no small part of the economic improvement was due to the government's tax policy combined with monetary ease. With the unemployment rate still close to 5 per cent at the beginning of 1965, it seemed only fitting and proper to the managers of our national prosperity to press harder the general policy of economic stimulation that had proved so dramatically successful. The second installment of the income tax reduction for corporations and individuals became effective in January, but that was deemed insufficient. The President urged in addition a reduction of excise taxes, and this proposal evoked such enthusiasm in the Congress that only thirty-four days elapsed between the introduction of the excise bill and the President's signature. The new law aimed to reduce excises by $2.2 billion in the fiscal year beginning July 1965, and by nearly $5 billion on a full-year basis when all the reductions would take effect. These tax reductions were not yet the whole of the fiscal stimulus applied in 1965. With the war in Vietnam intensifying and new civilian programs clamoring for governmental favor, the fiscal philosophy enunciated in the preamble of the Revenue Act of 1964 was quickly forgotten. By the last quarter of 1965, the annual rate of federal cash expenditure was already $12 billion higher than in the first quarter.

These fiscal expedients imparted, of course, a fresh stimulus to economic expansion. Since the economy was now booming, governmental revenues rose despite the new tax reductions. Nevertheless, the deficit increased during 1965, and this need for finance was reinforced by a tremendous upsurge of borrowing by business firms and consumers. On their part, the monetary authorities made sure that the growing demands for credit would be met. In fact, they supplied the commercial banks with reserves so generously that the banks were able to add to their investments in securities, besides adding abundantly to their loans. Indebtedness to commercial banks rose by $25 billion during 1965, in contrast to $16 billion during 1963 and $18 billion during 1964. Total debt, both public and private, grew by $96 billion during 1965, in contrast to about $77 billion during each of the two preceding years. With credit expanding all around, the money supply could not stand still. The nation's stock of money, which had grown at an average annual rate of less than 3 per cent between mid-1960 and mid-1964, rose at a rate of over 4 per cent between June 1964, and April 1965, and at a rate of nearly 6 per cent the rest of 1965. Thus, as the economy approached full employment, monetary policy became increasingly expansionist. And so, too, did fiscal policy. The full-employment surplus, which had become the official measure of fiscal stimulus, moved irregularly between 1961 and 1963, fell in 1964, and was nearly wiped out by the end of 1965.

The accelerating use of monetary and fiscal stimuli served to narrow very quickly the remaining gap, as the Council of Economic Advisers reckoned it, between the nation's actual and potential output. As 1965 drew to a close, the nation could rejoice that the unemployment rate was finally down to 4 per cent—the level which the Council had previously adopted as a reasonable target for full utilization of resources. But the widespread upsurge of public and private spending produced also other and less welcome results—in wholesale markets, prices that were 4 per cent higher than in mid-1964; in consumer markets, prices that were nearly 3 per cent higher; in the labor market, wages that were beginning to rise at an increasing rate; and in the money and capital market, interest rates that were moving up sharply, despite an enormous expansion in the supply of credit. These evidences of strain on the economy's resources became stronger during 1966. By the fall of the year, wholesale prices rose another 2.5 per cent, consumer prices over 3.5 per cent, while interest rates reached their highest level in about forty years.

Worse still, the economy became seriously distorted by 1966. In the first place, as bottlenecks on the supply side became widespread, the hectic advance of physical production could not continue. Crosscurrents in the economy therefore multiplied and the high expectations of many businessmen were frustrated. Second, a large gap between the rate of growth of business investment in fixed capital and the rate of growth of consumer spending had already lasted three years, and this imbalance in the structure of production could also not long continue. Third, concern over possible shortages and slow deliveries caused inventories to rise faster than sales in the early months of 1966. Later in the year, as the growth of sales weakened, inventories began to pile up involuntarily. Fourth, profits became vulnerable as a result of the divergent movements of prices and wages. The advance of wholesale prices abated after mid-1966, mainly because of weakness in farm and industrial materials prices, while the rise of consumer prices quickened. With profits high, the demand for labor strong, and the consumer price level rising at a disconcerting rate, the upward push of wages accelerated. Meanwhile, numerous factors slowed down the advance of productivity—among them, the poorer quality of newly hired labor, more rapid labor turnover, lesser diligence of employees, accumulating fatigue of workers and their managers, slower and less dependable delivery of materials and equipment, the need to keep much high-cost equipment in use, and the need here and there to bring obsolete equipment back into use. The net result was that the rate of increase of output per man-hour not only slackened, but fell below the rate of increase of wages per hour. With demand pressures, particularly in the consumer sector, beginning to wane, while unit labor costs were rising all around, a cost-price squeeze developed in the world of business.

These forces internal to the boom, which were now causing readjustments in the economy, were heavily influenced, but in conflicting directions, by governmental policy. Federal cash expenditures moved up with extraordinary rapidity, and reached an annual rate of $156 billion in the second half of 1966, in contrast to a rate of $130 billion a year earlier. Tax revenues also rose rapidly in 1966, largely, but by no means entirely, as a result of the boom. Higher social security taxes that had previously been legislated went into effect at the beginning of the year. A little later, some excises were raised and a speedup of tax payments was ordered. In the fall the investment tax credit was suspended. Nevertheless, as estimates of the full-employment surplus indicate, fiscal policy taken as a whole became even more expansionist in 1966 than in 1965.

But if fiscal policy was still highly stimulative, monetary policy became severely restrictive. As signs of inflation multiplied in 1965, the monetary authorities became concerned that their policy of active credit ease was being carried too far. They were troubled by the deterioration in the basic condition of the balance of payments as well as by domestic developments. As characteristically happens during a boom, imports were now rising much more swiftly than exports. Besides, the war in Vietnam was causing large and increasing foreign exchange costs. In December 1965, the monetary authorities finally overcame their hesitation and raised the discount rate, despite strong opposition from the White House; but they continued for another few months to allow bank credit to grow at practically the same rate as before. By the spring of 1966, when it became apparent that the stimulative thrust of fiscal policy was not abating, they shifted bluntly to a policy of credit restriction, thus repeating a familiar pattern. Many businesses, even large and well established corporations, that sought to borrow from their commercial banks, now discovered that they would have to get along with less credit or try to find credit elsewhere. But other financial institutions—life insurance companies, mutual savings banks, and particularly the savings and loan associations—could not extend significant relief, since they were even more hard pressed than the commercial banks. In this constricted environment of finance, not only did interest rates move up rapidly from a level that was already abnormally high, but the public market for debt instruments became disorganized for a while, and total private borrowing in the final quarter fell to the lowest level for that season since 1962.

The credit squeeze reinforced the gathering forces of readjustment in the economy. The homebuilding industry, which is peculiarly dependent on credit, became the outstanding casualty of financial stringency. Many real estate firms and small businesses in other lines of activity were injured. Moreover, the high interest rates brought depression to the bond market, and became a major negative influence on the stock market as well. Tight money, however, was not the only factor now disciplining the boom. With the scope of economic expansion narrowing, labor costs rising, profit margins shrinking, construction costs running well above investors' estimates, uncertainty about the course of federal finances growing, and the business mood gradually becoming less exuberant, powerful forces besides tight money operated to bring the investment boom to a close. Consumer markets also lost their vigor as many families began practicing stricter economies in order to cope with the rising cost of living. In the meantime, inventories soared and the need to bring them into closer relation to sales cast a cloud on the economic outlook for the months immediately ahead.

VI

The recent sluggishness of the economy has inevitably led to much questioning of governmental policy. In particular, the monetary authorities have been blamed for bringing on a damaging credit shortage and unacceptably high interest rates last year. The critics are undoubtedly right if they mean that the shift from easy to tight money need not have been so blunt. But the complaint of some goes deeper; namely, that the government should have seen to it that interest rates remained at the moderate level that ruled until mid-1965. It is doubtful whether such a result could have been achieved. If the monetary authorities had attempted to peg interest rates, the boom would have become still more intense and the demand for credit would have risen still faster. The resulting open inflation, quite apart from other grave consequences, could have made interest rates rise eventually even more than they did. After all, when the price level is going up fast and constantly, lenders will in the end seek to be compensated for the depreciation of money during the period of the loan, and no central bank can force lenders to do anything else. As it was, the advance of interest rates before April 1966, merely reflected the fact that the demand for credit had become so intense that it rose even faster than the extraordinary rise in the supply of credit. It was only then that the authorities stepped bluntly on the credit brake.

The fiscal authorities also have not escaped criticism. In view of the scale of federal spending and the escalation of the war in Vietnam, they have been repeatedly blamed for not raising income tax rates early in 1966. It seems likely that if defense costs had not been greatly underestimated, income taxes would actually have gone up. In that event, monetary policy would probably have been less restrictive, the homebuilding industry would have fared better, and some of the gyrations in financial markets would have been avoided. On the other hand, since retail trade was already beginning to display some signs of sluggishness, higher income taxes on individuals might well have accentuated the slackening rate of expansion. The case was perhaps stronger for a temporary increase in the corporate income tax or a suspension of the investment tax credit; but any such measure would also have come at an inconvenient time—that is, when profit margins were already beginning to recede. As things happened, the suspension of the investment tax credit did not become law until November, the very month when the Federal Reserve authorities had already begun relaxing the credit restraints.

The fact is that prompt or really good solutions are rarely, if ever, available for the imbalances generated by inflation. Once forces of inflation have been released, it becomes very difficult to bring them under control without some sizable readjustments in the economy. Mistakes in economic policy were undoubtedly made in 1966 as in every year; but they largely derived from the fateful policies of 1965 when, despite the larger spending on defense, practically every weapon in the arsenal of economic stimulation was brought into use—greater monetary ease, lower income tax rates for individuals, lower income tax rates for corporations, lower excise taxes, and larger spending on programs of the Great Society. All this happened when moderate measures of restraint rather than accelerated stimuli were needed, so that the expanding economy could retain its balance. And so we finally come to the agonizing question: Why did the nation's policymakers, who for years had succeeded so well in monitoring a business expansion under difficult conditions, finally unleash the forces of inflation? Why did men who showed the ability to profit from experience succumb to one of the oldest weaknesses of governmental practice?

One reason, I think, is that they were misled by the very success that for a time attended their efforts. Economic expansion was continuing, and the level of costs and prices was remaining steady. Even the disequilibrium in the balance of payments no longer seemed so formidable. The export surplus had risen steadily since 1962 and, disagreeable though it would be to do so, the adverse capital movement could be handled by special measures—such as the interest equalization tax of 1963 or new guidelines for foreign loans and investments. With production, employment, personal incomes, and corporate profits going up steadily, and the consumer price level rising less rapidly than in earlier years, the nation's electorate returned the administration to power with an overwhelming vote of confidence in November 1964. Economic policies for and during 1965 were shaped in this atmosphere of success, to which the Council of Economic Advisers had made a very notable contribution. The massive tax cut was its bold conception, and the enactment of such a measure at a time when the economy was advancing smoothly was a triumph of the "new economics."

The central doctrine of this school is that the stage of the business cycle has little relevance to sound economic policy; that policy should be growth-oriented instead of cycle-oriented; that the vital matter is whether a gap exists between actual and potential output; that fiscal deficits and monetary tools need to be used to promote expansion when a gap exists; and that the stimuli should be sufficient to close the gap—provided significant inflationary pressures are not whipped up in the process. The magnitude of the stimulus to be applied in any particular case involves, of course, difficult estimating and forecasting, but the Council's forecasts were apparently improving. Its economic forecast for 1962 was wide of the mark; it was better for 1963 and it was nearly perfect for 1964. In judging economic prospects for 1965, the diminished slack in the economy could not be ignored. But if the margin for expansionist policies appeared smaller on this account, the guidelines for prices and wages could increase it. That, indeed, was their basic purpose. Originally presented as a contribution to public discussion, they had by now been shaped into crisp rules that might lead to censure of violators or worse. With the price level nearly steady and unemployment still well above 4 per cent, it thus seemed tolerably safe as well as desirable to resort to fiscal and monetary stimuli on a larger scale than before. But as later experience demonstrated, neither trade unions nor business firms will act often or long in a manner that is contrary to their economic interests. Once slack in the economy was significantly reduced, expectations of stable prices began to fade, inflationary pressures reappeared, and their initial symptoms were already visible in 1964, as I previously noted.

The policymakers paid slight attention to these cyclical

symptoms, for their thinking was focused on bringing down the rate of unemployment—an objective to which the government was rightly committed. An unemployment rate of 4 per cent, or possibly somewhat less, had always been the objective of the administrators of the Employment Act. But in 1961 the figure of 4 per cent became official for the first time, and this inevitably added to public pressure for its prompt realization. However, the economic significance of any particular figure of unemployment does not stay fixed in a dynamic environment. In recent times, the labor market has changed profoundly as the numbers working part-time or intermittently grew relative to the stable full-time labor force, as voluntary unemployment became a larger factor in the total, and as job opportunities for the unskilled declined. These structural changes in the labor market tended to make it harder to reach an unemployment rate of 4 per cent merely by stimulating aggregate demand. But if this was the case, it was desirable by 1965 to shift the emphasis of economic policy from expanding aggregate demand to the correction of structural maladjustments. The administration read the evidence differently, and it did so in part because of the theoretical apparatus of the Council of Economic Advisers. Since the Council identified an unemployment rate of 4 per cent with a condition of practically full employment, this figure served as a constant in the equation for computing the potential output. The gap between actual and potential output, in turn, was attributed to a deficiency of aggregate demand; so that, in effect, any unemployment in excess of 4 per cent called for correction of an alleged demand shortage. This was a dangerous shortcut in analysis, since the gap could obviously arise, in whole or in part, from obstacles on the side of supply or from a failure of the constituent parts of demand and supply to adjust sufficiently to one another. To analyze the labor market on these principles, the Council would have needed comprehensive statistics on job vacancies. Unfortunately, such statistics did not—and still do not—exist. Faulty statistics compounded the difficulties of the policy-makers. When industrial markets tighten, list prices for a time are apt to remain unchanged, while effective prices are raised by reducing special concessions or charging a premium. Since these common departures from list prices are largely ignored in the official index of wholesale prices, the rise that it registered in 1964 and 1965 undoubtedly understated the actual rise. Another statistical deficiency was still more mischievous. As originally calculated by the Department of Commerce, the annual rate of increase in the gross national product during 1965 was consistently too low, quarter after quarter, by amounts varying from about $2 to $5 billion. This cumulation of errors left its mark on economic thinking by underestimating the growth that was taking place, and therefore also exaggerating whatever gap may have still existed between actual and potential output.

Thus, the psychology of success, the novel guidelines for prices and wages, technical economic analysis, and its statistical accoutrements, all played their role in moving the nation to a more expansionist economic policy during 1965. But the role of philosophic views and political factors, which are always and inevitably present, may well have exceeded everything else. The main drive for an expansionist policy came from the executive establishment. The Congress generally acquiesced, and so too for a while did the Federal Reserve Board which still had some misgivings about the degree of caution that it had exercised in the past. Nowadays, the view is widely held in economic and political circles that a little inflation is tolerable because it can lead to a reduction of unemployment and some alleviation of poverty. The longer-run relations of inflation, unemployment, and poverty are less well understood. Thus, with prosperity increasing, it seemed only proper to the President and his advisers to take bolder steps in behalf of the sectors of the economy that had been left behind by the march of progress. With income taxes already lowered, it seemed only just to reduce excises and thus aid both merchant and consumer, whether rich or poor. The growing involvement in Vietnam came gradually and it was not expected to be a major factor financially. As the year advanced, it became evident even to many of those who supported the guidelines policy that trade unions and business corporations either would not or could not discharge adequately the responsibility of holding back the tide of inflation which the government, in effect, had asked them to assume. Indeed, by mid-1965, the Federal Reserve authorities had already become gravely concerned about the course of events; but they were reluctant to take immediate measures that would run counter to the policy of the executive—the main source of governmental power. Time is always needed to carry out a significant shift of policy by a far-flung government of divided powers, particularly when the move requires restraints on expansion. In this instance, the difficulty was magnified by the political cost of returning to orthodox policies for fighting inflation.

Theories have a power that administrators, no matter how able, cannot fully control. By and large, economic policy during 1965 was still governed by the theory that stimulation of activity was reasonably safe as long as a gap existed between actual and potential output, no matter how small the gap was becoming or how rapidly it was being closed. When small inflationary signs appeared, they were at first not believed or dismissed as trivial. By the time a change in policy was attempted, it had already been pushed into greater stimulation than was intended. Thus, deliberately expansionist measures were carried along passively for a time as the desirability of a shift in policy and how it might best be executed were being pondered by the managers of our prosperity.

VII

The course of economic policy in the United States in recent years, despite some disturbing misadventures, remains impressive. Since 1960 we surely have made progress in moving toward our national objectives. Production and employment rose substantially, the advance of prosperity became widely diffused, full employment was reestablished, and new doors of economic opportunity were opened up to underprivileged citizens. The government played a vital part in bringing about these gains by its imaginative, and yet pragmatic, approach to the nation's problems. When increases of federal spending failed to produce desired results, it shifted boldly to tax reduction, and thus made the psychology of confidence its ally in the quest for economic improvement. When structural maladjustments in the labor market became clearer, it proceeded to build on the modest beginnings of the Manpower Development and Training Act. And when inflation broke loose, it finally recognized that orthodox financial measures were better suited to our nation's genius than legal props for the badly bruised wage and price guidelines.

However, this willingness to learn from experience came much too slowly at times, and in any event recent years have brought disappointments as well as successes. Certainly, extensive unemployment lasted much too long, the disequilibrium in the balance of payments escaped correction, the federal government continued to run a deficit even when full employment was reestablished, the nation experienced another round of inflation and this, together with the large fluctuations in financial markets, resulted in a redistribution of wealth that injured

284 The Business Cycle in a Changing World

many defenseless citizens. Economic policy cannot escape a part of the responsibility for these failures, some of which may yet haunt us in the future.

Thus, governmental policies for dealing with the problem of full employment and economic stability have moved along a rocky road in recent years as in the past. Since the 1930's, economic policymakers have indeed demonstrated a capacity to learn from past mistakes. Too often, however, their memories have grown dim with the passage of time. Economic generals, not unlike their military counterparts, sometimes forget which war they are fighting, nor do they always know which war to fight. Nevertheless, significant progress has been made and we must try to extend it.

The needs are many, and so too are the opportunities. We need to become better aware of the limitations of the art of economic forecasting even as we try to improve it. We need to develop comprehensive data on job vacancies, so that it will no longer be necessary to guess whether or when a deficiency in aggregate demand exists. We need to improve our measures of prices and costs, so that inflationary pressures can be recognized more promptly. We need to develop quarterly projections of federal revenues and expenditures, similar to the information now compiled by the government on business sales expectations and investment intentions, so that the changing requirements of fiscal policy can be better evaluated than in the past or at present. We need to learn more about the subtle forces that shape the state of confidence. We need to develop policies for dealing with seasonal unemployment—a problem that we have largely ignored since the 1920's.

We need to learn to act, at a time when the economy is threatened by inflation, with something of the sense of urgency that we have so well developed in dealing with the threat of recession. We need to learn to make necessary shifts of economic policy more promptly, so that they may be gradual instead of abrupt. And most important of all, we need to learn better than we yet have the basic truth that, while stability of the general price level will not of itself bring prosperity in the years ahead, we cannot very well maintain international confidence in the dollar or have sustained prosperity without it.

ELEVEN

The Perils of Inflation

INFLATION is not a new problem for us, any more than it is a new problem for the peoples of other nations. During the decade of the 1940's, the purchasing power of the dollar was cut in half. Since 1950, we have experienced several lesser but still very troublesome spurts of inflation.

My purpose is to discuss the causes and consequences of the current inflation. Let me begin by calling several major facts about this inflation to your attention.

First, the general price level—that is, the price level of our total output of goods and services—has already risen 10 per cent since mid-1964.

Second, while individual price advances have been uneven, they have been diffused throughout the price system. Every major category of prices in both wholesale and consumer markets has experienced an appreciable advance.

Third, not only has the price level been rising, but the rise has also been accelerating. Between the first quarter of 1964 and the first quarter of 1965, the general price level rose 1.9 per cent. The next year it rose 2.1 per cent. The year after, 3.1 per cent. During the past year, the increase was 3.5 per cent.

Fourth, the advance of wages has also been accelerating.

Address given at Town Hall, Los Angeles, California, April 23, 1968. Reprinted from Tax Foundation's *Tax Review*, May 1968.

The average increase in the initial year covered by collective bargaining settlements came to 3.2 per cent for the agreements negotiated during 1964. The corresponding increase was 3.8 per cent during 1965, 4.8 per cent during 1966, and 5.7 per cent during 1967.

Fifth, the wage-price spiral has lately been working along classical lines, with every rise in prices spurring increases in wages and every rise in wages setting the stage for further increases in prices.

So much for the bare facts concerning the new inflation. Let us turn next to its causes. To what factor or factors in the overall situation can this inflation be attributed?

One popular notion attributes the inflation to the war in Vietnam. The Council of Economic Advisers has put this explanation as follows: "Around mid-1965, the growth of demand for industrial products suddenly accelerated as the direct and indirect consequence of the enlarged commitment of U.S. forces in Vietnam . . . The upward pressures on prices and wages in this period . . . tripped off a price-wage spiral." This explanation has an element of plausibility, but it cannot be readily accepted.

In the first place, the new inflation started before Vietnam was of any financial or economic consequence. Prices of raw materials began moving up in spirited fashion as early as the fall of 1963. By June of 1964, the average level of all wholesale prices began rising. Between that month and June 1965, the wholesale price index rose 3 per cent.

Moreover, price advances spread out over the economy well before mid-1965. During the second half of 1964, twelve of the fifteen major groups of commodities covered by the official index of wholesale prices registered advances. During the next six months, fourteen of the fifteen groups showed price increases. Clearly, inflation had already taken hold and become widespread many months before Vietnam began adding appreciably to aggregate monetary demand.

In the second place, total federal expenditures, as estimated in January, show an increase of $53 billion between mid-1965 and mid-1968. Less than half of this increase, that is, about $25 billion, is attributable to the war. Hence, if the war expenditures are regarded as a cause of the recent inflation, then non-war expenditures must be considered a still more important cause.

In the third place, while it is true that spending for Vietnam added powerfully to aggregate demand after mid-1965, this effect could surely have been offset by reducing nondefense spending or by raising taxes or by making credit more expensive and less readily available to private borrowers. The simple explanation that the recent price-wage spiral is attributable to the war in Vietnam must therefore be rejected.

Another popular explanation of the recent inflation is that business firms have lately found it expedient to use their market power—which is a polite term for monopolistic power—more aggressively. If this were actually the case, it would be reasonable to expect profit margins to rise. That, however, has not happened during the past two years. On the contrary, profit margins in American industry, taken as a whole, declined in 1966 and declined again last year.

The main reason for the narrowing of profit margins is that, on the average, prices of late have risen less than unit labor costs of production. And this brings me to a third popular explanation of the inflation, namely, that trade unions have been using their market power irresponsibly during the recent years of low unemployment.

There can be little doubt that some trade unions have lately been able to achieve extraordinary increases in wages, just as some business enterprises have been able to raise prices out of proportion to the increase in their costs. But the theory of labor monopoly does not hold up any better than the theory of business monopoly.

Between 1966 and 1967, wages rose all around. But where did the sharpest increases take place? Not in manufacturing, mining, or transportation—all of which are heavily unionized. In these industries, the percentage rise was below the national average. On the other hand, in agriculture—where trade unions play practically no role—wages rose most. Abnormally large increases occurred also in retail trade, wholesale establishments, service trades, financial institutions, and the construction industry. Except for the latter, these are industries in which trade unions are notoriously weak.

The pattern of wage increases between 1964 and 1966 was very similar to that from 1966 to 1967. The behavior of wages in recent years cannot, therefore, be explained in terms of monopolistic power, unless one is prepared to argue that trade unions have been using their power to restrict rather than to intensify wage increases.

What has happened of late in the wage sphere can, however, be explained quite simply in terms of a competitive market. As the aggregate demand for goods and services kept growing, the labor market became increasingly tight. Workers in low-wage industries, such as agriculture and the service trades, saw an opportunity to get jobs in high-wage industries, such as manufacturing. The outflow of labor from the low-wage industries therefore tended to raise substantially the wages in those industries, while the movement of workers to the high-wage industries served to moderate the wage increases in that sector. Such shifts in demand, supply, and relative wages express the normal workings of a competitive market.

There is an additional fact that we should bear in mind.

Contrary to a widespread impression, the real income of the average American worker has not improved at all during the past two or three years. Once wages are adjusted for the rise in consumer prices and for social security and income taxes, what we find is that the weekly earnings of the average worker in private nonagricultural employment were actually a trifle lower in 1966 than in 1965 and again a trifle lower in 1967 than in 1966.

Let me turn to still another explanation of the recent inflation, namely, that the Congress is responsible because it has failed to accept the President's repeated request for a 10 per cent surcharge on income taxes. If the Congress had done what the President wanted, so the argument goes, the increase in aggregate demand would have been curbed and the advance in prices would have been much slower.

This explanation again ignores much of recent history. Apart from the suspension of the investment tax credit, which became effective in November 1966, the President did not ask for an increase in taxes before January 1967. By that time the wholesale price level had already been rising two and one-half years. And when the President did ask for higher income taxes, he asked merely for an increase of 6 per cent, to become effective at mid-year. In the face of an explosive increase in federal spending, this request did not convey any great sense of urgency.

Moreover, within a few weeks of asking for a tax increase in the interest of restricting the growth of aggregate demand, the Administration actually stepped up its efforts to stimulate demand. Substantial funds for housing and highways, which had only recently been impounded, were released by March of 1967. In March, also, the President requested the Congress to reinstate the investment tax credit for machinery and equipment. This meant, of course, that the President was now asking for a substantial tax cut for business firms instead of the tax increase he had suggested a few weeks earlier.

The abrupt shift in early 1967 toward a more liberal fiscal policy was accompanied by a shift to a more liberal monetary policy. The Federal Reserve authorities lowered the discount rate. They reduced reserve requirements on time and savings deposits. Most important of all, they now pumped reserves into the commercial banks at so fast a rate that the money supply during 1967 grew more than 7 per cent. This was a faster rate of growth than in any year of the entire period since World War II.

Thus, despite the war in Vietnam, the government acted during much of last year as if a recession were under way, instead of coming to grips with the menacing reality of inflation.

True, in August 1967, the President made another switch in fiscal policy. Announcing that the nation was threatened by ruinous inflation, he then requested from the Congress a 10 per cent, instead of the earlier 6 per cent, surcharge on income taxes. By this time, however, the Congress as well as the rest of the nation was quite confused about the direction and purpose of national economic policy.

Many Congressmen asked: Why is the nation being whipsawed by sudden and apparently capricious shifts in tax policy? Has the danger of inflation now really become more acute? If so, did not the Administration bring on this difficulty by its aggressively expansionist policy since February? If the Administration was wrong then, can its judgment be trusted now? And if the Administration is really so concerned about inflation, why does it not curb the projected increase of federal spending and thereby reduce the need for a tax increase? It is largely because the Congress has not been satisfied with the answers that it has received to these questions that no increase in taxes has yet taken place.

The delay on the subject of taxes may be regrettable. I happen to think that it is very regrettable. But if Congress is to be blamed for the inflation which we are experiencing, the Administration's entire monetary and fiscal policy must be blamed much more.

When President Kennedy took charge of our government in January 1961, there was considerable slack in the economy, but the price level was steady. In fact, it had been quite steady for two years.

The new administration proceeded to shape its economic policy on the basis of an ingenious theory, namely, that by adjusting taxes or its own rate of spending, the government would be able to keep the aggregate demand for goods and services closely adjusted to what our economy can produce at full employment. According to this theory, as long as a gap existed between actual output and potential output, it was the responsibility of the government to stimulate demand by increasing its expenditures or by cutting taxes, but maintaining in either case an easy monetary policy.

The proponents of this theory realized that inflation could create an imbalance between production and sales or between business investment and consumer spending, and thereby lead to a recession before the gap between actual and potential output was closed. They believed, however, that price increases could be staved off by getting workmen to accept wage increases that equaled the over-all increase in output per manhour and by getting businessmen to set prices so that the ratio of the price of a commodity to its labor cost of production would be constant.

The Administration's economic policy therefore came to rest

on two articles of faith: first, that monetary and fiscal stimuli would serve to expand employment and close the gap between actual and potential output; second, that wage and price guidelines would serve to keep the price level stable while these stimuli were being applied.

This theory worked reasonably well as long as our factories and mines had considerable idle capacity and unemployment was moderately large. Under such conditions, an aggressive fiscal and monetary policy could be pursued without resulting in a wage-price spiral. By 1964, however, the gap between actual and potential output had narrowed substantially. As demand began pressing on available resources, bottlenecks developed and prices rose.

The new wave of inflation did not come without warning. By the late summer of 1964, a large increase had already occurred in the number of business firms reporting slower deliveries. By the end of 1964, the average workweek in manufacturing was already at the level reached during the Korean war, and price increases in wholesale markets—as I previously mentioned—had already become general.

The price increases, however, were as yet small and the Administration paid no attention to them. The official view was that the government's economic policy was working out as expected, that fiscal and monetary stimuli were narrowing the gap between actual and potential output, and that the guidelines were keeping wages and prices in check.

Indeed, since its policy of economic stimulation seemed to be working so well, the government felt it was desirable to push this policy more energetically. Thus, during 1965, when the economy was already advancing rapidly of its own momentum, the government accelerated the application of monetary and fiscal stimuli, instead of moving gradually toward a policy of restraint.

Practically every weapon in the arsenal of economic stimulation was released during 1965. In that year, we had the second installment of the cut in personal income taxes enacted in 1964. In that year, the second installment of the cut in corporate income taxes became effective. In that year, a significant reduction of excise taxes was enacted. In that year, spending on programs of the Great Society was enlarged. In that year, the rate of increase of the money supply and of bank credit was stepped up sharply. All this happened despite the expansion of federal spending on account of Vietnam.

This aggressively expansionist policy did indeed help the nation reach full employment by the end of 1965, but that was not the only result. By that time, wholesale prices were already 4 per cent higher than in mid-1964, and the rise of wages was already accelerating. As experienced observers had predicted, the price-wage guidelines proved a fragile barrier to inflation once labor and commodity markets tightened.

The architects of the policy that produced these results had promised that once full employment was approached, governmental policy would assure that aggregate demand rose no faster than the nation's productive capacity. This promise has not been fulfilled. In these recent years of prosperity and full employment, the federal budget deficit has continued to mount.

The yardstick on which economists nowadays rely to gauge the degree to which federal finances exert a stimulating or restraining influence on the economy is, however, the full-employment deficit or surplus rather than the actual budget deficit or surplus. This yardstick of the economist indicates that the fiscal stimulus applied by the federal government to our economy has grown progressively, year after year, since 1963.

The record of monetary policy has not been much better. True, over an interval of some seven or eight months during

1966, the Federal Reserve authorities pursued a restrictive monetary policy. In the past three or four months, they have also moderated the expansion of the money supply and credit.

However, the broad thrust of monetary policy during the past few years has been more and more expansionist. Between mid-1960 and mid-1964, the money supply grew at an annual rate of only 2.7 per cent. This rate was stepped up to 4 per cent between mid-1964 and the spring of 1965, and to 6 per cent over the next year. During 1967, as already noted, the rate was above 7 per cent.

It is this combination of an accelerating growth of the money supply and an increasingly expansionist fiscal policy that is the basic cause of the wage-price spiral that we have lately been experiencing. It may, perhaps, be debated how much of the responsibility for the recent inflation is to be attributed to the Congress and how much to the Executive Branch. But there can be no escape from the conclusion that the federal government has pursued an increasingly expansionist policy in the face of practically full employment and a soaring price level.

Now, as in other times of inflation, the administration in power has been blaming greedy businessmen, irresponsible trade union leaders, and unruly Congressmen. But the new inflation is mainly the result of the excessively rapid creation of new money and of our unbalanced federal budgets.

Let me now turn, briefly, to the effects of this inflation on our economy.

In recent years, we have discussed extensively the need to reduce the poverty which still exists in our land of plenty. This is an objective that practically all Americans share. Unhappily, much of the public as well as private effort to reduce poverty is being nullified by inflation.

There can be little doubt that poor people, or people of

modest means generally, are the chief sufferers from inflation. Poor people rarely know how to protect themselves against inflation. What little savings they have are apt to be in the form of bank deposits, life insurance policies, or government savings bonds, the purchasing power of which keeps eroding when the price level rises.

Moreover, since bad health, unemployment, irregular work habits, and poverty often go together in life, the incomes of poor people are apt to fluctuate more than the incomes of the well-to-do. Last year, for example, the number of low-income families suffering a loss of dollar income nearly matched the number that experienced a gain. Once we take account of the advance in prices, it appears that the proportion of low-income families whose real income has lately declined may well exceed the proportion whose income has risen. This is a grave injustice.

The injustice of inflation is not confined to poor families. Inflation affects adversely everyone whose money income fails to respond to the rising cost of living or whose savings take the form of fixed dollar assets.

Besides these effects, the recent inflation has worked havoc with our money and capital markets. Last year the Federal Reserve authorities made a strong effort to create monetary ease and to bring interest rates down. They were, however, entirely unsuccessful. Not only did interest rates fail to come down, but some rates—notably, government and corporate bond yields—rose to the highest level in several decades. This rise in interest rates is proving a burden on many home buyers and others who find it necessary to borrow.

One major reason for the upsurge in interest rates is that many prospective borrowers have been fearful that governmental policies would create so great an expansion in aggregate demand that, high though interest rates were, they would soon be higher still. By anticipating some of their credit needs, businessmen and state and local borrowers have tended to push interest rates up.

Another reason for the upsurge in interest rates is the widening expectation that inflation will continue. Feeling this way about the future, not a few businessmen have been borrowing on the comfortable expectation that they can repay their loans later in cheaper dollars. However, since suppliers of loan funds have likewise been anticipating inflation, they have become less willing to lend at the going interest rate. A 6½ per cent interest rate on a triple-A bond may seem terribly high; but sophisticated lenders know that when the price level rises 3½ per cent a year, the real yield of such a bond is merely 3 per cent.

The recent inflation has had another serious effect on our economy: it has hurt our foreign trade.

In the early 1960's our price level was steady, while much of the rest of the world practiced inflation. In the last two or three years, European countries have been making a moderately successful effort to restrain the advance of prices, while we have been experiencing a new wage-price spiral.

This change in international price trends, combined with the reduced rate of growth of the world economy, has affected adversely our foreign trade. In 1964, we had a surplus on merchandise trade of nearly $7 billion. The surplus shrank to $4.8 billion in 1965, to $3.7 billion in 1966, to $3.5 billion in 1967. During the past few months, the surplus expressed as an annual rate has been less than $2 billion.

This vanishing export surplus is a major reason for the deterioration in our balance of payments. Other factors, of course, have contributed to the deterioration—notably, the large and increasing foreign-exchange cost of the war in Vietnam.

The sorry condition of our balance of payments has led the

government to place restrictions on how private citizens can use their money. In January, the President issued an executive order which limits severely the investments that American firms can make in their foreign subsidiaries or branches. Commercial banks and other financial institutions are now also operating under regulations which restrict the loans that they can make to foreigners.

The decline of economic freedom that we are experiencing may not stop with lending and investing. As you well know, control of foreign travel by Americans has been under active consideration recently.

In spite of such drastic measures to limit the outflow of dollars, there is less confidence now in the external value of the dollar than at any time since 1933. Much has been said in recent weeks about the gold crisis. What we have been experiencing, of course, is an international crisis of confidence in American financial policy.

With inflation proceeding at an accelerating pace in our country, with the balance of payments deteriorating, and with the federal budget deficit likely to exceed $20 billion, it was only natural for holders of dollars to become increasingly concerned about the possibility that the dollar would soon be devalued, just as the British pound was last November.

The flight from the dollar took on such vast proportions that our stock of gold, which was still close to $13 billion last November, fell to about $10½ billion in March. As a consequence, the London gold pool, which had kept the market price of gold close to the official price of $35 an ounce, was discontinued. For a few days in March, Americans abroad found that some banks, hotels, and merchants were unwilling to honor their dollars or traveler checks. They were unprepared for this humiliation.

Fortunately, the leading central banks of the world acted quickly to shore up the dollar in the hope of preserving the present international monetary system. But the dual price of gold which they established is a very tenuous arrangement. Even in the short-run, its viability will depend on how we conduct our national finances. Other governments now have a larger voice in our public policies, both domestic and foreign. They will not cooperate with us in the monetary sphere unless they deem our over-all performance acceptable.

The dual price of gold gives us some time to put our national finances in order, but it does not give us much time. And so I finally come to the critical question: What is the prospect of bringing our inflation under control and of reestablishing equilibrium in the balance of payments?

In view of the recent run on the dollar, our governmental authorities at last recognize that general price stability and the balance of payments deserve a higher priority in our economic policymaking than they have yet received. The Federal Reserve System is now moderating the growth of the money supply. The Administration is also showing some willingness to curb expenditures in the interest of inducing the Congress to accept the 10 per cent surcharge on income taxes.

It is by no means clear, however, that our government is even now ready to adopt the measures of austerity that are needed to slow down the inflation materially.

The tax surcharge has large symbolic significance, but its real power to restrain aggregate demand has been exaggerated in current discussion. Not many corporations will revise downward their capital expenditure plans just because of a temporary 10 per cent increase in their income tax. The effect of the tax surcharge will be greater on consumer spending. But in view of the high savings rate during the past year and the revival of the propensity to spend in recent months, a large part of the increase in personal tax payments will probably be at the expense of savings.

A reduction in governmental expenditures is a much more potent device for restraining aggregate demand than a temporary increase in taxes, but there is little prospect of cutting expenditures in the present political climate. Even if spending plans are cut back by $5 or $6 billion, Federal spending in the next fiscal year is still expected to rise about $10 billion above this year's level.

The fiscal measures that are now being seriously considered might well have achieved their purpose of curbing inflation if they had been adopted a year ago or even six months ago. Meanwhile, the inflation has reached a more advanced phase, the budget has moved further out of balance, and confidence in the dollar has greatly diminished. In view of the prevailing political sentiment, it seems doubtful to me that our government will practice monetary and fiscal austerity on either the scale now needed or over a sufficiently long time to subdue inflationary expectations and restore full confidence in American financial policy.

But if we shun the path of real austerity, how will we deal with the stubborn deficit in the balance of payments? One possibility would be to subject foreign transactions to additional controls and perhaps apply controls to domestic prices and wages as well. If we travel this road, other countries will retaliate with protectionist devices of their own, the efficiency of our economy will suffer, and the broad result is likely to be a constriction of world trade and a lower rate of growth of the world economy.

Whatever we do about additional controls, unless the deficit in our balance of payments is soon corrected, the new dual price system for gold will probably collapse. In that event, we may have to choose between raising sharply the official price of gold or letting the dollar find its own value on the foreign exchange market.

Either answer would mean devaluation of the dollar and further damage to our international political prestige. If the price of gold is raised, the dollar will be devalued with respect to gold. On the other hand, if the dollar is allowed to float, it will be devalued with respect to other currencies, unless foreign governments choose to support the dollar in the interest of protecting their own export trade.

Foreign support of a floating dollar is conceivable, but it is unlikely to last. After all, a foreign country has an alternative to accumulating dollars that it does not want; namely, it can let the dollar depreciate and protect itself by restricting imports from the United States. In the end, a floating dollar would probably result in extensive unsettlement of business, new restrictions on international transactions, and political turmoil.

On the other hand, an increase in the price of gold would leave the present system of foreign exchange rates virtually intact, so that business could go on as before. This expedient is subject, however, to political criticism, since Russia, China, France, South Africa, and thousands of private speculators to boot, would reap a windfall profit. Moreover, while a substantial increase in the price of gold would give us time to work toward a policy of financial prudence, it will not give us elbow room indefinitely. Once the dollar has been devalued with respect to gold, the financial community will be very alert to the possibility of a second devaluation.

I would like to think that we will be fortunate enough to escape such unhappy developments. Perhaps, the war in Vietnam will come to an end soon and bring larger relief both to the federal budget and to the balance of payments than now seems likely. Perhaps, foreign countries will step up their own rates of inflation and thereby aid our balance of payments. Perhaps, we will even be willing to practice real austerity.

We cannot count, however, on such favorable developments, and we need to ponder realistically the choices before us. The uncertainties are great. But as far as I can now judge, if we are unwilling to practice austerity on a sufficient scale, then an increase in the price of gold may be the wisest course open to us.

One thing is clear. When a nation permits its economy to become engulfed by inflation, policymakers no longer have any good choices. That is the tough legacy and also the chief peril of inflation.

TWELVE

Heller's "New Dimensions of Political Economy"

THE GODKIN Lectures that Professor Walter Heller gave at Harvard University in March 1966 are expanded in his lively book on "New Dimensions of Political Economy." Its central theme is the use of economics in the formation of national policies during the 1960's—a period and subject of which Professor Heller has exceptional firsthand knowledge. The first chapter deals with the role of economists, particularly the Council of Economic Advisers, in shaping economic policies and in advancing the President's program. The second chapter discusses the tools and achievements of the "new economics" since 1961 and "the promise of modern economic policy" for the future. The third and final chapter is devoted to a close examination of the opportunities that growing federal revenues provide for strengthening the fiscal foundations of hard-pressed state and local governments. Clearly, Professor Heller deals with issues of large significance for the modern world.

His book has other notable qualities. It is humane in spirit and is concerned with the business of life, not merely economic improvement. It presents a lucid and stirring account of the

Review of *New Dimensions of Political Economy*, by Walter W. Heller. Reprinted, by permission, from *The National Banking Review*, June 1967.

"new economics" in action. It argues eloquently for a strongly activist economic policy, particularly in fiscal matters. It is informed by a thorough understanding of the political process. It seeks to avoid ideological conflict or commitment. And it yields interesting glimpses of the two presidents whom Professor Heller served so ably as Chairman of the Council of Economic Advisers. For all these reasons the book deserves to be read widely.

Not all of the book, however, deserves to be remembered, and the main reason is the author's neglect of history. Governmental concern with economic growth is hardly an offspring of the "new economics." In the nineteenth century, economic growth was a paramount objective of our nation's policy—as the debates and legislation on tariffs, internal improvements, banking and currency, land settlement, conservation, and the state of competition testify. With industrialization and urbanization proceeding rapidly, the business cycle naturally became a subject of large public concern toward the end of the century. Much attention was therefore directed in succeeding decades, first to the prevention of financial crises, later to the moderation of fluctuations in the general price level, still later to the prevention of mass unemployment. After World War II, as the nation's resolve to deal with unemployment became stronger and as evidence that the business cycle was moderating accumulated, interest shifted again to economic growth and economic policy became increasingly focused on the simultaneous achievement, as far as feasible, of full employment, a high rate of growth in productivity, and general price stability. The Economic Report of the President in January 1954 stated the modern view accurately: "The new concept that is emerging in the practical art of government . . . is to subject every act of proposed legislation or administrative decision, as far as that is humanly possible, to review from the standpoint of the contribution it is likely to make, whether in the immediate or a more distant future, to the attainment of an expanding economy with maximum employment and without price inflation" (Economic Report, p. 112).

Professor Heller brushes aside what happened before the 1960's. He conveys the impression that, at least during the 1950's, the "old mythology and wrong-headed economics" of the budget dominated economic policy (p. 36). He at no time mentions the huge tax cut, or the provisions for accelerated depreciation, or the highway legislation, or the reform of the social security program, or the concern with education and training programs during the Eisenhower years. He notes, to be sure, the restrictive financial policy of 1958–60, but does not refer to the urgent circumstances from which it arose. "At the 1966 Symposium on the Employment Act," he tells us, "there was much talk of the gradual evolution of economic policy . . . But evolution became revolution the moment we had Presidents—and now we have had two—with the Keynesian perception to welcome their responsibilities under the act and to use its mandate and the weapons of political economy to generate . . . prosperity" (p. 12). This vision of a revolution is indeed suggested by the very first sentence of the book: "Economics has come of age in the 1960's." Again, Professor Heller speaks of Presidents Kennedy and Johnson as "the first modern economists in the American Presidency" (p. 36)—a claim that appears to be largely based on their advocacy of a massive tax cut at a time when the economy was advancing and the budget was out of balance. This was undoubtedly a new, significant, and at the time a salutary departure in economic policy. But if the first modern economist in the presidency is to be identified at all, may not this title belong to President Truman who fought so valiantly for the passage of the Employment Act or perhaps to President Hoover who, de-

spite his tragic inadequacy in a time of crisis, was the first in-
cumbent of the White House to deem it essential to use governmental power to moderate the ill winds of the business
cycle?

Between 1961 and 1966, production and employment in our
country rose substantially, the advance of prosperity became
widely diffused, full employment was reestablished, and new
doors of economic opportunity were opened to underprivileged citizens. Professor Heller stresses these achievements and
he is right in claiming that the federal government played a
vital part in bringing about these gains. However, he glosses
over the disappointments of the '60's—the fact that extensive
unemployment lasted much too long; the fact that disequilibrium in the balance of payments escaped correction; the fact
that governmental finances continued to show a deficit even
when full employment was reestablished; and the fact that
governmental policy released forces which eventually resulted
in a new round of inflation.

Professor Heller properly assigns a high role to fiscal policy,
particularly the tax cut of 1964, in the prosperity of recent
years. But his view that the expansion was "fiscally spurred"
(p. 68) is an oversimplification which fails, in particular, to
recognize the strongly expansionist thrust of monetary policy
from 1961 to 1965. He claims that the "chief reliance" (p. 95)
of fiscal policy during 1961–65 was tax reduction, when in
fact expenditure increases came to a much larger total than tax
reduction. He conveys the impression that President Kennedy's
proposal to cut income tax rates worked out precisely as
planned, but fails to mention that the tax proposal was accompanied by a plan to raise federal expenditures by nearly $5 bil-
lion and that the Congress accepted the former but rejected
the latter. And he is surely mistaken in suggesting that Vietnam is responsible for the recent inflation. Many months be-

fore Vietnam was of any financial consequence, evidence of economic strain began to appear—particularly, although by no means exclusively, in the markets for raw materials and skilled labor. Signs of incipient pressure on the nation's available resources, which were already plain during 1964, were ignored or overlooked by the policymakers. In fact, during 1965, with Vietnam beginning to hurt and the economy approaching full employment, the federal government unleashed practically every weapon of economic stimulation—greater monetary ease, lower income tax rates for individuals, lower income tax rates for corporations, lower excise taxes, and larger spending on programs of the Great Society.

The theory of the "new economics" has a fascination for the modern generation because of its intellectual elegance and scorn of evil—the evil of inflation no less than the evil of unemployment. In Professor Heller's words, the "success of the 'new economics' . . . requires willingness to shift or reverse gears" (p. 99). More precisely, "flexibility of program calls for a readiness to move taxes and interest rates up as inflation pressures mount and down as demand ebbs" (p. 100). But this fine rule of symmetry was practiced unevenly by policymakers during the 1960's—as it had indeed been before them, thereby strengthening the fears of many that the "new economics" may in practice be just another engine of inflation. Even now, Professor Heller does not stop to ponder or even to note the fact that the wholesale price level rose 4 per cent between mid-1964 and the end of 1965. Even now, he believes that economic conditions required "overt fiscal stimulus" (p. 95) during 1965. Even now, while he takes pride in the boldly expansionist policy that was pursued when unemployment was extensive, he explains the hesitations of fiscal policy during 1966 on the simple ground that "the economic calculus was clouded by uncertainty" (p. 88).

Professor Heller professes little interest in the business cycle. "Gone is the countercyclical syndrome of the 1950's," he announces in the Preface. Later, he explains that closing of the gap between actual and potential output "rather than the smoothing of the business cycle became the main preoccupation of policy" (p. 64); and that "the main instrument for dethroning the cyclical model and enthroning the growth model has been the GNP or performance gap" (p. 62). Apart from language, I am unaware of any real difference between "gap-closing" and "smoothing of the business cycle" provided, of course, that the smoothing is substantial and occurs at a high level of the employment rate. There is no real difference here between the objectives of economic policy during the 1960's and the objectives during the 1950's. However, "enthroning the growth model" cannot of itself rid the economy of the processes stressed by business-cycle theory—for example, the imbalance that normally develops between capital investment and consumption or between costs and prices as the economy moves toward full employment. The "cyclical model" therefore serves a diagnostic purpose and its neglect can prove serious, as it indeed has. Fortunately, "the countercyclical syndrome of the 1950's" is not yet entirely "gone." It has not even been entirely abandoned by Professor Heller, for he too recognizes the need "to avoid the excesses that destroy expansions" (p. 49).

The unique function of the Council of Economic Advisers, in Professor Heller's well-chosen words, is "to put at the President's disposal the best facts, appraisals, and forecasts that economic science, statistics, and surveys can produce" (p. 16). But, as he explains, the activities of the Council extend beyond giving advice to the President himself. Professor Heller discusses perceptively the activities of the Council since 1961, but he again fails to do justice to earlier history. He conveys the impression that prior to 1961 the Council pursued a "detached,

Olympian, take-it-or-leave-it approach to Presidential economic advice" (p. 15).[1] This description may fit the brief period when Dr. Nourse was Chairman of the Council. Otherwise, it is simply untrue. During 1953–56, for example, the Chairman of the Council had weekly scheduled meetings with the President—a privilege that only one other member of the government, the Secretary of Defense, enjoyed. He had full access to the President at other times and he used it when necessary. He represented the Council at weekly Cabinet meetings, made frequent reports on current and emerging policy requirements, and participated actively in Cabinet debates on economic matters. He served as Chairman of various Cabinet committees and used the opportunity to advance the Council's program. He worked closely with the Secretary of the Treasury and the Chairman of the Federal Reserve Board. He and his Council colleagues spent a good part of practically every day striving for a consensus on policy issues with representatives of the various departments and agencies. The Council thus fought tirelessly within the Executive establishment for the policies that it deemed needed and proper. The Council did not, however, take to the stump and fight in the public arena for the President's program. It refrained from this essential political activity because it felt, by and large, that professional economists should stick to their knitting, that economic counseling and political advocacy could get in one another's way, and that economists should not devote their precious time to do what politicians—who at least then were not in short supply—can do better.

In other periods, both before and after President Eisen-

[1] Professor Heller has written me as follows: "Because of the context in which they were put, these words apparently conveyed the wrong impression. They were meant to apply to Dr. Nourse's well-known, but unique, concept of Presidential economic advice."

hower's first administration, the Council did indeed choose to play a large and active public role. Since 1961, as Professor Heller explains in detail, the Council has considered its advisory responsibility to include public advocacy of the President's program and even the occasional release of trial balloons in his behalf. It may not be easy to decide, on the basis of evidence yet available, whether such activities seriously interfere with the objectivity and receptiveness to new thought and fresh evidence that the Council needs to have. It is still useful, however, to remember that political activities on the part of the Council nearly led to its destruction not too many years ago.

Whatever view one may take of Professor Heller's treatment of the past, his views concerning the future are always important. His plea for revenue sharing with the states and localities is well reasoned and well documented. It has already aroused wide interest in the Congress and will inevitably become a subject of lively debate once the pressure of Vietnam on the federal budget eases. Professor Heller also makes an impressive plea for flexibility and speed in fiscal action. Since changes in tax rates affect swiftly the income structure, he feels that "high-speed income tax legislation, quickly translated into changes in withholding and quarterly payment rates, would give the Federal Reserve Board a run for its money in timely stabilization policy" (p. 102). This is difficult to achieve under our form of government, and the subject deserves the most careful thought and study—as Professor Heller urges.

Candor compels me to add that my enthusiasm for high-speed tax legislation, which was once considerable, has waned in recent years. I am not at all confident, by way of example, that fiscal policy in early 1966 would have been less hesitant if "pushbutton procedures or Presidential authority for temporary tax increases" (p. 98) had been available. With such devices at hand, we might very well have had a "quickie tax cut" in the summer of 1962, such as the Council then recommended (p. 33). But in that event, would we have gotten the judicious and well-balanced Revenue Act of 1964 which became law only after Congress had worked long and conscientiously on the economic, ethical, and administrative issues surrounding the income tax? Besides doubts of this character, I do not think that economic forecasting is as yet sufficiently accurate to justify fine fiscal tuning. I also fear that if it ever becomes governmental policy to move income taxes up or down at brief intervals, this rule of fiscal behavior will become a normal part of expectations and the effectiveness of fiscal policy in inducing needed changes in investment and consumer spending will therefore be drastically reduced. Thus, if a tax reduction is deemed to be temporary, it will affect economic activity only through its effect on current disposable income and the spending response may be quite small. On the other hand, if the tax reduction is expected to be permanent, both individuals and corporations will not only be more willing to commit their larger disposable income, but they are also apt to use their brains, their energy, their liquid resources, and even their credit to take advantage of the new environment in which business is to be done. These considerations argue against frequent changes, but not necessarily against speedy changes, of tax rates. It would be helpful to learn what we can from the experience of Great Britain, Canada, and perhaps other countries where quick tax legislation has been practiced.

Let me say, in closing, that Professor Heller's optimism and his compassionate concern with both the present and future are perhaps the most engaging features of his book. His faith in the power and promise of the "new economics" is strong. The following is a typical utterance: "I count on our growing economic maturity to keep on lowering the political barriers to sound economic decisions" (p. 97). But Professor Heller is realistic enough to recognize that the path of the "new economics" is strewn with rocks in practice. His warning that "if fiscal and monetary policies are consistently less vigorous in checking overexpansion than in combatting underexpansion, the resulting inflationary bias could in part discredit the 'new economics'" (p. 50) is timely and constructive.

THIRTEEN

Economic and Social Impact of the Defense Sector

IN HIS FAMOUS farewell address, President Eisenhower warned the nation to remain vigilant of what he called "the military-industrial complex." This warning needs to be remembered and pondered by thoughtful citizens. An age of nuclear weapons leaves no time for assembling the military and industrial forces needed to repel an aggressor. Once a nation is attacked, it can be practically destroyed in a matter of minutes. For this reason, as well as because of the unhappy state of our relations with the Communist bloc, "normalcy" for us has come to include since 1950 a formidable military establishment in a state of constant readiness, if need be, for war. But "the conjunction of an immense military establishment and a large arms industry," as President Eisenhower has observed, "is new in the American experience. The total influence —economic, political, even spiritual—is felt in every city, every statehouse, every office of the Federal government." My purpose today is to consider with you some of the ways in which the emergence of a massive and permanent defense sector has

Moskowitz Lecture at New York University, Nov. 20, 1967, originally published in *The Defense Sector and the American Economy*, New York University Press, 1968. Reprinted by permission of the publisher.

already changed and is continuing to change our economic and social life.

I

To begin with, the defense sector has revolutionized governmental finances in our generation. In fiscal year 1948, federal expenditures came to $36 billion. In fiscal 1964, well before Vietnam became a significant financial burden, spending on national defense alone amounted to $54 billion, or half as much again as the total budget in 1948. In the current fiscal year, the defense budget may amount to about $80 billion, but this huge sum still does not indicate the full financial cost of defense activities. The federal government expects to spend another $5 billion on international programs and also $5.25 billion on space research and technology. These activities, of course, are mainly pursued in the interests of our national security. Moreover, the federal budget allows $10.5 billion for interest on the public debt and over $6.5 billion for veterans' benefits, the former being preponderantly and the latter entirely a legacy of past wars. Thus, defense-related expenditures will probably come this year to over $100 billion—a sum that represents more than $500 for every man, woman, and child of our population.

The large and rising cost of defense activities would have caused financial problems even if other costs of government had not changed. In fact, as we all know, the range of governmental activities has greatly increased. Since the end of World War II, the American people have come to expect their government to maintain economic conditions that are generally conducive to full employment. The federal government has been also under increasing pressure to enlarge social services—that is to say, improve the nation's schools, help support uni-

versities, improve hospitals and medical facilities, facilitate
home ownership, reduce urban slums, promote safer and faster
air travel, raise social security and related welfare benefits,
train manpower for the needs of industry, seek ways of reducing air and water pollution, and even concern itself with problems of traffic congestion and police protection. These expanding interests of the federal government are a political response
to the increasing urbanization of modern life, the new opportunities opened up by advances in technology, and the growing impatience for better living on the part of many citizens
who have been left behind by the march of progress. Thus, at
the very stage of history when demographic, technological,
and political trends have been releasing powerful forces to
raise the costs of government, the defense sector likewise became an increasing burden on the Treasury. The inevitable
result has been a vast growth of federal spending—from $36
billion in fiscal 1948 to $120 billion in 1964, and probably $175
billion, if not more, this fiscal year.

The upsurge of federal spending on defense and on civilian
activities has naturally resulted in much higher taxes. To be
sure, we have recently become accustomed to deficits when the
economy is booming as well as when the economy is depressed. The role of deficits in governmental finance, however,
is commonly exaggerated. From mid-1946 to June, 1967, the
cumulative revenue of the federal government covered all but
2 per cent of its expenditures, so that federal taxes have in fact
grown just about as rapidly as expenditures. Our economy has
also grown substantially during this period, but not enough to
prevent taxes from siphoning off an increasing portion of the
national income. In fiscal 1940, federal revenues came to about
7 per cent of the gross national product, in 1950 to 15.5 per
cent, in 1960 to 19 per cent, last year to 20 per cent. Meanwhile, state and local taxes have also moved up—indeed, they

have grown even more rapidly during the past ten or twenty years than federal taxes. According to the national income accounts, the combined revenue of all governmental units amounted in the past fiscal year to about 29 per cent of the gross national product and 32 per cent of the net national product; and even the higher figure may understate the tax burden, since it makes inadequate allowance for the capital used up in the process of producing goods and services.

This year, with the war in Vietnam escalating and social expenditures also rising, the federal budget deficit may well exceed $20 billion unless steps are taken to raise taxes and curb expenditures. To reduce the enormous deficit now in sight, President Johnson has proposed a 10 per cent surcharge on income taxes, but the Congress has thus far failed to adopt the proposal. Some members of Congress feel that the tax burden is already so heavy that it would be wiser to cut governmental expenditures than to raise taxes. Others would be willing to accept higher taxes provided substantial reductions in expenditures were simultaneously made. With financial markets disturbed and interest rates rising above last year's abnormally high level, a great debate is now raging both within and outside governmental circles about the relation of the federal budget to economic activity, interest rates, and inflation. What is critically at issue in this debate is not whether federal spending should be permitted to rise, but the size of the reduction—if any—in the projected scale of spending on nondefense programs. No matter how this issue is resolved, spending in the aggregate will still go up, and—if history is any guide—taxes will follow; so that we now face the prospect of higher income taxes besides higher social security taxes and assorted increases of state and local taxes.

We also face the prospect of paying more for foodstuffs, clothing, automobiles, and whatever else we buy. The causes of inflation are complex, and it is never strictly true that an increase in spending on defense or on business equipment or on any other category is the sole cause of inflation. In principle, the government can always adjust its monetary and fiscal policies to economic conditions so as to keep the price level reasonably stable. If the government had foreseen how rapidly the cost of the Vietnam war would mount and if it had taken promptly the restraining measures needed to keep the aggregate demand for goods and services from outrunning the nation's capacity to produce, the new round of inflation that we have experienced since 1964 could have been prevented. But if we blame the government for its lack of foresight or courage in this instance, we should also bear in mind that the theoretical ideal of price stability has rarely, if ever, been closely approximated under wartime conditions.

When demand presses hard on a nation's resources, as it generally does at a time of war, it becomes very difficult to adjust tax, credit, and expenditure policies on the scale needed to prevent advances in the price level. The doubling of wholesale prices between 1940 and 1950 was obviously linked to the enormous expansion of military spending during World War II. Since then, the trend of prices has continued upward at a much slower pace, and no single factor stands out so prominently among the causes of inflation. Indeed, prices have risen less in our country since 1950 than in most others, despite our exceptionally large military burden. It is nevertheless true that the greater part of the recent advance in both wholesale and consumer prices came in three spurts—between 1950 and 1952 when the Korean war was raging, between 1955 and 1957 when a fairly rapid increase of military contracts for newly developed weapon systems paralleled a booming trend of business investment in new plant and equipment, and since mid-1965 when our ground forces shifted to an active role in

Vietnam. It thus appears that the sudden surges within the defense sector have contributed to the inflationary trend which has been gradually eroding all savings accumulated in the form of bank deposits, life insurance, savings bonds, and other fixed-income assets, besides complicating life for everyone whose money income fails to respond to the rising cost of living.

The defense sector has also contributed to the deficit in our balance of payments. Since 1950 the receipts from our sale of goods, services, and securities to foreign countries have run considerably below the sums that we need to pay foreign countries. One reason for this persistent deficit is the large expenditure that is required, year in and year out, to maintain our military forces abroad. Foreign assistance programs have also been adding to the deficit, although their foreign exchange cost is now much smaller. Since the revenue derived from our foreign transactions has been insufficient to cover the required payments, our stocks of gold have shrunk from $24.5 billion at the beginning of 1950 to about $13 billion at present. Meanwhile, the dollar balances that are held here by foreigners have also grown, so that the United States finds itself in the position of a banker whose short-term liabilities are steadily rising while his reserves keep dwindling. In order to check the deterioration in our international financial position, the Department of Defense has lately been favoring domestic over foreign suppliers even at cost differentials of 50 per cent. More disturbing still, the government has found it necessary to impose restrictions on the outflow of capital—an interference with private investment that is contrary to our national traditions. Even so, the deficit in the balance of payments has persisted, and—at least partly as a result of the war in Vietnam—it is larger this year than last. International confidence in the dollar, which is of such immense importance to America's political leadership as well as to our economy and that of the rest of the world, is still strong, but we can no longer count on it as we did ten or twenty years ago.

II

I have been concerned thus far with the financial aspects of national defense—its impact on governmental expenditures, taxes, the price level, and the balance of payments. Financial transactions and the price system, however, are merely mechanisms for putting a nation's resources to work and for distributing what is produced among people and their government. The resources that we devote to national defense are not available for making consumer goods or for adding to the stock of industrial equipment or for public uses in the sphere of education, health, or urban redevelopment. To the extent that we allocate labor, materials, and capital to national defense, we cannot satisfy our desires for other things. The civilian goods and services that are currently foregone on account of expenditures on national defense are, therefore, the current real cost of the defense establishment.

This cost has become very large, as my observations on governmental finance have already suggested. Its magnitude can perhaps be grasped best by considering the amount of labor devoted to national defense. In fiscal 1965, the armed forces numbered close to 2.75 million. They were supported by over 900,000 civilian workers attached to the Department of Defense and by another 2.1 million civilians employed in private industry who worked, directly or indirectly, on military supplies. Thus the total employment on defense goods and services amounted to 5.75 million, or to 86 out of every 1,000 employed workers in the country. Two years later—that is, during the fiscal year which ended June, 1967—the number was nearly 7.5 million, or 103 out of every 1,000 employed workers. The employment currently attributable to national security expenditures is still larger; for the figures that I have cited, besides not being fully up to date, take no account of the activities of the Atomic Energy Commission, the National Aeronautics and Space Administration, or other defense-related efforts.

A mere count of numbers, moreover, does not convey adequately the drain of the defense establishment on the nation's work force. Men differ in quality, and we need to take account of the fact that those involved in the defense effort are, on the average, superior from an economic viewpoint to workers engaged in civilian production. Military technology and operations have become very sophisticated in our times. The armed forces now have a highly skilled core and are very selective in accepting men for service. Indeed, the proportion of personnel who completed high school is much larger in the armed forces than in the comparable age group of the civilian population, while the proportion of college graduates is not materially lower. Training and skill count even more heavily among the civilians involved in defense activities. Last year, professional workers accounted for nearly 16 per cent and skilled blue-collar workers for 21 per cent of the civilians employed on defense work, in contrast to about 13 per cent for each of these groups in the total working population. One out of every five of the nation's electrical and mechanical engineers in civilian jobs, two out of every five airplane mechanics, two out of every five physicists outside of teaching, and three out of every five aeronautical engineers were employed on defense goods during the past year. And even these figures understate the skill dimension of defense employment, for they again leave out of account the highly technical activities originating in the Atomic Energy Commission and the Space Administration.

The heavy emphasis on skill and brainpower in defense employment reflects, of course, the explosion of military technology to which modern science has been contributing so much of its finest energy. Since the Korean war, defense contractors have been devoting themselves not only to the production of extremely complex weapons but also to developing entirely new weapon systems that no one as yet knew how to produce. Much of the defense sector of our economy has come to consist, therefore, of research and development work. The President's budget for this fiscal year, for example, allots about $16 billion to research and development, of which $9 billion is to be devoted to defense and another $5 billion to space activities. Since 1960 defense and space programs have consistently accounted for over 80 per cent of the rapidly increasing federal funds devoted to research and development. More important still, they have amounted to about 54 per cent of the expenditure on research and development carried out in the entire nation—that is, by the federal government, industry, universities and colleges, research centers affiliated with universities, and other nonprofit institutions. During the 1950's the proportion of the nation's research and development effort devoted to defense-related activities was only a little lower.

By diverting to its interest so much manpower, especially scientific and engineering skills, the defense establishment has left its mark on both the structure and the functioning of our economy. The effects are all around us. Some defense-oriented industries—notably, the aerospace group, electronics, and communications—have become a major factor in the economy, and their development has favored many communities—for example, Los Angeles, San Diego, Seattle, Baltimore. Some large firms have acquired marvelous technological competence from their work on defense or space contracts and this rather than any immediate profit has commonly been their chief reason for wanting the contracts in the first place. Not a few of the scientists and engineers who received their training in the more sophisticated enterprises have moved into traditional lines of activity, bringing something of the spirit of research and innovation with them. Many of the men released by the armed forces have been able to put the technical skills acquired during their military service to effective use in civilian jobs. Nondefense activities have shared in the increased supply of engineers, scientists, and technicians that has been stimulated by the defense-related demand. And not a few of the processes or products developed for the military have found application in civilian life—for example, jet transports, advanced computers, radar, miniaturized components, and nuclear power plants.

But if the defense sector has stimulated economic development in some directions, it has retarded growth in others. Many civilian-oriented laboratories of business firms have found it difficult to match the salaries or the equipment that subsidized defense firms offer to scientists and engineers. Research and development work in behalf of new products and processes for the civilian economy has therefore been handicapped. Small firms have derived little benefit from military or space contracts. The draft has added to the labor turnover of all businesses, large and small. The lack of opportunity in the defense sector for poorly educated and unskilled workers has not helped the rural Negroes who have flocked into the cities in recent years in search for jobs and a better life. Moreover, a new class of business executives has arisen, consisting of men whose understanding of marketing and cost controls is often deficient, but who know how to negotiate effectively with government officials handling military or scientific problems. While knowing the right people or having friends in the right places can sometimes advance the interests of an enterprise better than plain business ability, the nation's economic efficiency is not likely to reap a corresponding advantage.

In any event, the economic growth of a nation is a blind concept unless we consider what is produced as well as the rate of growth of what happens to be produced. During the decade from 1957 to 1966, our nation spent approximately $520 billion on defense and space programs. This sum is almost two-and-one-half times as large as the entire amount spent on elementary and secondary education, both public and private. It is two-and-three-quarter times as large as the amount spent on the construction of new housing units. It exceeds by over a fourth the expenditure on new plant and equipment by the entire business community—manufacturing firms, mining concerns, transportation enterprises, public utilities, and all other businesses. To be sure, an extra billion dollars' worth of bombs or missiles will increase current production just as much as an extra billion of new equipment for making civilian goods. Bombs or missiles, however, add nothing to the nation's capacity to produce, while new equipment serves to augment production in the future. The real cost of the defense sector consists, therefore, not only of the civilian goods and services that are currently foregone on its account; it includes also an element of growth that could have been achieved through larger investment in human or business capital. But even if we assumed that the conflicting influences of the defense sector on economic growth canceled out, its real cost is still enormous.

Unhappily, we live in dangerous times which make large national security expenditures practically unavoidable. Nevertheless, there are always some options in a nation's foreign and military policy, and we therefore must be alert to the opportunities that our military establishment forces us to forego. For example, if the resources devoted to military and space activities during the past decade had been put instead to civilian uses, we could surely have eliminated urban slums, besides adding liberally to private investment in new plant and equipment as well as to both public and private investment in human capital.

III

It follows from our analysis that the military-industrial complex, of which President Eisenhower spoke so perceptively in his farewell address, has not only been enlarging the scale of governmental operations and thereby complicating financial problems. By changing the thrust of economic activity and by making the economy more dependent on government, it has also been affecting profoundly the character of our society. Nor have the social effects been confined to the kinds of goods that we produce. Hopefulness about the future, optimism about success of new undertakings, impatience to complete satisfactorily whatever is begun—these psychological qualities have been peculiarly American characteristics, and they account in far greater degree than we may realize for the remarkable achievements of our economic system and the vigor of our political democracy. These qualities are deep-rooted in American experience and they continue to sustain us. Nevertheless, the development and spread of thermonuclear weapons, the frustrations of the cold war, and now the brutal struggle in Vietnam have left us, despite our awesome military power, more anxious about our national security than our fathers or grandfathers ever were.

Adults whose habits were formed in an earlier generation may put the dangers of nuclear catastrophe out of mind by losing themselves in their work or by seeking solace in religion. That is more difficult for our children who increasingly wonder what kind of world they have inherited by our doings. There can be little doubt that the lively competition among the great powers in devising instruments of terror is one of the underlying causes of the restlessness of modern youth.

Moreover, young men of military age are bearing a disproportionately large part of the defense burden. That is unavoidable at a time of war, but our generation has institutionalized compulsory military service even when the nation is at peace. It is undoubtedly true that many young men derive deep satisfaction from helping to protect their country by serving as soldiers, sailors, or aviators. Not only that, many have also found useful careers in the armed forces, or have benefited in their civilian jobs from the skills and discipline acquired during military service, or have gained a larger understanding of life by associating with men of widely different backgrounds or by being stationed abroad for a time. But just as these benefits deserve recognition, so too does the fact that the draft has by and large proved to be a seriously upsetting factor in the lives of young people. Not knowing when they would be called up for military service or whether they would be accepted, many have found themselves marking time. Those who are accepted have often had to interrupt their schooling or careers, perhaps alter plans with regard to marriage, and in any event be content with substantially lower pay than they could earn as a rule in civilian work. Moreover, the administration of the draft over the years, particularly the handling of student deferments, has raised troublesome moral questions in the minds of young people—and, for that matter, in the minds of older citizens as well.

The emergence of our country as a great military power, having world-wide political responsibilities, has also affected our educational system. Greater emphasis on science, mathematics, and modern languages in secondary schools and colleges, new area institutes and schools of international affairs in the universities, advanced courses in the esoteric languages and customs of the Far East and Africa—these educational developments not only reflect the widening scientific and geographic interests of modern business; they are also a response to urgent requirements of national security. But it is in the area of research, rather than teaching, where the impact of the defense establishment on our universities has been particularly felt. Colleges, universities, and research centers associated with universities spent in the aggregate $460 million on the performance of research and development in 1953, with something over half of this sum financed by the federal government. Last year, the sum so spent was six-and-one-half times as large, and the federally-financed portion rose to 70 per cent. Clearly, federal funds are mainly responsible for the extraordinary growth of research activities in universities, and the chief—although by no means the sole—reason for this governmental involvement is the intensive search for new knowledge on the part of defense-related agencies. During 1963–1966, the Department of Defense, the Atomic Energy Commission, and the Space Administration together accounted for five-eighths of the dollar value of federal grants for research and development to institutions of higher learning, and their proportion in immediately preceding years was even larger.

The huge influx of governmental research funds has served to enrich the intellectual life of numerous colleges and universities, especially in the larger institutions where the grants have been mainly concentrated. By virtue of research grants, professors have better equipment to work with and more technical assistance than they had in former times. They also travel more, keep in closer contact with their counterparts in other universities, and mingle more freely with government officials, business executives, and scientists working for private industry. The gulf that previously separated a university from the larger interests of the community and the nation has therefore narrowed very significantly.

However, governmental research grants have created problems for universities as well as new opportunities for useful service. The greater interest of a faculty in research is not infrequently accompanied by lesser devotion to teaching. No little part of the time set aside for research may in practice be consumed by travel and conferences of slight scientific value. However welcome grants from military and space agencies may be, their concentration on the physical and engineering sciences makes it more difficult for a university to maintain the balance among various branches of learning that is so essential to the intellectual and moral improvement of man. Some military contracts involve classified research, and the secrecy which attends such work introduces an entirely foreign note in institutions that have traditionally taken a strong pride in completely free and uninhibited communication among scholars. Not less serious is the tendency, which appears to be growing among university scholars, to forsake the research to which they are drawn by intellectual curiosity in favor of projects that have been designed by, or contrived to suit the tastes of, government officials or others who take care of the financing. All universities and many of our colleges are struggling with this and other problems that the defense sector has created or accentuated.

The danger of diminished independence is not confined to research activities. If college or university presidents no longer speak out as vigorously on national issues as they did a generation or two ago, one major reason is that the institutions over whose destiny they preside have become heavily dependent on federal contracts and subsidies. Even professors who are benefiting from federal research grants or consulting relationships, or who expect to be able to do so in the future, have been learning the occasional value of studied reticence. And if discretion is tempering the spirit of forthright questioning and criticism in our universities, its power is all the stronger in the business world. It is hardly in the interest of businessmen to criticize their customers publicly, and by far the largest customer of the business world is clearly the federal government itself. Some firms sell all and many sell a good part of what they produce to the federal government, and there are always others that hope to be in a position to do likewise in the future.

To be sure, the great majority of business executives, even those who manage very large enterprises, prefer commercial markets to governmental business; but they have become so sensitive nowadays to the regulatory powers of government that they rarely articulate their thoughts on national issues in public. Trade union leaders are typically more candid and outspoken on governmental issues than business executives; but they too have become dependent in varying degrees on the goodwill of government officials and therefore often deem tact or reticence the better part of wisdom. Not only that, but it is no longer unusual for the government in power, whether the administration be in Democratic or Republican hands, to suggest to prominent businessmen, trade union leaders, attorneys, journalists, or university professors that they support publicly this or that administration proposal. And men of public distinction at times comply regardless of their beliefs, perhaps because they are flattered by the attention accorded them, or because they vaguely expect some advantage from going along, or simply because they feel that they dare not do otherwise. Thus the gigantic size to which the federal government has grown, for which the defense sector bears a heavy but by no means exclusive responsibility, has been tending to erode perceptibly, although not yet alarmingly, as the open discussion of the war in Vietnam indicates, the spirit of rational and constructive dissent without which a democracy cannot flourish.

The huge size of military budgets and incomplete disclosure concerning their management carry with them also the danger of political abuse. Since money spent in the interest of national security necessarily has economic effects, the government in power may sometimes be tempted to ease domestic problems by adjusting the scale or direction of military spending. For example, raw materials may be stockpiled beyond the minimum military target, or the target itself may be revised upward, in order to grant some relief to a depressed industry. Or at a time of general economic slack, the government may begin to look upon military spending as if it were a public works program. Worse still, considerations of political advantage may play a role in deciding whether contracts are placed in one area rather than another, or with this firm instead of that. Such practices confuse military officers, lead to waste, and might even exacerbate international relations. Nevertheless, they are not entirely unknown to history, including our own. Fortunately, our government officials have generally been reluctant to tamper with something so fundamental to the nation as its defense establishment; and even on the rare occasions when they have strayed from virtue, the sluggishness of a governmental bureaucracy in carrying out any plan has kept down the scale of mischief. But if politics is ever effectively computerized, as some students believe it will be, we may have less protection against political abuse within the defense sector in the future.

Any enlargement of the economic power of government, whether brought about by military expenditures or through other causes, can eventually result in some infringement of liberty. However, because of the sense of urgency in troubled times, the requirements of national security may lead more directly to restriction of freedom. Necessary though the draft may be, it still constitutes compulsion of the individual by the state. Necessary though security clearances may be, they still constitute an invasion of privacy. Necessary though passport regulations may be, they still restrict the freedom of individuals to travel where they choose. Fortunately, the vitality of our democracy has thus far proved sufficient to limit restrictions of freedoms such as these. Not only that, it has enabled us to put an end to the nightmare of McCarthyism, to suppress the interest of the Central Intelligence Agency in our colleges and universities, and even to fight the war in Vietnam without imposing price and wage controls. We cannot take it for granted, however, that our formidable defense establishment will not give rise to more serious dangers to our liberties and the democratic process in the future.

IV

Throughout the ages, philosophers and religious teachers have lamented the horrors of war and searched for the keys to peace. Yet their noblest thought has been frustrated by the course of human events. Our country has been more fortunate than most, but we have had our share of the destruction of life and property that is the universal coin of warfare. Every American of age fifty or over has lived through two world wars, the Korean war, and now the smaller but still very costly and protracted struggle in Vietnam. When this war ends, military expenditures will probably decline for a while, as they have in fact after every war in our history. We cannot look forward, however, to demobilization on anything like the scale experienced after World War I or World War II, when the military budget was reduced by about 90 per cent within three years.

The reason for the difference, of course, is that the cold war is still with us, just as it was when the Korean hostilities ended. After the cessation of that conflict, the defense budget was reduced merely by a fifth. If the cost of the Vietnam war remains at approximately the current rate, it is doubtful whether a cease-fire will be followed by a reduction of even the Korean magnitude. A return to the defense budget of fiscal 1964 or 1965 would indeed involve a cut of roughly 35 per cent from this year's expenditure; but in the absence of a dramatic change in our international relations, this is quite unlikely. In the first place, prices are higher at present than they were in 1964 or 1965, and they will probably be higher still when the war phases out. In the second place, it may well be necessary for us to keep many more troops in Vietnam after a cease-fire than was the case in Korea and also to become more heavily involved in the task of reconstruction. In the third place, while stocks of military equipment were built up during the Korean war, they have been seriously depleted—particularly for the Reserve and National Guard units—by Vietnam. They will need to be rebuilt when hostilities come to an end, and this demand will be reinforced by the deferred procurement of newer models to replace equipment now in inventory.

Nevertheless, a sizable reduction of military spending will take place in the year or two after the cease-fire, and we will have the opportunity to concentrate more of our resources on the arts of peace. In the past, the American economy has demonstrated a remarkable ability to adjust speedily to cutbacks in military spending, and we can be confident of doing so again. After World War I the conversion from war to peace was carried out with only a mild and brief setback in total economic activity. The like happened after World War II, despite the fact that more than two-fifths of our nation's resources were devoted to military uses at the peak of the war. Between 1945 and 1946, spending on the manufacture of defense goods dropped drastically and the number of men in the armed forces declined from 11.5 million to 3.5 million. Nevertheless, the unemployment rate remained below 4 per cent. The termination of the Korean war was followed by a recession but the return of peace was not its sole cause. In any event, unemployment during this recession was less serious at its worst than during the recession which came just before or just after it. With the experience that our country has gained during the past two decades in coping with economic fluctuations, with both the Executive and the Congress obviously eager to prevent unemployment, and with plans for dealing with post-Vietnam problems already beginning to take shape, there should not be much difficulty in adjusting federal tax, expenditure, and credit policies so as to maintain aggregate monetary demand at the level needed to assure reasonably full employment when hostilities cease. Some sizable adjustments will still need to be made by numerous communities and industries; but even they should prove manageable since the military cutbacks are likely to be largely concentrated on items produced by business firms that are closely oriented to our diversified and resilient civilian markets.

The highly specialized aerospace, electronics, and communications industries will probably not bear much of the burden of post-Vietnam cutbacks. Indeed, once the curve of military spending turns upward again, as it well may two or three years after the cease-fire, these are the very industries that are likely to benefit most from the dynamism of modern technology. To maintain a sufficient strategic superiority to deter any aggressor, we have been devoting vast sums to research and development, as I have already noted. The fantastic new weapons and weapon systems devised by our scientists and engineers soon render obsolete some of the existing devices, which themselves were new and revolutionary only a short time ago. But until the new devices are ready, those that were only recently new cannot be abandoned and may even need to be augmented. Meanwhile, strategic concepts may shift, as they did during the sixties from reliance on massive nuclear deterrents to developing a capability for limited warfare and counterinsurgency operations. One way or another, therefore, costs tend to multiply all around. The Soviet Union, of course, will not stand still while our military prowess increases. On the contrary, it is striving through a remarkably enterprising and inventive military-industrial complex of its own to establish military parity, if not actual supremacy. For example, we have recently learned of the deployment of an anti-ballistic missile system around Moscow and Leningrad, of a novel ship-to-ship missile of Russian origin fired in the Mediterranean, and of the apparent development of an orbital bomb capability by the Soviet Union. Communist China has also been developing, and with greater speed than was generally anticipated, the ability to make and deliver sophisticated weapons. In turn, our military establishment, besides innovating vigorously on its own, keeps devising countermeasures to what the Russians or Chinese have or may have in hand. Both its reaction and its fresh challenge to potential aggressors can be expected to become stronger once Vietnam no longer requires top priority.

As we look beyond the cessation of hostilities in Vietnam, we therefore need to recognize that the scale of defense expenditures has, to a significant degree, become a self-reinforcing process. Its momentum derives not only from the energy of military planners, contractors, scientists, and engineers. To some degree it is abetted also by the practical interests and anxieties of ordinary citizens. Any announcement that a particular defense installation will be shut down, or that a particular defense contract will be phased out, naturally causes concern among men and women who, however much they abhor war and its trappings, have become dependent for their livelihood on the activity whose continuance is threatened. With a large part of our economy devoted to defense activities, the military-industrial complex has thus acquired a constituency including factory workers, clerks, secretaries, even grocers and barbers. Local politicians and community leaders may not find it easy to plead for the extension of activities that no longer serve a military purpose. Many, nevertheless, manage to overcome such scruples. Indeed, candidates for the Congress have been known to claim that they are uniquely qualified to ward off military closings or even to bring new contracts to their districts, and their oratory has not gone unrewarded by the electorate. The vested interest that numerous communities have acquired in defense activities may therefore continue to run up costs on top of the rising budgets generated by the momentum of competing military technologies.

If this analysis is at all realistic, the military-industrial complex will remain a formidable factor in our economic and social life in the calculable future. It will continue to command a large, possibly even an increasing, part of our resources. It will continue to strain federal finances. It will continue to test the vigor of our economy and the vitality of our democratic institutions. It will continue to confuse understanding by suggesting to many foreign citizens, as it sometimes does even to our own, that our national prosperity is based on huge military spending, when in fact we could be much more prosperous without it. For all these reasons, while we need to recognize the high and honorable national purpose of our military-industrial complex, we also need to remain continually vigilant of its activities and seek to protect ourselves against its possible abuses, just as we long ago learned to guard the public interest against business monopolies and as we are beginning to protect ourselves against labor monopolies.

V

The scale and activities of our defense sector are now being subjected to a searching public discussion. Two major schools of political thought have become locked in a contest for the mind and soul of America. One school draws much of its strength from the revolution of military technology, the other from the revolution of rising expectations. One school tends to regard communism as a centrally directed conspiracy that threatens our survival as a free people. The other school believes that communism is breaking up into independent national movements, and sees the main threat to free institutions in the deterioration of our cities and the sickness of our society. One school seeks overwhelming military power to deter fresh Communist adventures, and is willing to risk war in order to prevent the geographic expansion of communism. The other school seeks wider social justice and better economic conditions for Negroes and others who have not participated fully in the advance of prosperity, and holds that the force of moral example can contribute more to our national security than additional bombs or missiles.

Both schools have focused attention on the federal budget and neither has been satisfied by the treatment accorded its claims. From 1955 to 1965, federal spending on nondefense activities increased faster than spending on defense. Since then, defense expenditures have gone up more rapidly, though not much more rapidly. Looking to the future, professional economists never tire of pointing out that our growing economy will make it possible to have more butter and, if they are needed, also more guns, even as we have been managing to do while the war in Vietnam is being waged. Their reassurance, however, does not satisfy those who feel that our national security requires not just more guns, but many more guns, and that we therefore need to give up some of our butter. Nor does it satisfy those who feel that we need not just more butter, but much more butter, and that our statistics of the gross national product are misleading us by their failure to allow for the pollution of our water, the poisons in our air, the noise of our streets, the rats in our slums, the rioting in our cities, and the destruction of life on our highways. Debate along these lines has reached a high pitch of intensity and even bitterness as the war in Vietnam has dragged out. It has become a divisive force, and it has brought anguish to our people. Its effect on the conduct of the war, however, is likely to count for less than its effect on the general direction of our foreign and military policy in the future.

For the debate is demonstrating to thoughtful citizens that our national security depends not only on awesome military forces. It depends also on the strength of our economic system, on the wholesomeness of our social and political life, and particularly on how well governmental objectives express the national will and purpose. As this lesson sinks in, we will want to try far harder than we ever have, both in our personal capacity and through our government, to bring the armaments race under decent control. And if the cracks of freedom within the Communist system of tyranny widen, as they well may in coming decades, we can count on being joined in this quest by the people of the Soviet Union and eventually by the people of mainland China as well. That, at any rate, is the only real basis for hope of saving ourselves and the entire human family from catastrophe.

Index

volume of, 33
of wholesalers and retailers, 22
Saulnier, Raymond, 89
Savings
during recession, 113
and inflation, 296
and tax increases, 300
Savings and loan associations, 157
Schumpeter, Joseph A., 12
Seasons
and business cycle, 5-6, 219
and unemployment, 207
Securities and Exchange Commission, 170
Service industries
and business cycles, 48
future gains in, 125
per cent of labor force engaged in, 110
Small business
and credit restraint, 169, 174
loans obtained by, 169-171
Small Business Administration, 145-146, 169-170
loan funds available to, 174
Social security system, 214
changes in, 107
effect on business cycle, 47-48
and Kennedy Administration, 263
Social security taxes, 274
Soil Bank Program, 145
South Africa, increase in price of gold and, 301
Soviet Union, 256, 336
economic fluctuations in, 8
increases in price of gold in, 301
military-industrial complex of, 333
Space programs, cost of, 323
Specific cycles, 8-9
aggregate of, 73, 86, 94
business cycle as consensus of, 60-66

dispersion of, 56-60
distribution of turning points of, 56-57, 59, 91-92
exceptions to, 56
nature of, 19
State and local governments
expenditures, 152-154
and federal revenues, 303, 310
financing difficulties of, 168-169
taxes of, 106, 315-316
Statistics
before World War I, 10
on gross national product, 229-230
on unemployment, 228
on job vacancies. See Job vacancy statistics.
Steel companies
President Kennedy and, 265
and price guidelines, 231, 248-249
Stock market
crash of 1929, 43, 131
during Kennedy Administration, 265
in 1966, 275-276
prices
and aggregate activity, 74
and business cycle movements from country to country, 44
cyclical amplitudes in, 23, 42-43
during recession, 36
and inflation, 143
Structuralist school, 193, 210-211, 225-226
Sweden, contracyclical policies of, 50

Tax policies
cuts, 271, 278-279
as contracyclical measure, 141